The College History Series

Florida Institute of Technology

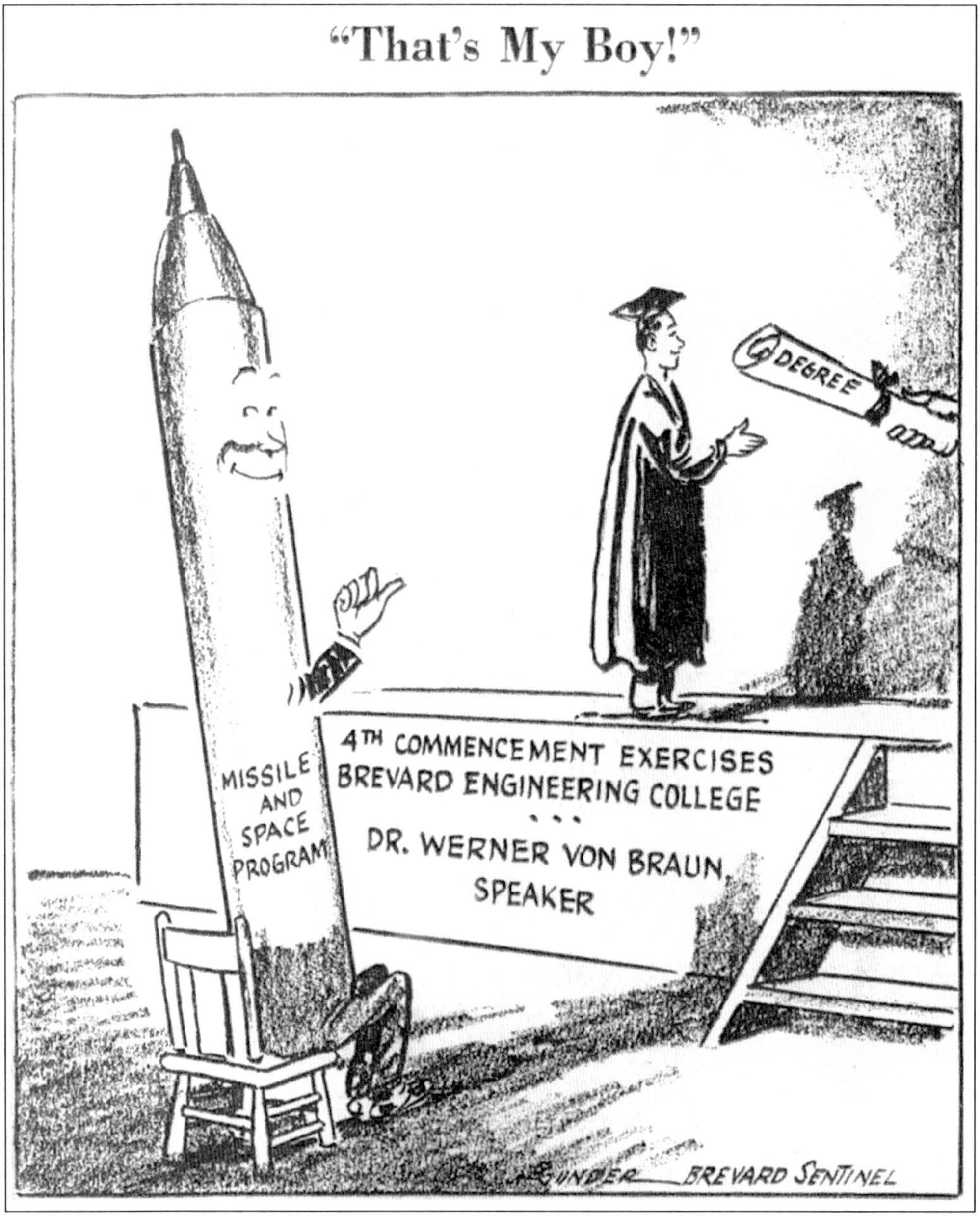

In 1964, Werner von Braun spoke at Brevard Engineering College's (later Florida Institute of Technology) fourth commencement. The German-born scientist who led America's drive to land a man on the moon told the graduates that this college "will someday become one of the top engineering colleges in the nation." This cartoon appeared in the Brevard Edition of the *Orlando Sentinel*.(Courtesy of *Orlando Sentinel*.)

Cover Photo: Lift-off of Bumper 8 on July 24, 1950.

The College History Series

FLORIDA INSTITUTE OF TECHNOLOGY

GORDON PATTERSON

ARCADIA PUBLISHING

Copyright © 2000 by Gordon Patterson.
ISBN 978-0-7385-0660-9

Published by Arcadia Publishing
Charleston, South Carolina

Printed in the United States of America

Library of Congress Catalog Card Number: 00-108556

For all general information contact Arcadia Publishing at:
Telephone 843-853-2070
Fax 843-853-0044
E-mail sales@arcadiapublishing.com
For customer service and orders:
Toll-Free 1-888-313-2665

Visit us on the Internet at www.arcadiapublishing.com

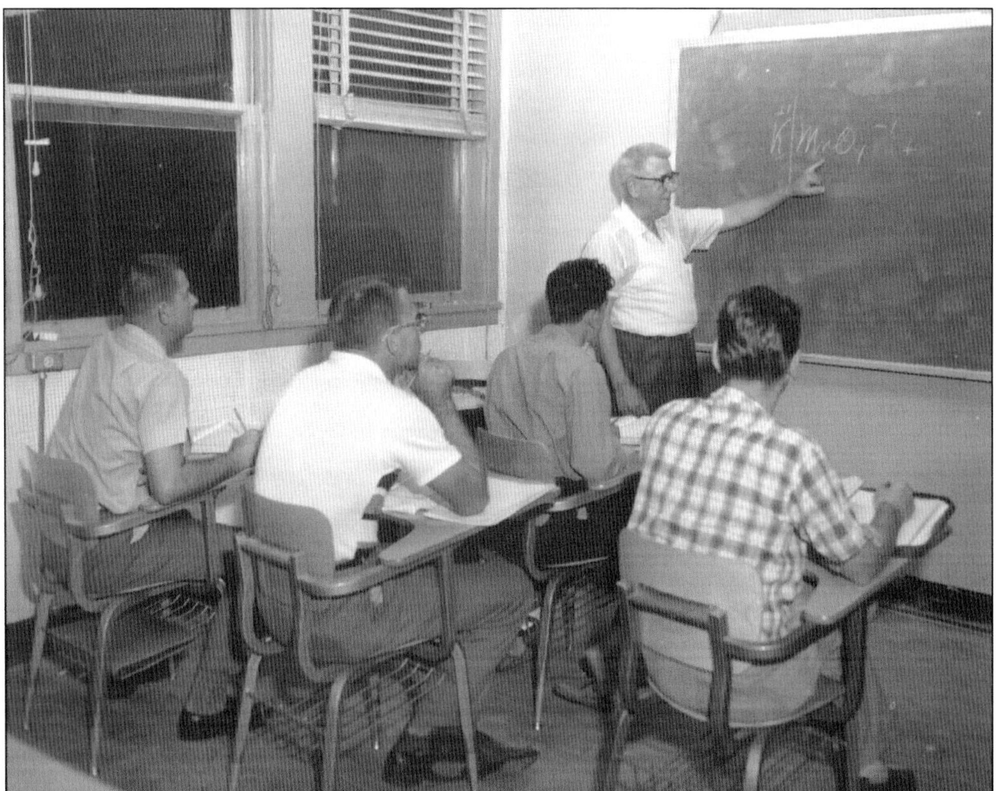

Professor Dan Dahle is shown here teaching a chemistry class in one of the classrooms in the Radiation Building in 1960. When he retired after a decade of service, Dr. Dahle was the first faculty member named professor emeritus. (Courtesy of Evans Library.)

Contents

ACKNOWLEDGMENTS

This book has been on my mind for several years. I am indebted to many people for their encouragement and help. Jerry Keuper, Jim Stoms, and Lynn Edward Weaver were always willing to answer my questions. Celine Alvey, Tom McFarland, Nancy Wallington, and the staff of the Evans Library gave me free access to the University's Special Collections. Marilyn Goravitch, Suanne Powell, and Sue Downing in the Humanities Department helped keep me on schedule. Bob Taylor and Bob Fronk offered sound advice. Emily Perry and Roger McCormick, Air Force Space and Missile Museum, provided valuable assistance. Dan Striby, Sterling Photo, allowed me access to his archive. Jim DeSantis supported this project throughout its development. Gordon Ring supplied much good advice. Jay Wilson, Karen Rhine, and Verna Layman checked facts and helped secure permissions to reprint photographs from published sources. University Publications' Judi Tintera, Rob Gribbroek, Kristie Nostrand, Rachele Ross, and Liz Tottenham were always ready with good advice. Florida Tech's Alumni Association's directors and past presidents Charlie McShane, Rob Phebus, Ken Revay, Paul Cecala, Lisa Turocy, Bob Arnold, Bill Creed, Neville Daruwalla, and Dale Dettmer encouraged this project. Andy Revay, Tom Bowman, Ed Kalajian, Dick Enstice, Bill Jurgens, Alan Rosiene, Carol Shehadeh, and Joy Patterson reviewed the manuscript and offered valuable criticism. This book would not, however, have been completed without the help of Joan Crutcher. Her talent and careful attention to detail are reflected on each page. Mistakes are my responsibility. All praise should go to the students, faculty, alumni, staff, and friends of the university.

INTRODUCTION

The story of Florida Institute of Technology is an improbable one. In 1958, a young physicist named Jerry Keuper, drawn to Cape Canaveral by the space program, decided to launch a university. Initially, Keuper and his confederates called their school Brevard Engineering College (BEC). The first contribution to the school was 37¢. Classes met in three rented junior high school rooms. In 1959, local school officials blocked the continued use of the rented classrooms because Florida Tech's faculty and students did not believe that segregation had any place in education. The college found a temporary home in an old church and a decommissioned Navy barracks. In 1961, the university moved to its permanent home in Melbourne.

Many thought the college would not succeed. Fortunately, there were a few men and women who disagreed. Werner von Braun was one. He called the university "Countdown College." Virgil "Gus" Grissom, one of the original Mercury Seven astronauts, was a cherished friend. In 1962, Grissom received the university's first honorary doctorate in space science at the June commencement exercises. In 1964, the Commission on Colleges of the Southern Association of Colleges and Secondary Schools (SACS) granted the college accreditation. In 1966, the college changed its name to Florida Institute of Technology.

During the 1960s and 1970s, Florida Tech grew at a phenomenal pace. Dormitories sprang up overnight. New programs in biology, chemistry, aeronautics, business, psychology, environmental studies, science education, oceanography, the humanities, and communication joined the flourishing engineering and science curriculum.

In the 1980s, leadership of the university passed to a new generation. Since 1988, Florida Tech has redoubled its effort to provide a quality education for its students. During the past decade, the university has committed itself to becoming a world-class center of research. The first signs of success are showing themselves in extraordinary work in medicine, pharmaceuticals, meteorology, and the engineering sciences.

There is something magical about this university. Florida Tech radiates a kind of energy and vision, passion and intensity. Florida Tech has made a tradition of confounding skeptics and realizing its dreams. It is my hope that this small book will allow readers a glimpse of Florida Tech's marvelous history.

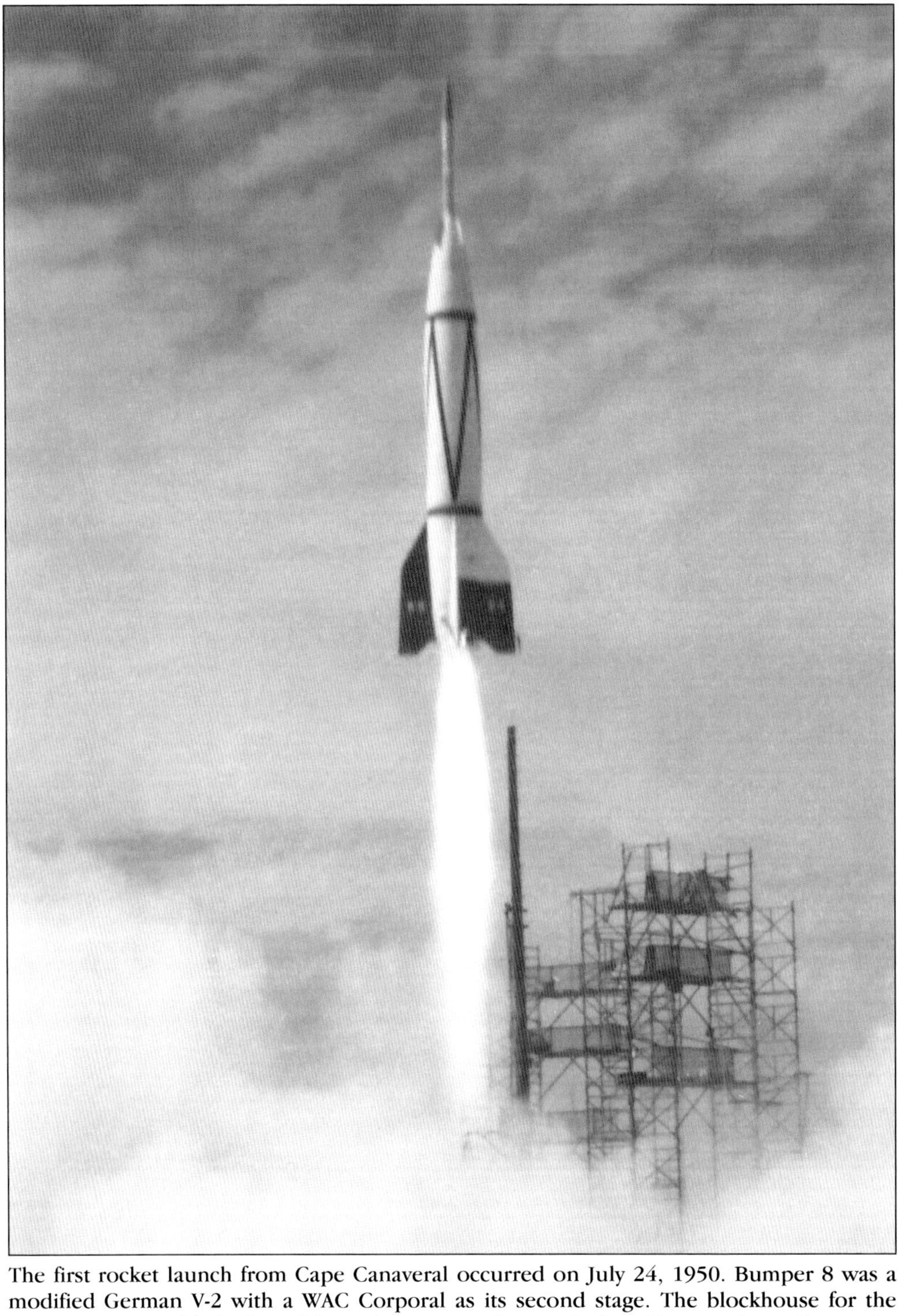

The first rocket launch from Cape Canaveral occurred on July 24, 1950. Bumper 8 was a modified German V-2 with a WAC Corporal as its second stage. The blockhouse for the mission was an old shed used by swimmers to change clothes. Twenty-nine miles to the south in Melbourne, people stopped in parking lots and watched the rocket streak into the heavens. (Courtesy of NASA.)

One

Countdown to College: 1950–1960

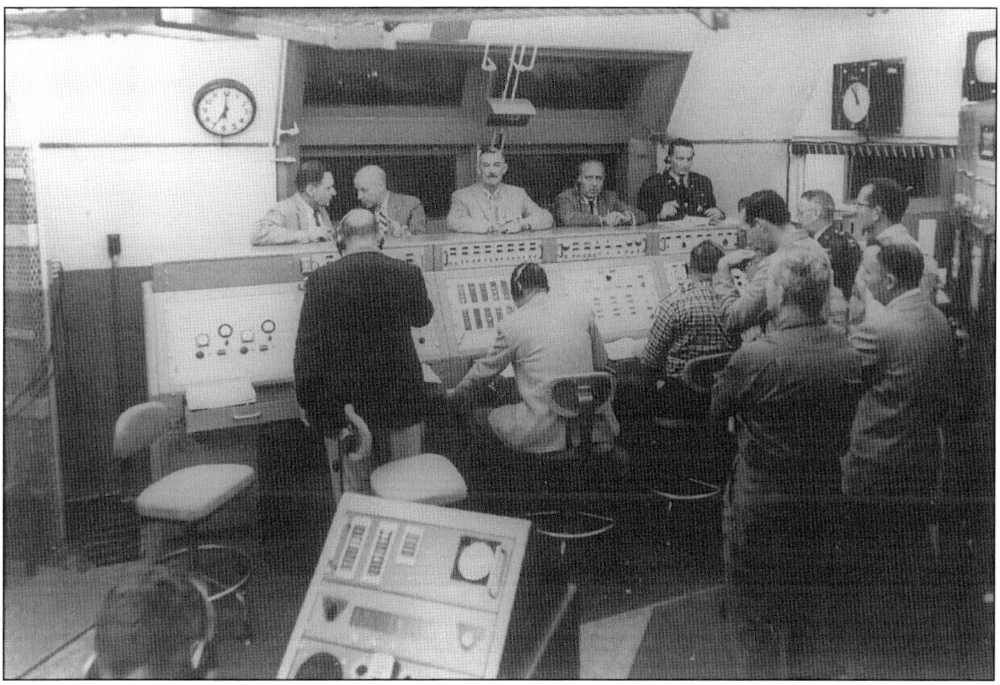

America's first satellite, Explorer I, was launched on January 31, 1958. This photograph shows pre-launch activities in the Firing Room at Complex 26 at Cape Canaveral Air Station. Technicians are monitoring the control consoles in the foreground. Gen. John Medaris (third from left) and Kurt Debus (fourth from left) are facing the camera. General Medaris was in charge of the Army Missile Project. (Courtesy of NASA.)

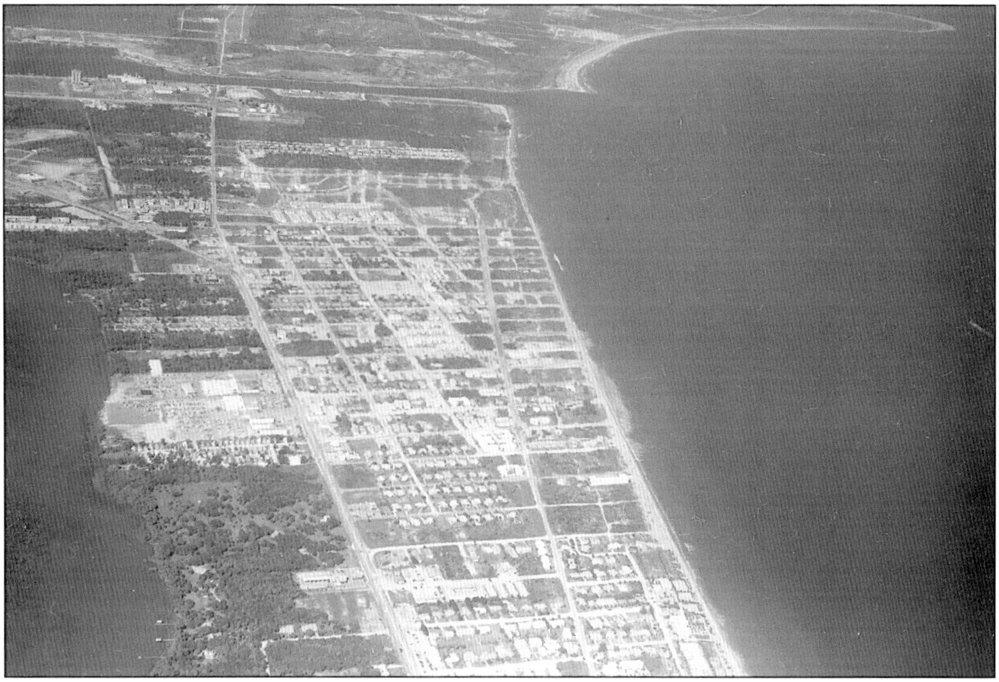

Ponce de Leon cruised past Cape Canaveral in 1513 in search of the fountain of youth. In 1948, the first "missilemen" (used to describe men and women) arrived at the sparsely populated Cape. The launch of Sputnik on October 4, 1957, started the space race in earnest. Edward Teller warned that Sputnik represented a "technological Pearl Harbor." (Courtesy of Sterling Photo.)

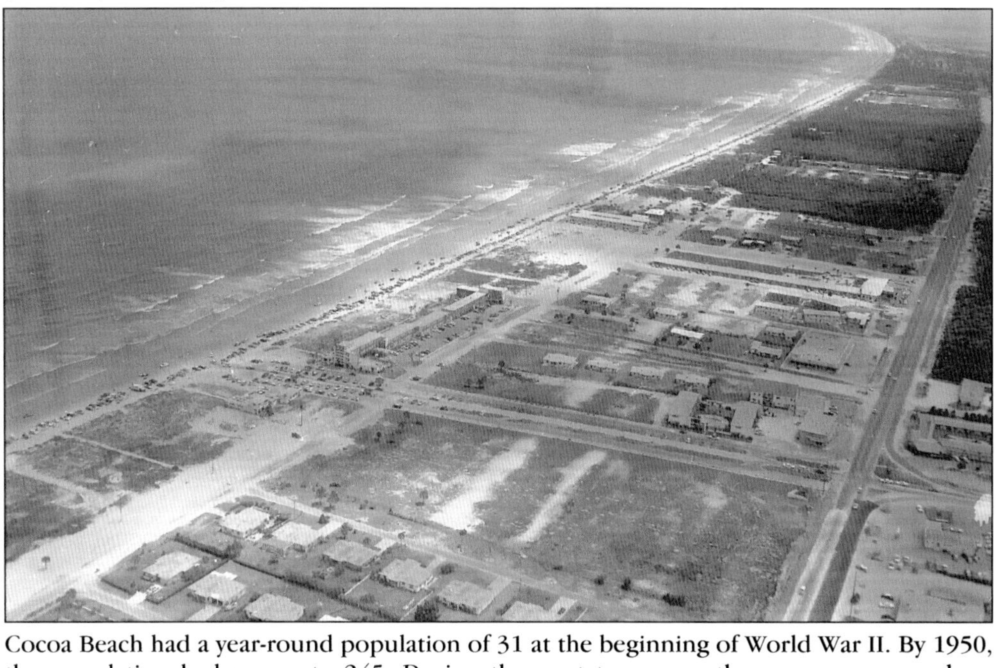

Cocoa Beach had a year-round population of 31 at the beginning of World War II. By 1950, the population had grown to 245. During the next ten years, the space program drew 75,000 new residents to Brevard County. (Courtesy of Sterling Photo.)

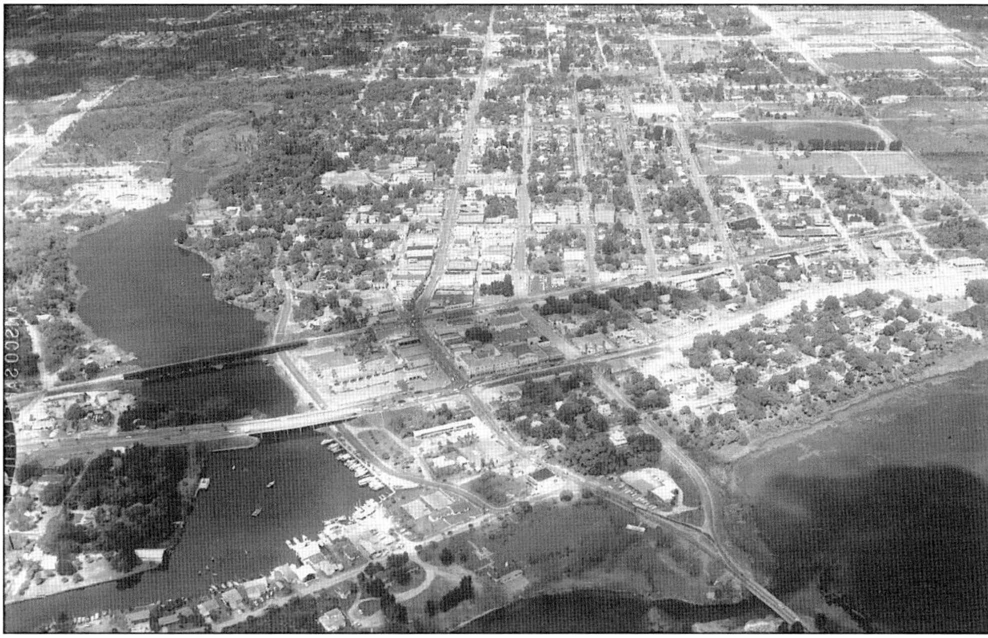

In 1950, Melbourne had a population of 4,223. The city grew rapidly in the 1950s and early 1960s because of its airport and reputation for outstanding schools. This 1963 photograph shows the city and the causeway across the Indian River Lagoon. (Courtesy of Sterling Photo.)

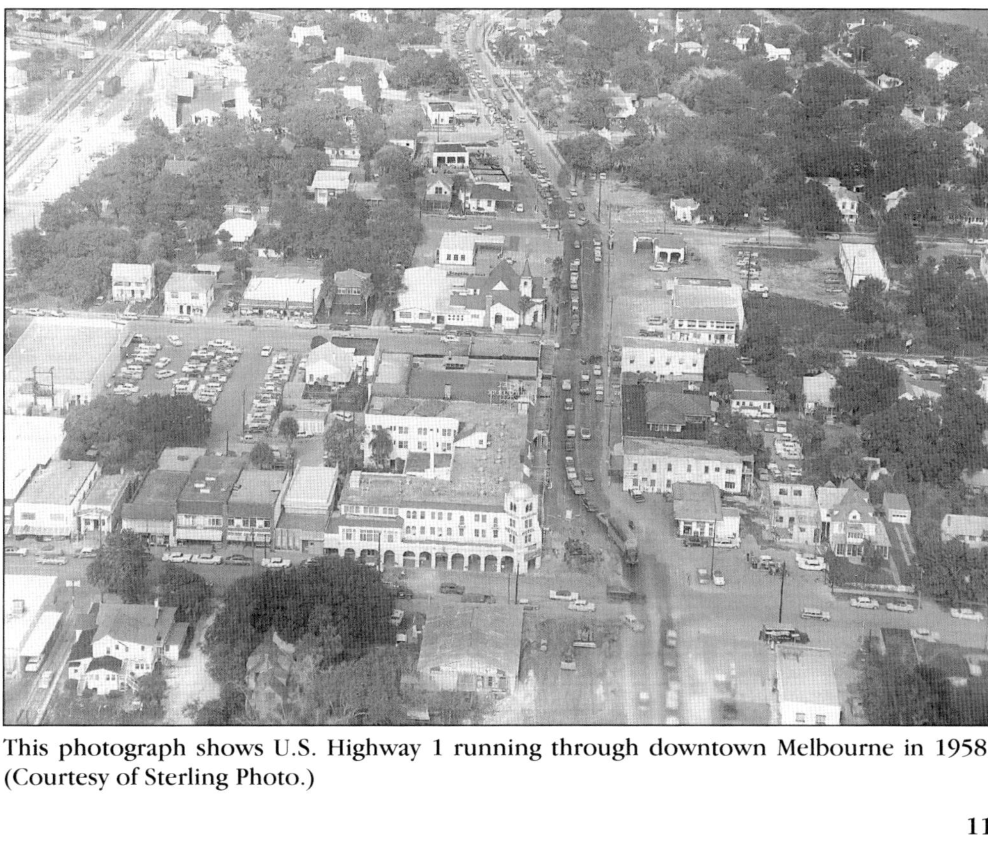

This photograph shows U.S. Highway 1 running through downtown Melbourne in 1958. (Courtesy of Sterling Photo.)

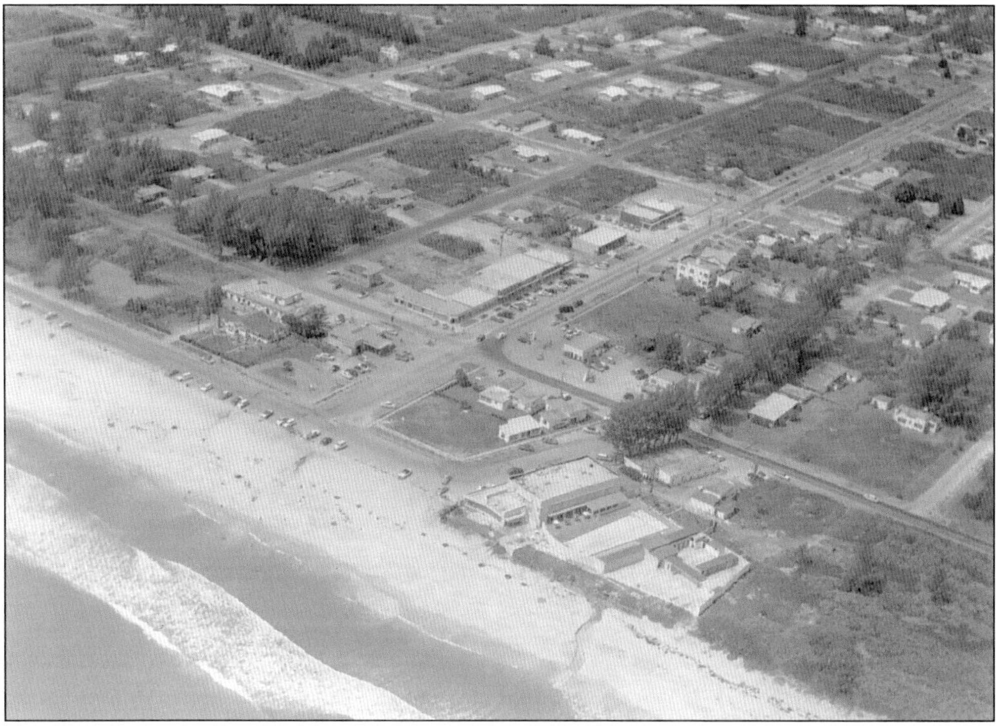

The Bahama Beach Club (lower right), located on the beach in Indialantic, was a favorite meeting place for missilemen festivities. Automobiles were allowed to park on the beach in July 1958 when this picture was taken. (Courtesy of Sterling Photo.)

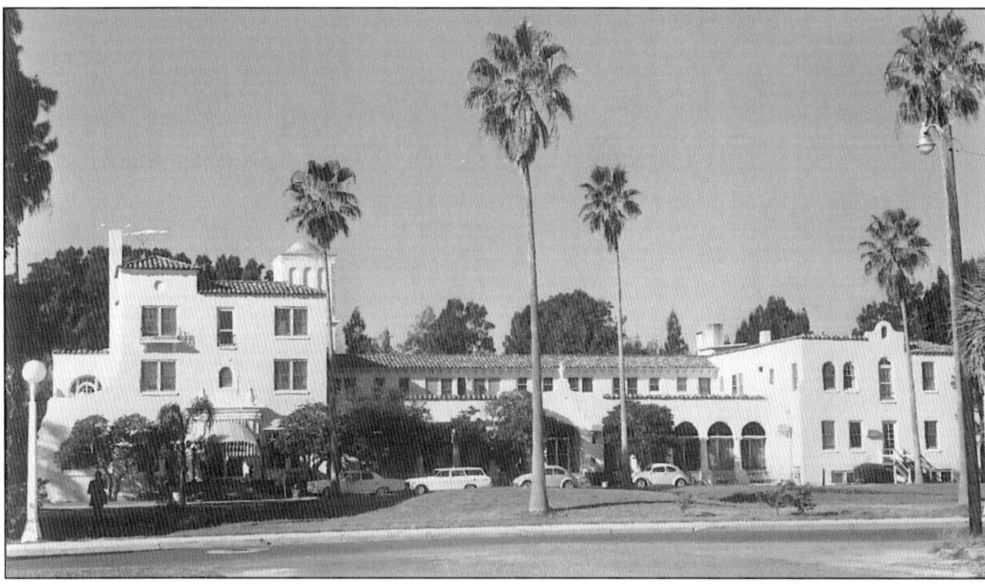

The Trade Winds Hotel (originally Hotel Indialantic) opened in 1926. Guests such as Charles Lindbergh, Jack Benny, and Werner von Braun found the hotel a "flash of Castillian fineness" on the "mosquito coast." Jerry Keuper and Harold Dibble organized an Engineer's Cotillion at the Trade Winds to rally support for the college on June 6, 1958. (Courtesy of University Publications.)

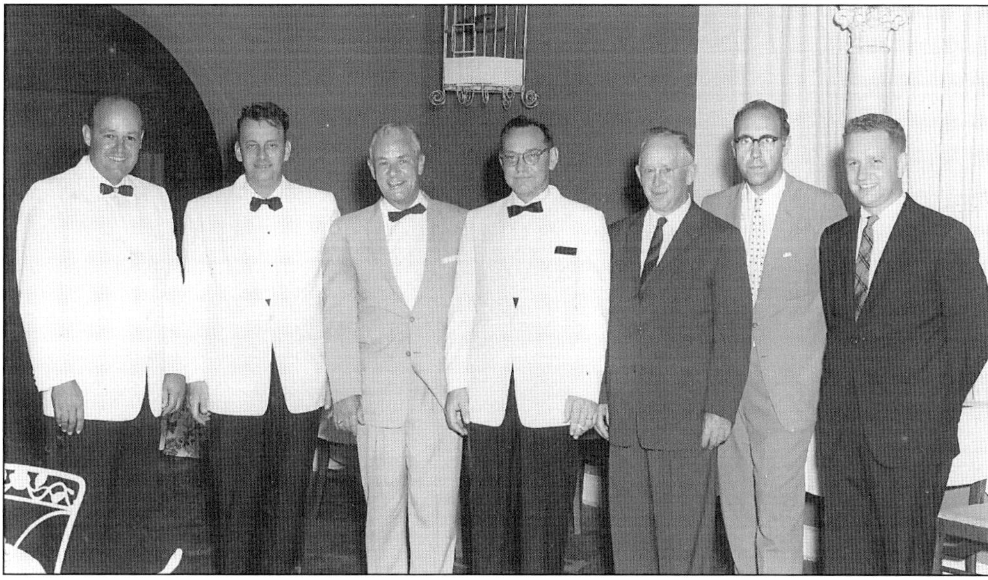

The Engineer's Cotillion provided money to pay for newspaper advertisements and class schedules for the college. Pictured, from left to right, are Jack Hazard, North American Aviation MTF Manager; Jerry Keuper, BEC president and scientist with RCA System Analysis Division; J. Spitznogle, mayor of Melbourne; Harold Dibble, vice president and dean of the college; D'Alton Meyers, Department of Business Administration; George Shaw, Radiation; and Garrett Quick, attorney. (Courtesy of University Publications.)

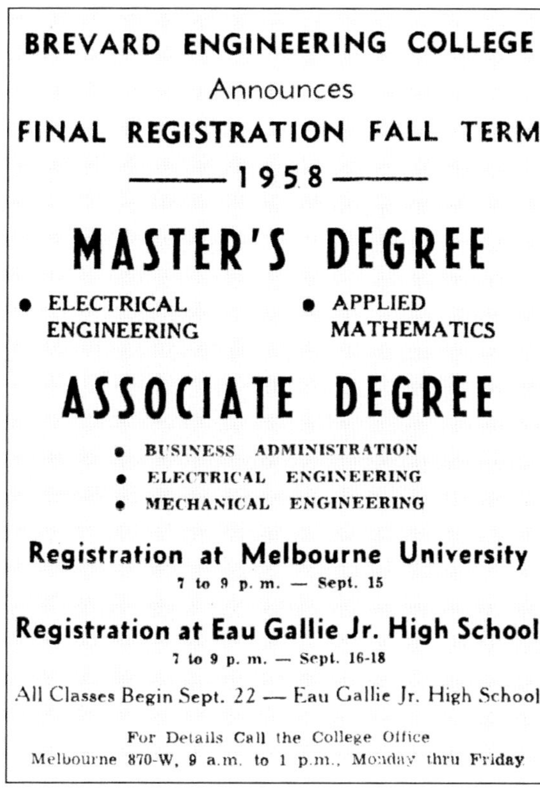

This announcement appeared after the Engineer's Cotillion. One hundred and fifty-four students signed up for classes. There were 148 male and 6 female students and the average age was 33. The University of Melbourne, an off-shoot of the American Homesteading Foundation, allowed Brevard Engineering College to use its building on Country Club Road as its college office. Gertrude Martin served as secretary for both institutions. (Courtesy of Evans Library.)

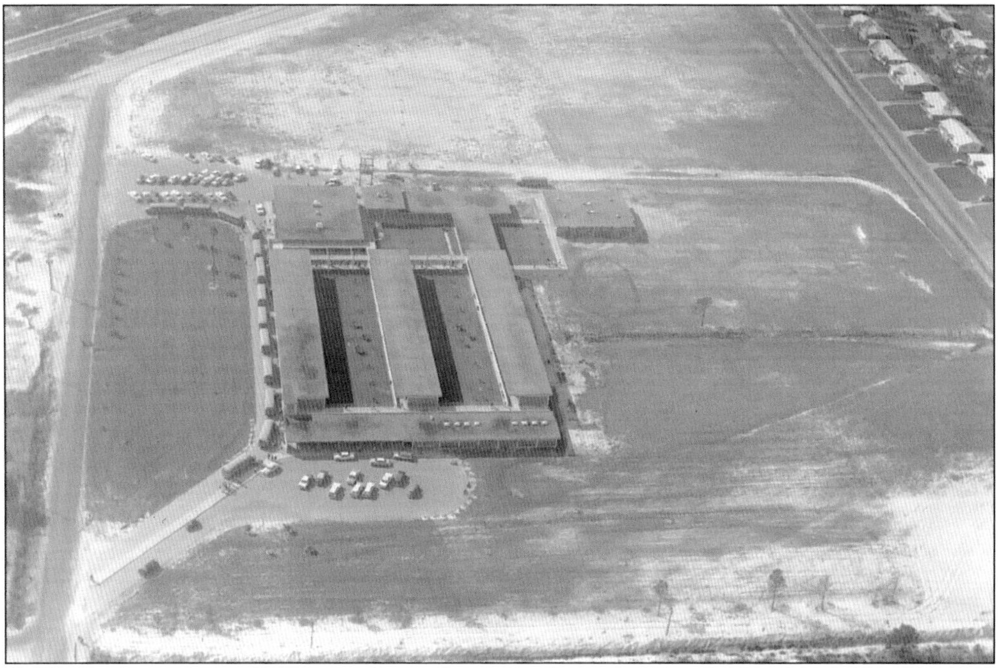

Classes were scheduled from 7 to 10 Monday, Wednesday, and Friday evenings in three rented classrooms at the newly built Eau Gallie Junior High School. Tuition was $35 for one course, $68 for two courses, and $96 for three courses. (Courtesy of Sterling Photo.)

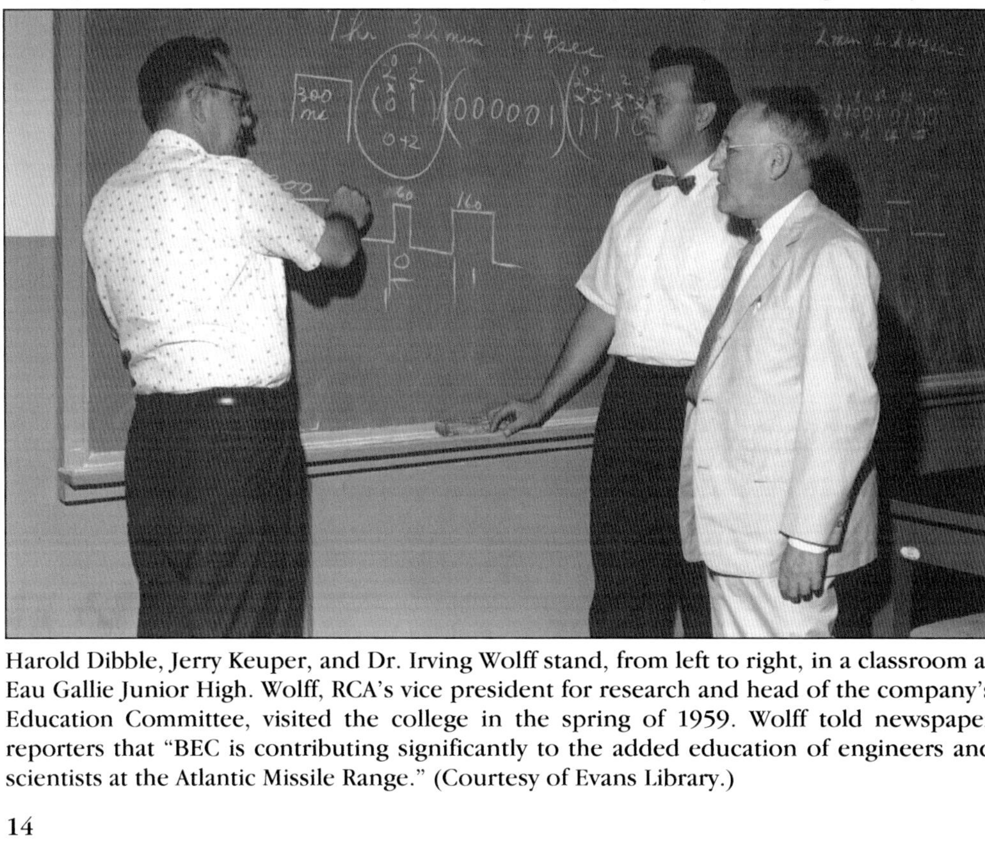

Harold Dibble, Jerry Keuper, and Dr. Irving Wolff stand, from left to right, in a classroom at Eau Gallie Junior High. Wolff, RCA's vice president for research and head of the company's Education Committee, visited the college in the spring of 1959. Wolff told newspaper reporters that "BEC is contributing significantly to the added education of engineers and scientists at the Atlantic Missile Range." (Courtesy of Evans Library.)

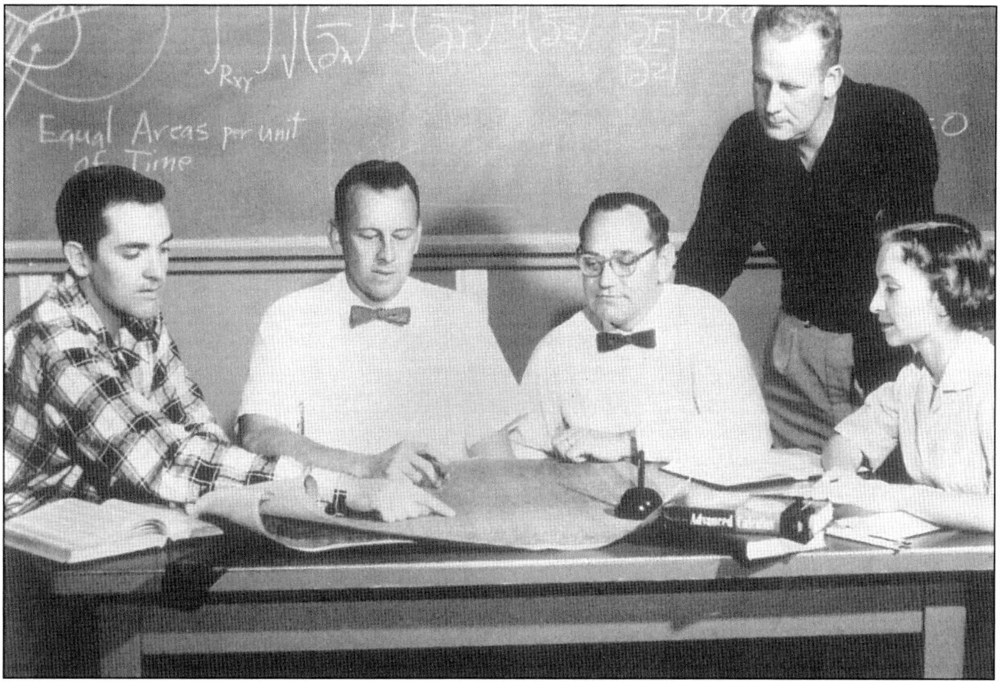

Wolff's endorsement led to RCA's paying for its employees' tuition. Seventy-five RCA scientists and technicians enrolled in BEC's first semester. Pictured here discussing their progress in early 1959 are, from left to right, Reagan DuBose, undergraduate and RCA technician; Jerry Keuper, president; Harold Dibble, dean; Ray Work, graduate student; and Donya Dixon, graduate student and RCA Quality Analysis scientist. (Courtesy of University Publications.)

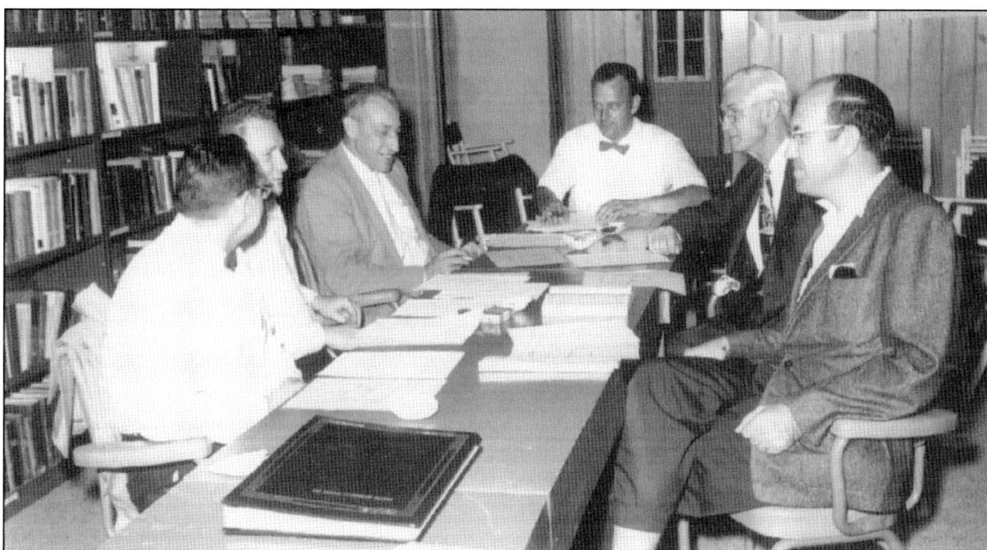

BEC's first board of trustees meeting took place on February 25, 1959, at the college's offices at the University of Melbourne building. Shown here, from left to right, are Harold Dibble, Garrett Quick, Clifford Mattox, Jerry Keuper, Norman Lund, and George Shaw. (Courtesy of Evans Library.)

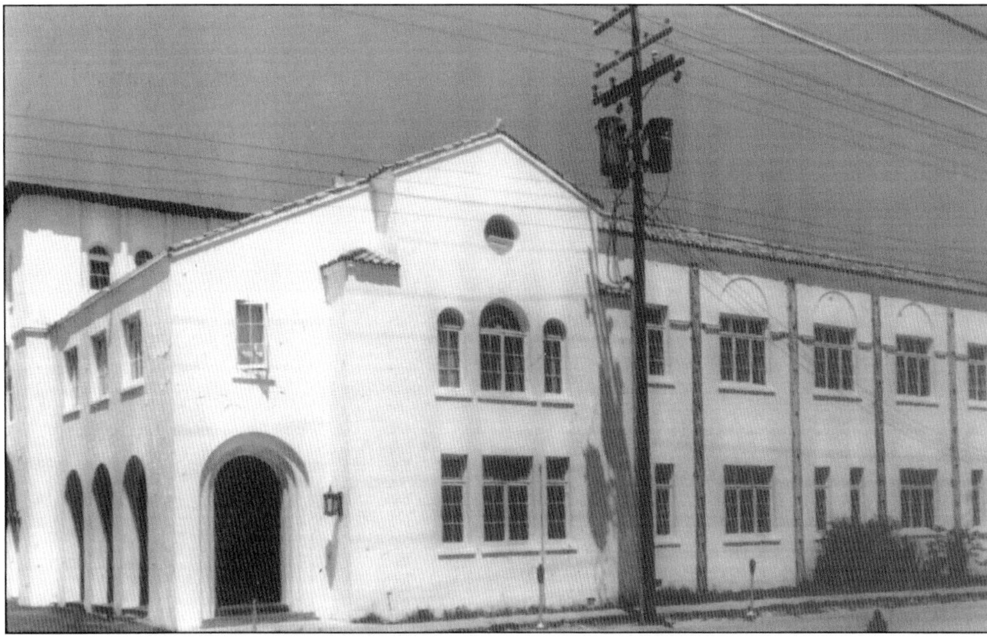

BEC was forced to relocate its classes to the old First Methodist Church Building at Waverly Place in Melbourne in June 1959. In March, BEC's leaders learned that classes would not be allowed in the junior high school after June. County school officials objected to the presence of African-American students at BEC. (Courtesy of Jerry Keuper.)

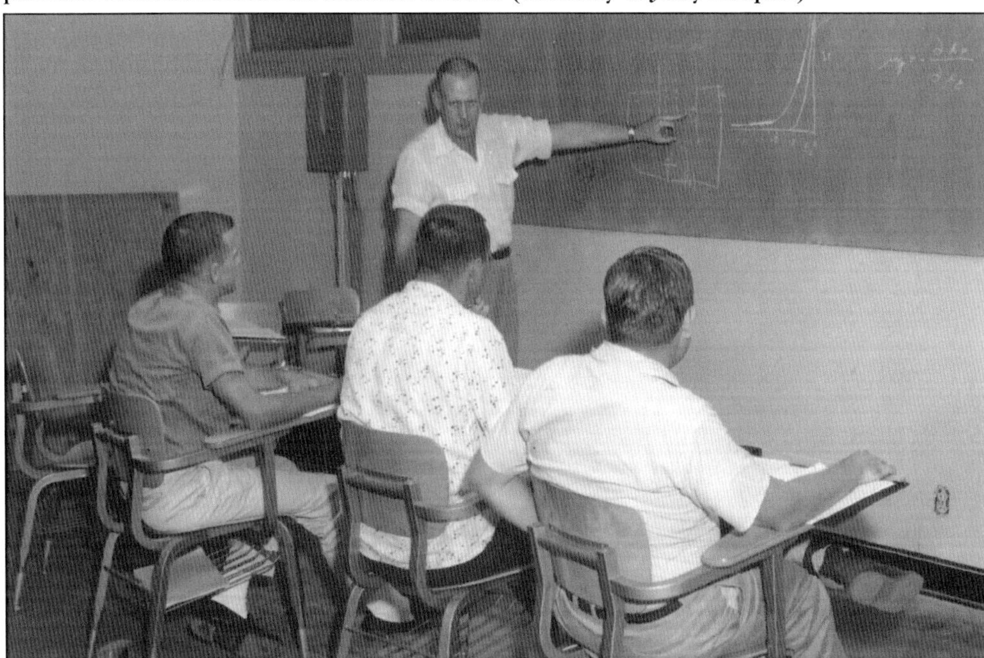

Ray Work is shown teaching an undergraduate electrical engineering course at the First Methodist Church Building in 1959. In addition to continuing his graduate studies, Work taught undergraduate courses and served as BEC's unofficial registrar at RCA. During its second year, BEC attracted more than 500 students. (Courtesy of Evans Library.)

In 1960, BEC moved to its third home at Radiation, Inc.'s Building No. 1 located adjacent to Melbourne's airport. Founded in 1950, Radiation, now known as Harris Corporation, was the brainchild of Homer Denius and George Shaw. Shaw, a BEC trustee, and Denius were committed to the university. Denius promised to donate 1,000 shares of Radiation stock to the school if it could find a permanent home in Melbourne. (Courtesy of University Publications.)

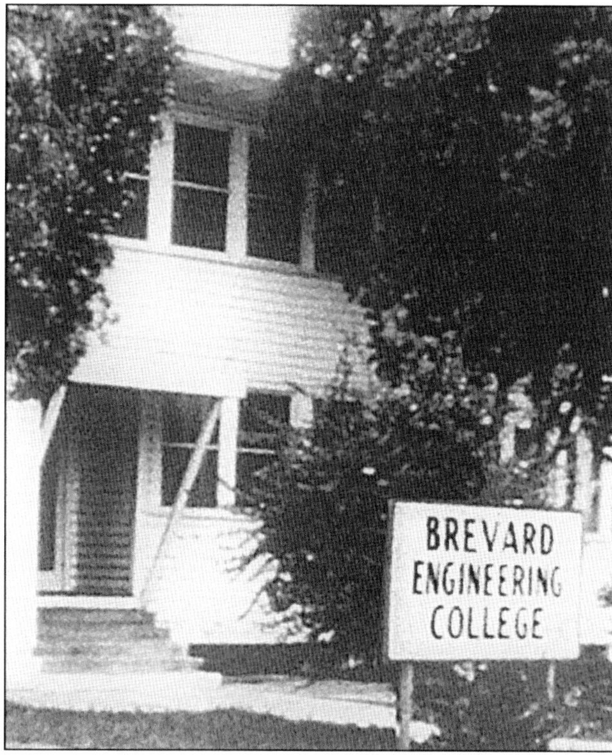

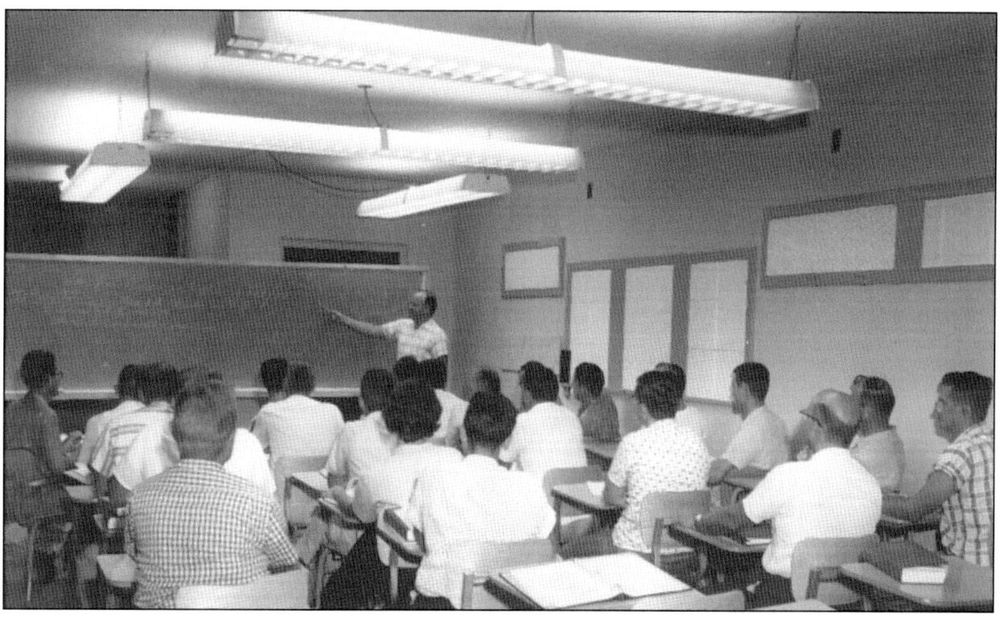

In July 1960, BEC expanded its curriculum to include the humanities. Day classes were added for the missilemen who worked nights. Here, Dr. Robert Lindemann, BEC's first chairman of the humanities program, is teaching an American history course in the Radiation building. Proposed courses included the history of science, English composition and literature, music, art appreciation, economics, logic, psychology, and philosophy. (Courtesy of Evans Library.)

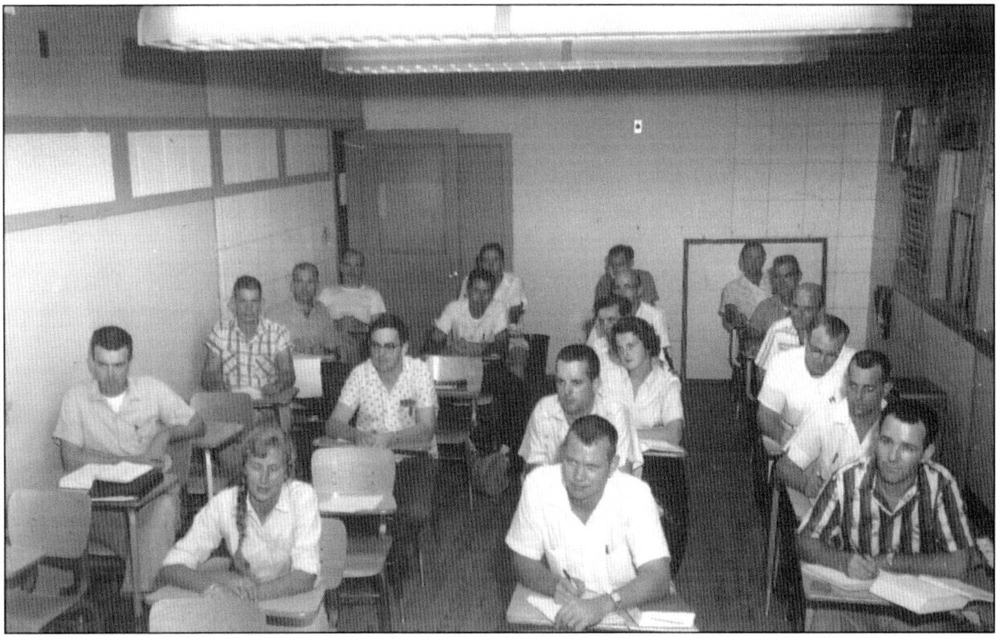

Shown here is an unidentified class meeting in 1960 at the Radiation building. The majority of the students were male and the average age of the student body remained in the mid-thirties. With two women students, this class was exceptional. (Courtesy of Evans Library.)

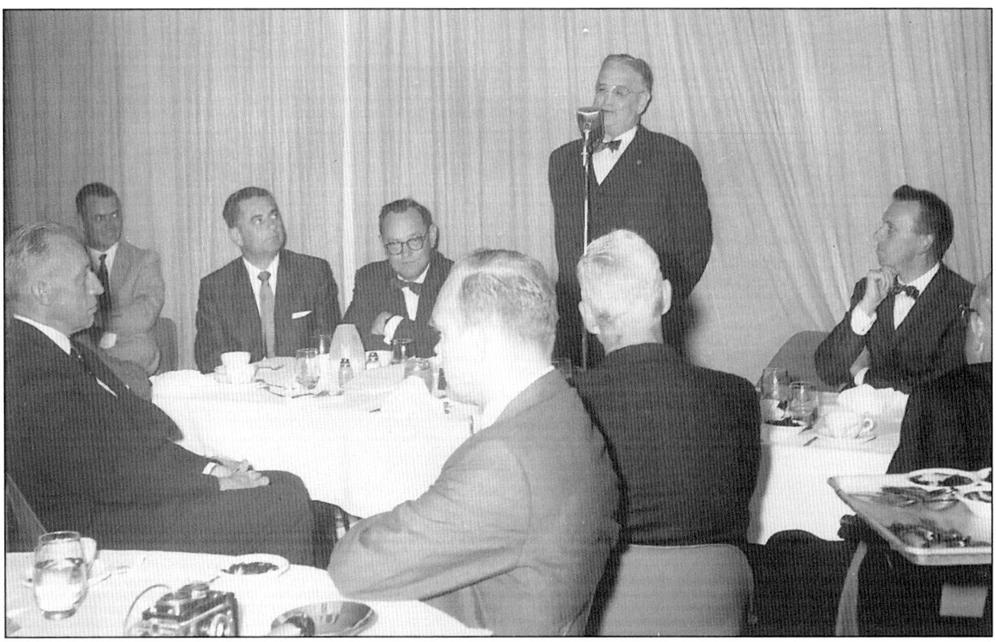

Massachusetts Institute of Technology professor and inertial guidance expert Charles Draper is addressing the November 1960 BEC faculty dinner at the Bahama Beach Club. Clifford Mattox, BEC trustee and president of the central Florida section of the Institute of Radio Engineers, and Jerry Keuper invited Draper to make the presentation in a Lecture Series on Space Technology held at Patrick Air Force Base. (Courtesy of University Publications.)

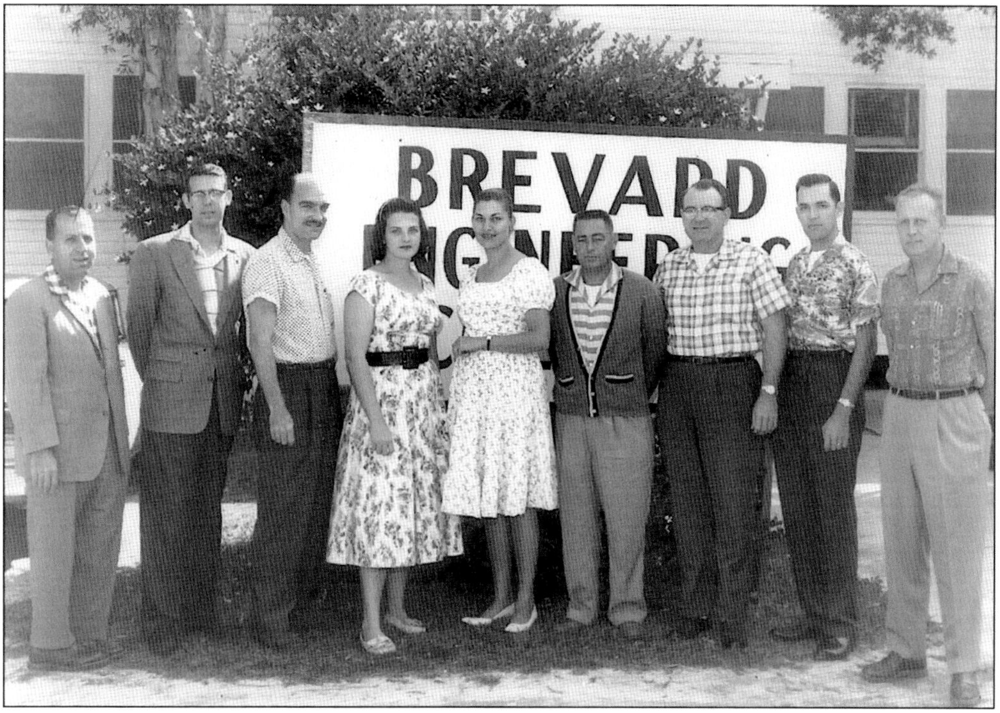

Pictured here is BEC's newly elected student body president George Sirbola, left. Sirbola, a missileman working for Pan American Range Planning, is shown here with student government officers, from left to right, John Alexander, Tom Farr, Margaret Connerly, Ann Benton, Tom Rutherford, Russ Connerly, Reagan DuBose, and faculty advisor Ray Work. (Courtesy of Jerry Keuper.)

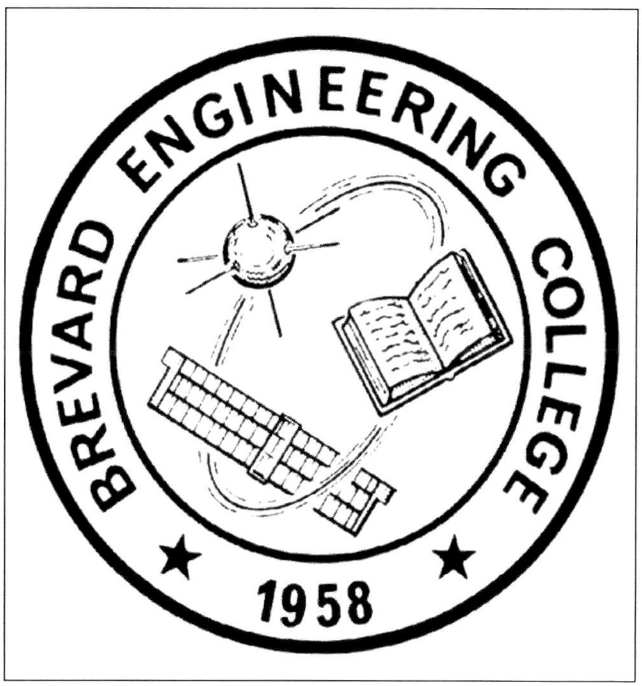

Students formed a committee in November 1960 to develop school spirit and encourage activities. The effort was spear-headed by John Dixon, George Sirbola, Margaret Connerly, Thomas Gibbons, Russ Connelly, Thomas Farr, and James Irvin. The students sponsored a contest to design a school seal. George Sirbola won the contest with a design showing a slide-rule, satellite, and book surrounded by the school's name. (Courtesy of Evans Library.)

Brevard Engineering College

Balance Sheet for Fiscal Year Ending August 31, 1960

* * * * * *

ASSETS

	Aug. 31, 1959	Aug. 31, 1960
CASH:		
Petty Cash	$ 2.50	$ 32.27
General Fund	1,740.91	3,016.42
Computer Fund	——	1,709.28
Reserve Fund	35.24	2,091.30
ACCOUNTS RECEIVABLE:		
Students	323.89	273.20 (1)
Other	297.91	341.50
BOOK STORE INVENTORY:		
(At Cost)	——	1,046.96
FURNITURE & EQUIPMENT		Note (2)
TOTAL ASSETS	$2,400.45	$8,510.93

LIABILITIES

	Aug. 31, 1959	Aug. 31, 1960
ACCOUNTS PAYABLE:		
Book Store	——	$ 615.03
Trade	$ 274.65	1,010.56
Students	34.50	——
TUITION & MATRICULATION FEES COLLECTED IN ADVANCE	——	140.00
TOTAL LIABILITIES	$2,400.45	$8,510.93
RESERVES:		
For Contingencies	——	$ 856.64
Unappropriated Reserve	$2,091.30	5,888.70
TOTAL LIABILITIES & RESERVES	$2,400.45	$8,510.93

* * * * * *

SUMMARY OF INCOME & EXPENSES

September 1, 1959 to August 31, 1960

* * * * * *

INCOME:

Tuition & Matriculation Fees	$50,608.96
Gifts	1,725.50
Book Store Income (Gross)	4,221.13
Computer Income (Gross)	5,020.37
Interest Income	28.93
West Palm Beach Ext.	6,000.00
Sale of Equipment & Supplies	266.46
Miscellaneous Income	362.20
TOTAL INCOME	$68,233.55

EXPENSES:

Faculty Salaries	$38,306.78
Office Salaries	1,925.20
Book Store Salaries	50.00
Computer Salaries	816.90
Miscellaneous Salaries	190.25
Rent & Maintenance	3,578.82
Utilities & Postage	1,746.56
Officee Supplies & Expenses	869.52
Computer Supplies & Expenses	100.85
Computer Rental	2,834.70
Books, Supplies & Exp. (Book Store)	3,501.02
Catalogue & Announcements	1,505.53
Advertising & Publicity	708.55
Administration Expense	393.94
Travel	292.58
Freight & Moving	355.11
B.E.C. Scholarships	358.00
Student Functions & Graduation	80.56
Bad Debt & Uncollectibles Expense	1,020.29
Miscellaneous	198.36
Furniture, Fixtures & Equipment	2,711.74
Library Additions & Subscriptions	211.88
Florida State Sales Tax	1.32
Dues & Society Memberships	387.00
West Palm Beach Ext. — Transportation, Books & Expenses	1,640.29
West Palm Beach Ext. — Rent	250.00
Reserves Expense	400.00
TOTAL EXPENSES	$64,436.15

* * * * * *

BEC was unique in its openness. The college published its 1960 Balance Sheet. Tuition provided 74% of the school's income. Faculty salaries were the largest single expense, accounting for 59% of the budget. Rent, maintenance, utilities, and postage accounted for 8% of the budget, while scholarships represented .5% of total expenditures. (Courtesy of Evans Library.)

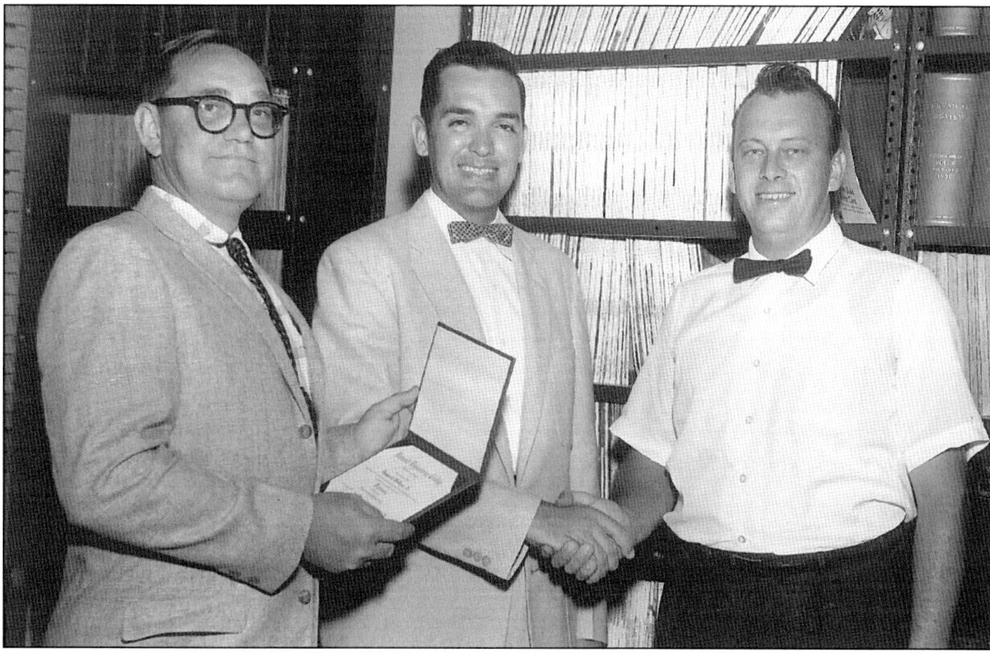

Harold Dibble (left) and Jerry Keuper (right) congratulate Reagan DuBose (center) on being BEC's first graduate. DuBose, a program engineer at Pan American at the Missile Test Center, received an associate degree in engineering in 1961. He completed his course work in five semesters. DuBose, married and the father of four, eventually went on to earn his B.S. in electrical engineering from BEC. (Courtesy of University Publications.)

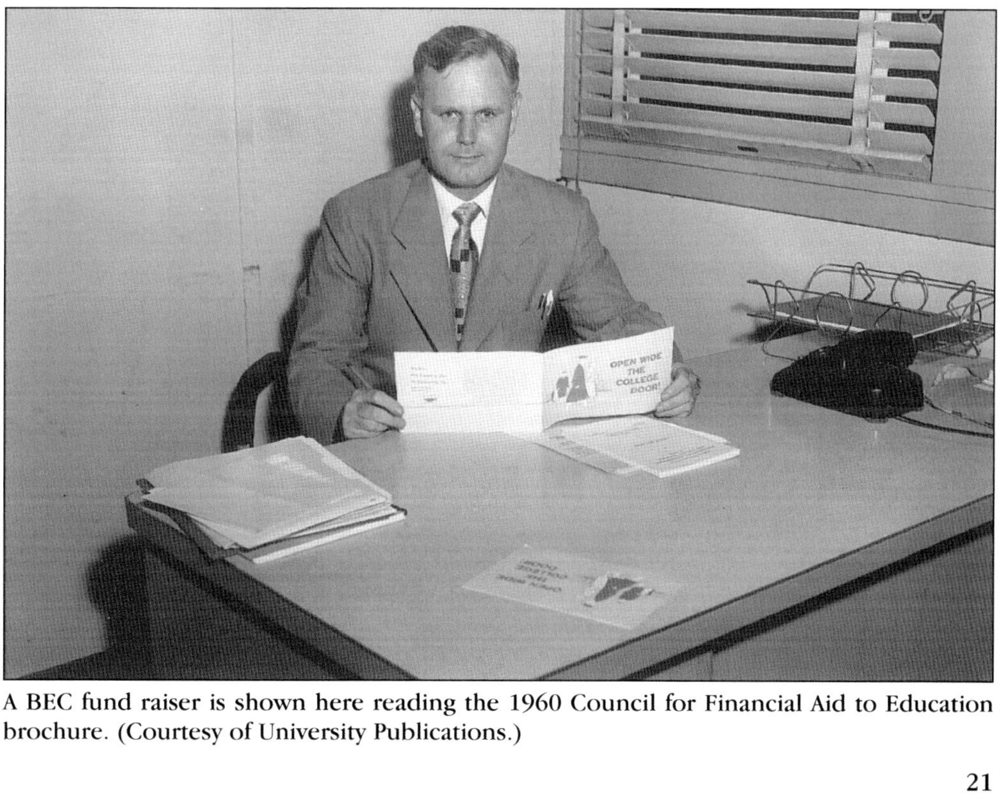

A BEC fund raiser is shown here reading the 1960 Council for Financial Aid to Education brochure. (Courtesy of University Publications.)

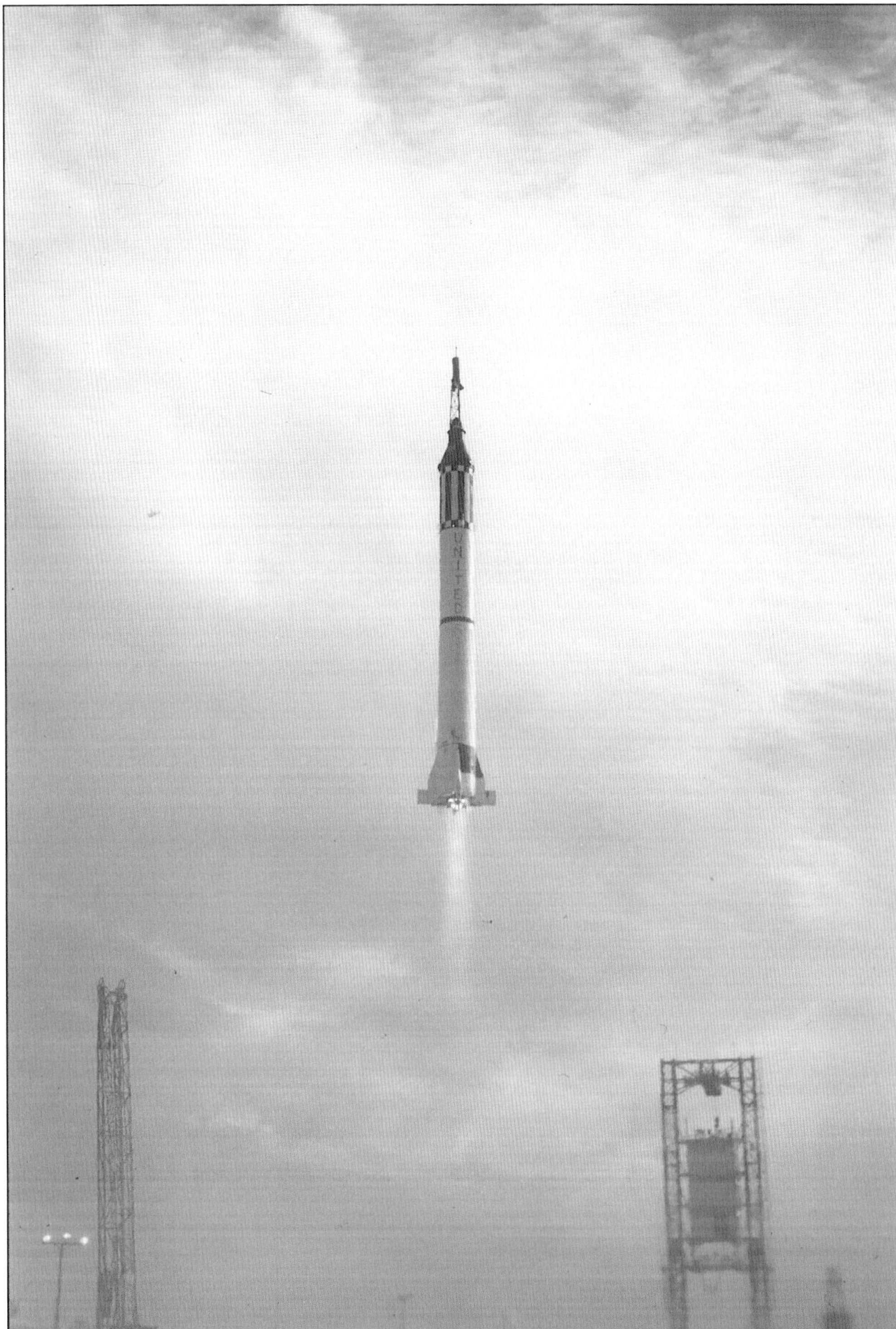

Pictured here is the Mercury Redstone 4 rocket lifting astronaut Gus Grissom into sub-orbital flight on July 21, 1961. (Courtesy of Air Force Space and Missile Museum.)

Two

Launching the University: 1961–1966

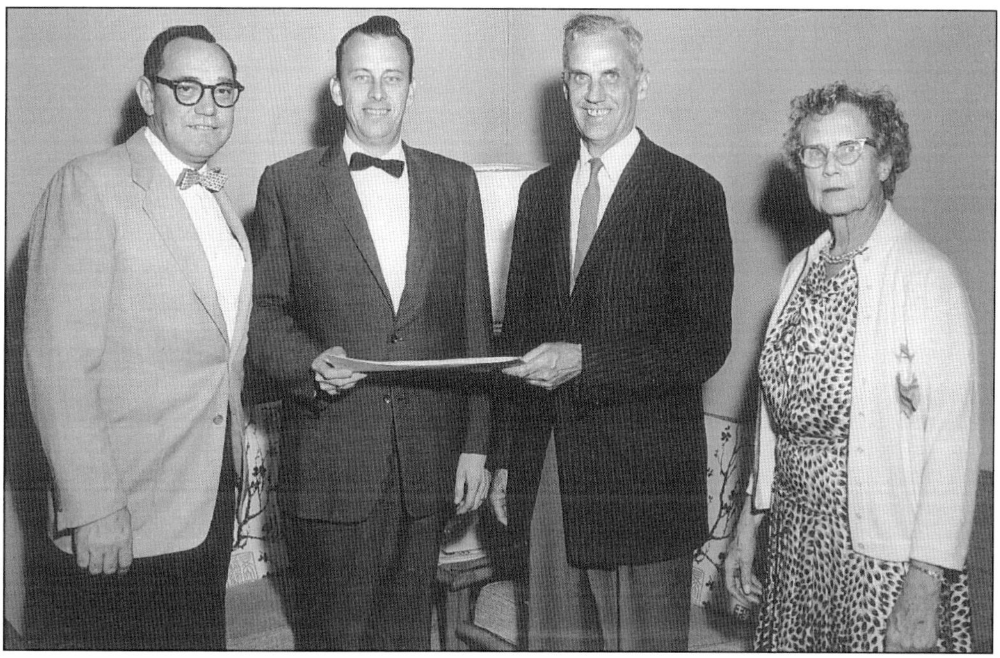

Brevard Engineering College's search for a permanent campus ended in January 1961. Pictured above, from left to right, are Harold Dibble and Jerry Keuper (representing BEC) and Hubert Normille and Elizabeth Wood (representing the University of Melbourne) examining documents transferring control of the University of Melbourne's 40-acre Country Club Road campus to BEC. BEC's first trustee, Clifford Mattox, was instrumental in making the agreement a reality. (Courtesy of University Publications.)

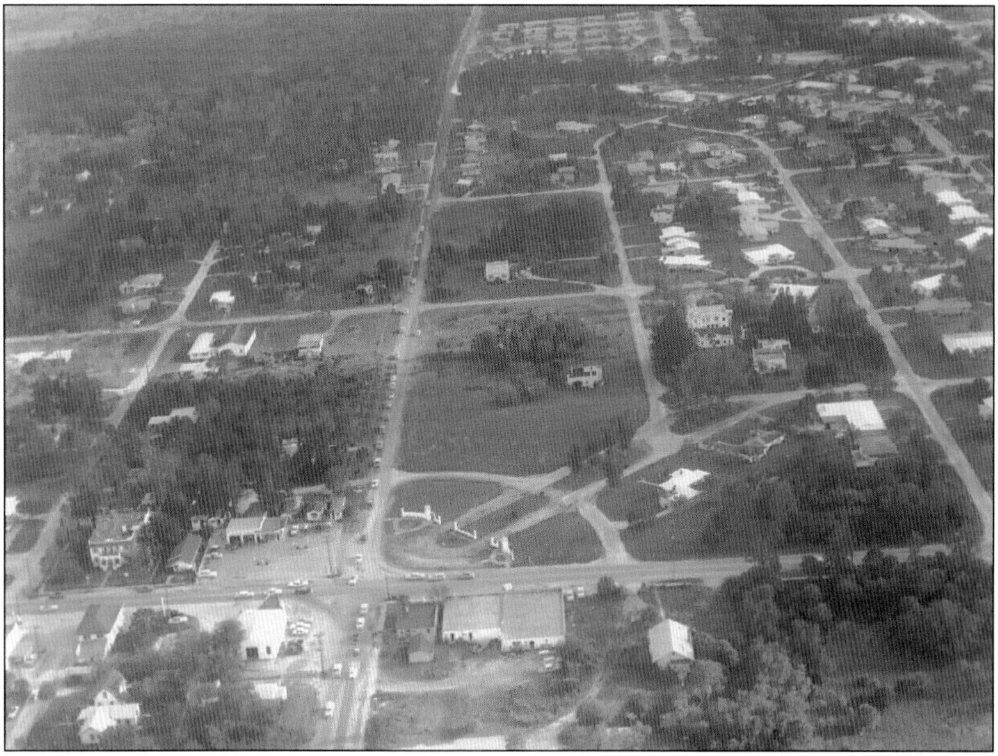

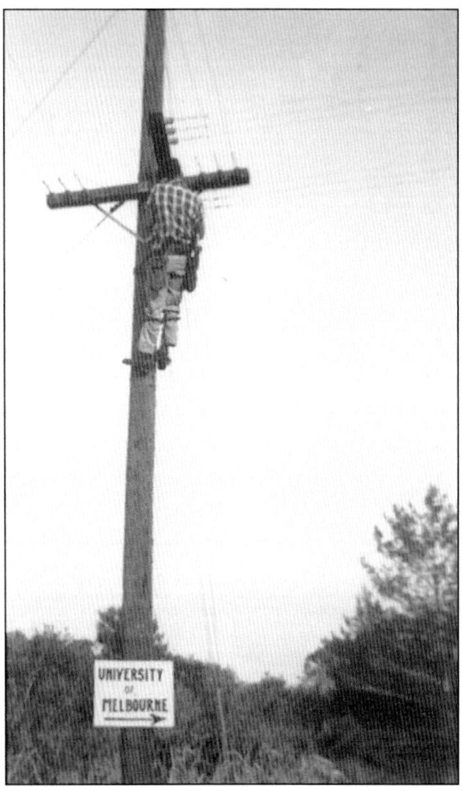

This photograph shows the intersection of Babcock and New Haven (State Road 192) shortly before the agreement between BEC and the University of Melbourne. The future home of BEC was located in the upper right hand corner of the photograph. (Courtesy of Sterling Photo.)

Pictured here in 1955 is a sign on Country Club Road identifying the University of Melbourne. The University of Melbourne was launched in January 1954 when a progressively minded group of individuals led by Ralph Borosodi decided to open a "small graduate school . . . a real university with a universal point of view, not simply a western one." Local businessman V.C. Brownlie donated 40 acres on Country Club Road for the campus. (Courtesy of Evans Library.)

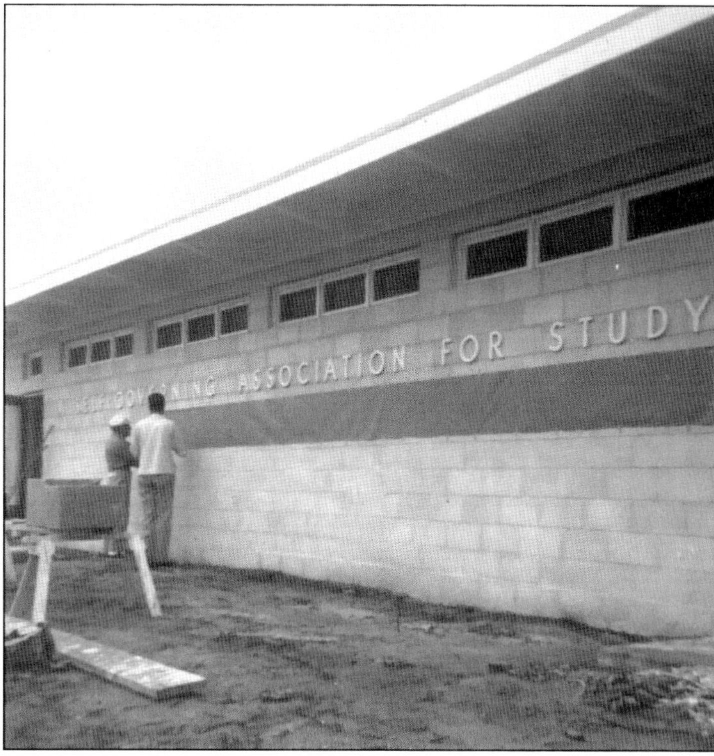

Work was completed on the University of Melbourne's single building in December 1955. Workers are shown inscribing the University's ambitious objectives on the structure's façade. The inscription read "Self-Governing Association for Study/ Institution for the Guidance of People/ Agency for Resolving the Problems of Civilization." Virginia Wood and Clare Borosodi contributed $25,000 apiece to the university's trust fund. (Courtesy of Evans Library.)

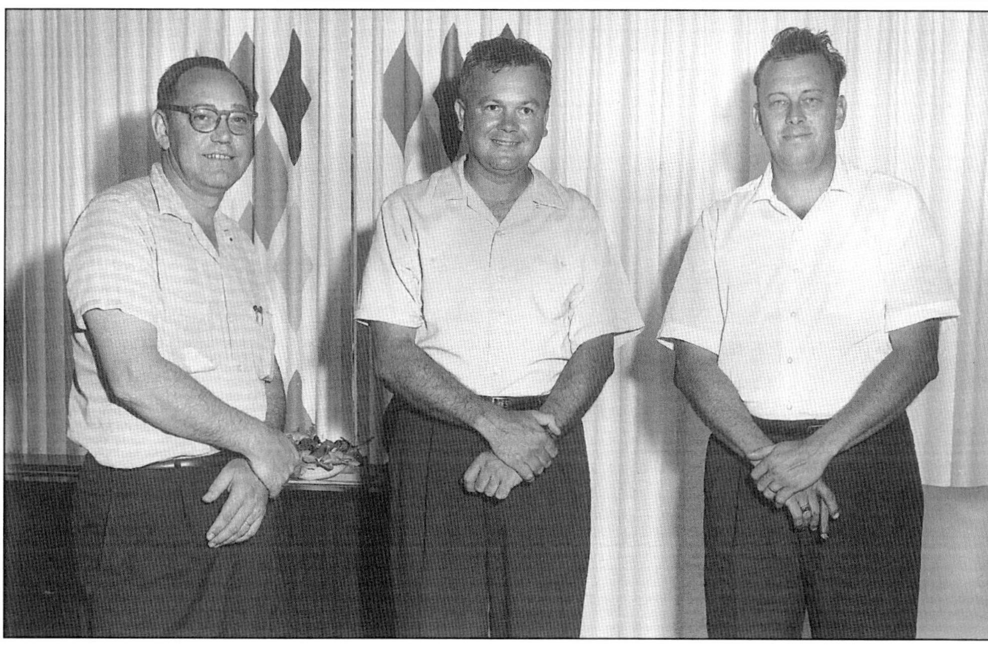

Ground was broken on BEC's first building in April 1961. Homer Denius (shown here standing between Harold Dibble and Jerry Keuper), president of Radiation, Inc., donated 1,000 shares of Radiation stock to help finance the administration building and first classrooms. The 9,285-square-foot structure cost $75,000. The first buildings were patterned after the Quad at Massachusetts Institute of Technology. (Courtesy of University Publications.)

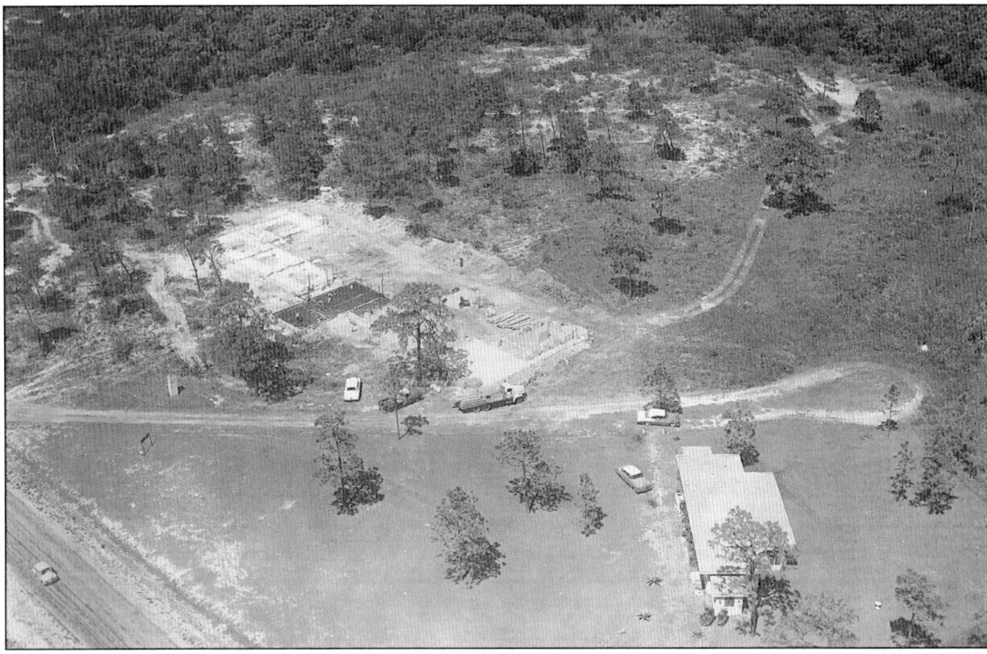

This 1961 aerial photograph shows the Country Club campus at the start of construction. The University of Melbourne's single building is located in the foreground. The concrete pad for the first building was poured in early April. Note that Country Club Road (lower left) was unpaved. (Courtesy of Sterling Photo.)

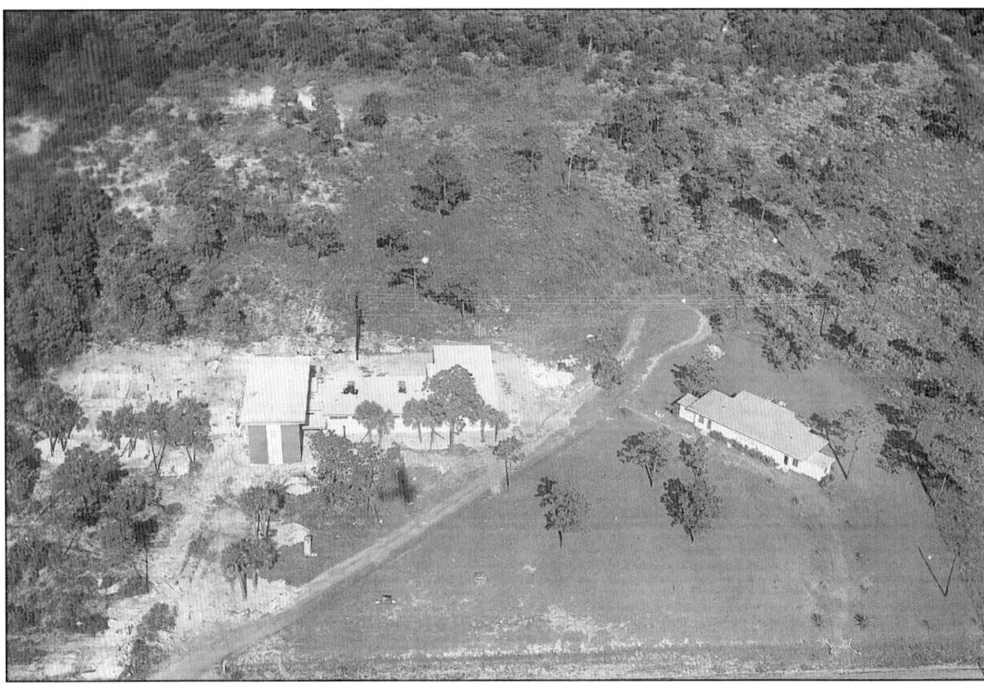

The Administration Building (later named the John Miller Building) and the first classrooms were completed in May 1961. The first classes met in the new facilities in June. (Courtesy of Sterling Photo.)

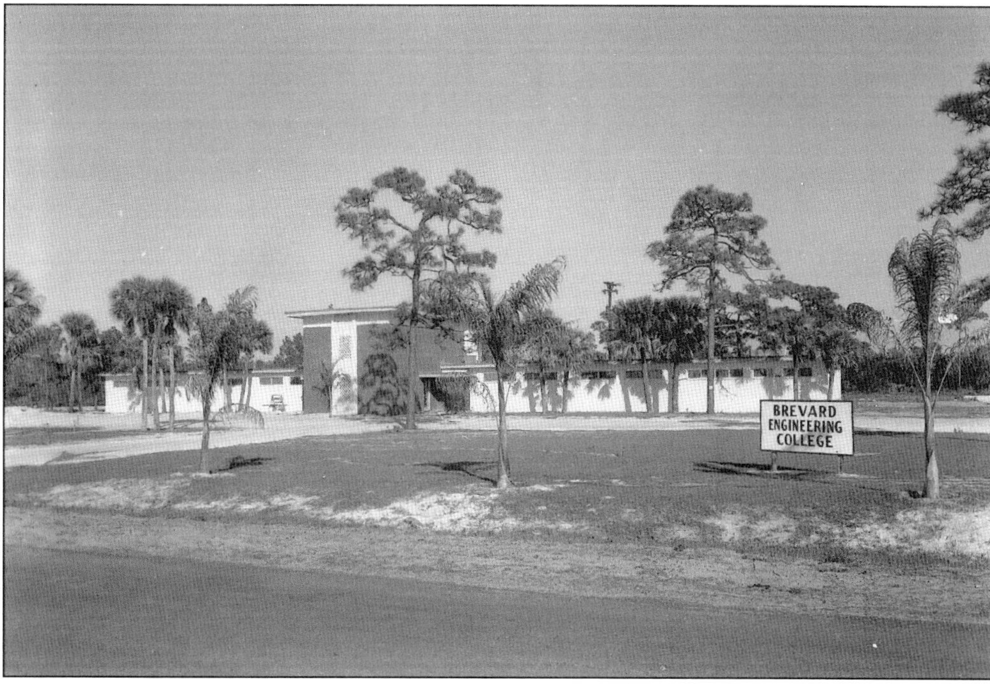

New classrooms (left side of photograph) were added in the fall of 1961 to complete the first part of BEC's Quad. (Courtesy of Sterling Photo.)

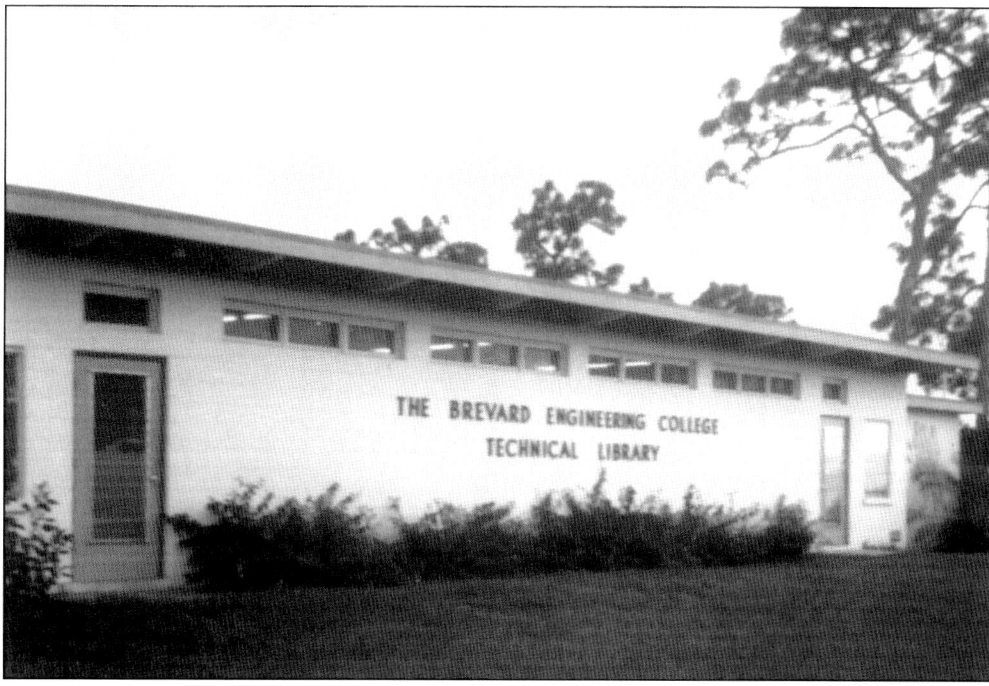

The old University of Melbourne meeting hall metamorphosed into BEC's Technical Library and bookstore in 1962. The library was open Monday through Friday evenings 7 to 10 and Saturday mornings between 9 and 12. The door to the library is on the right side of the picture. (Courtesy of Sterling Photo.)

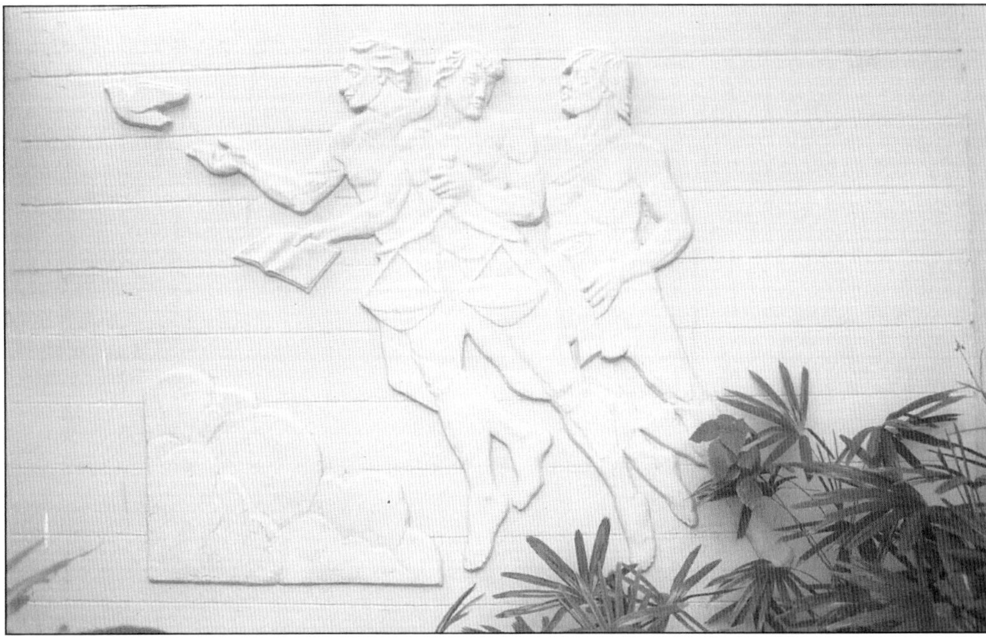

Pictured here is one of the two ornamental decorations that adorned the old University of Melbourne building. This bas-relief (west end of BEC Technical Library) shows three individuals representing different races, rising above the world. One holds a dove of peace, the second carries a pair of scales and a scroll, while the third bears a book. The relief embodies the idealism of University of Melbourne's founders. (Courtesy of University Publications.)

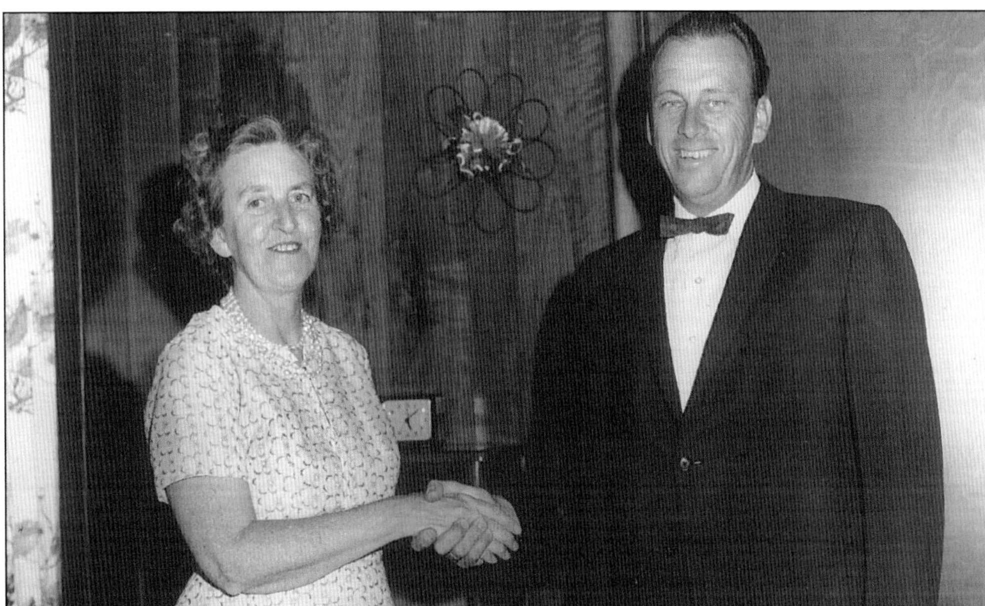

On May 10, 1961, Eileen Hall, formerly a senior librarian at Georgia State, became BEC's first librarian. Hall served as director of the library until 1972 when she was succeeded by Llewellyn L. Henson. (Courtesy of University Publications.)

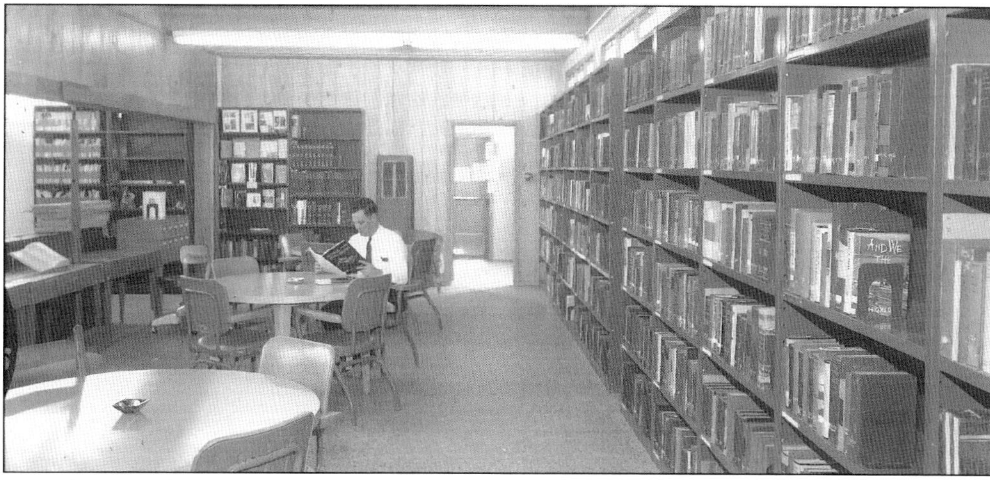

A student studies in the Technical Library. Most of BEC's library collection came from donations. Irving Wolff, director of RCA's Princeton Labs, arranged for periodicals such as the *Physical Review* to be sent to the college. Volunteers did the cataloguing and provided library services. Later, this building was used as the school's first student union and dining facility. (Courtesy of Sterling Photo.)

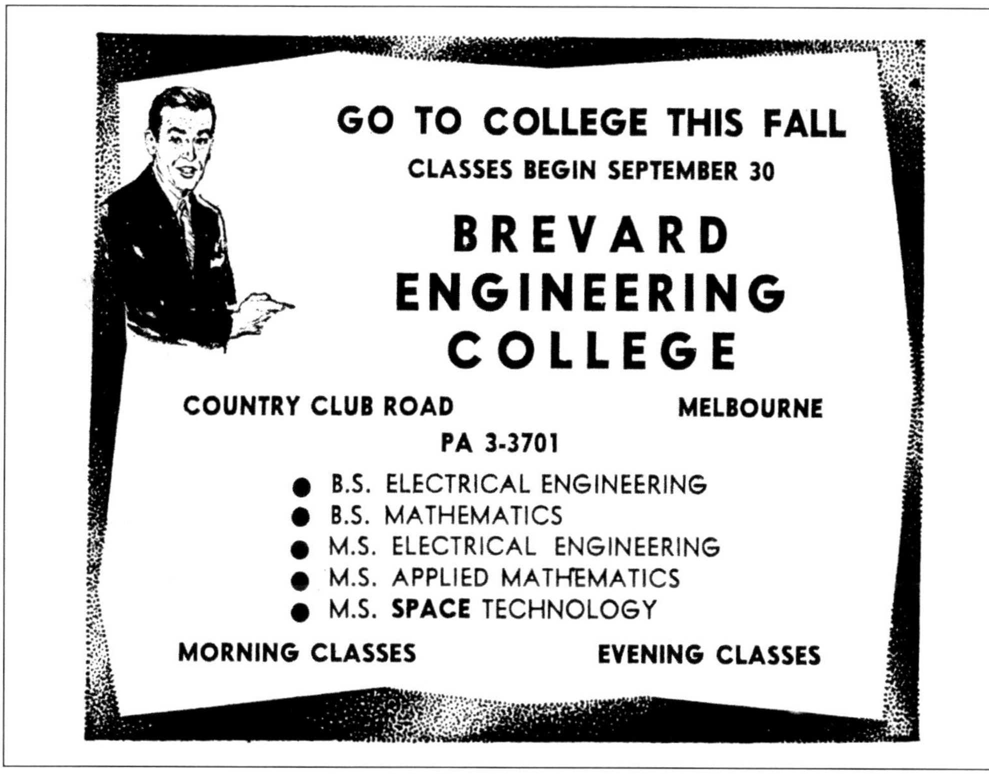

This advertisement appeared in the summer of 1961. During its early years, BEC was on the semester system. The majority of classes met in the evening. Day classes were offered to accommodate night shift workers. A reporter on the *Miami Herald* wrote "Just the name of the degree offered by the school—master of science in space technology—fires the imagination." (Courtesy of Evans Library.)

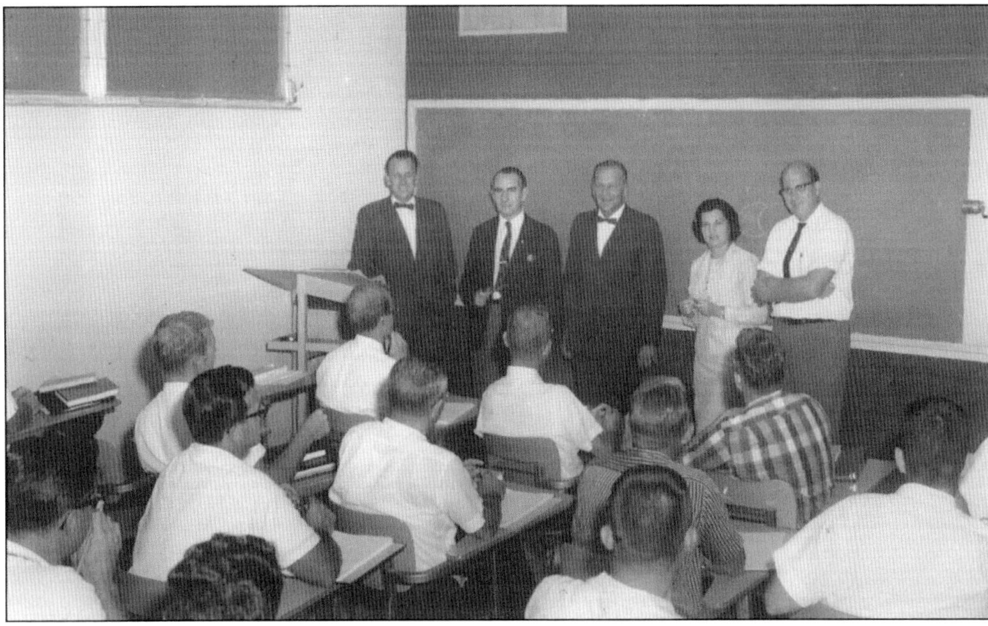

From left to right, Jerry Keuper (president), Charles Cummings (dean), and faculty members Ray Work, Norma Lindemann, and Bob Lindemann are shown here meeting with students in the new Quad classrooms. Harold Dibble, BEC's first dean, left the college in 1961. (Courtesy of Evans Library.)

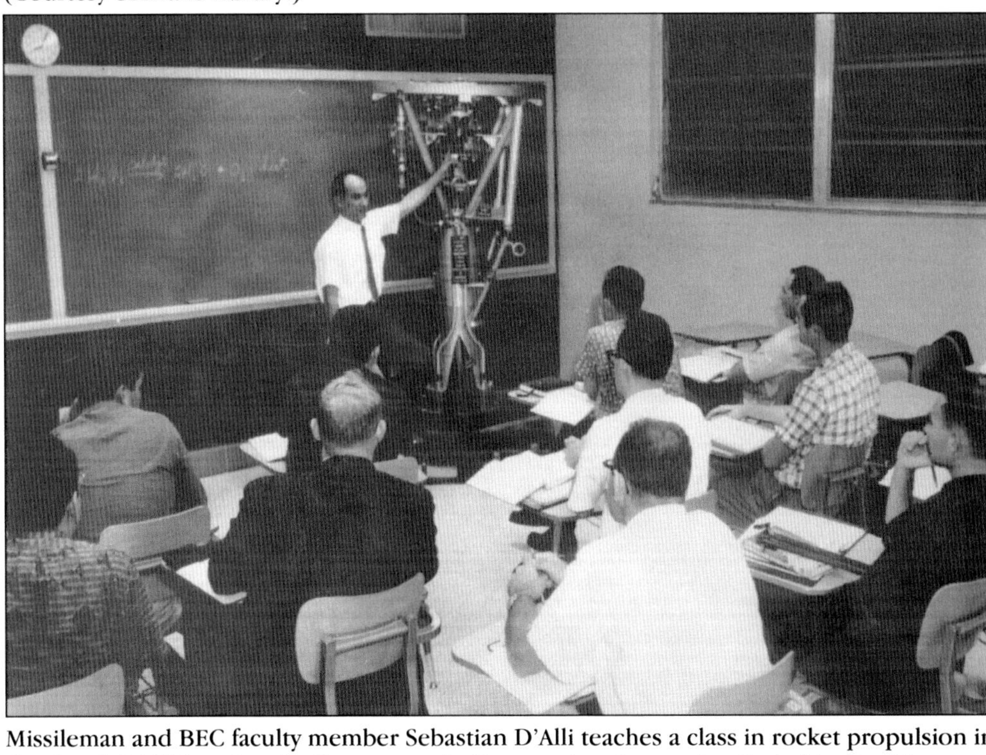

Missileman and BEC faculty member Sebastian D'Alli teaches a class in rocket propulsion in the Quad. D'Alli is using the first stage of a Vanguard rocket engine fueled by liquid oxygen and kerosene to illustrate his remarks. (Courtesy of Evans Library.)

BEC held its first commencement exercises at Melbourne High School in June 1961. Pictured here is Mercury Astronaut Gus Grissom receiving an honorary doctorate in space science from Jerry Keuper at BEC's second commencement in 1962. Tom Putnam, the school's first full-time employee, is adjusting Grissom's hood. Tom Adams, Florida's secretary of state, received an honorary doctorate in space education at the ceremony. (Courtesy of University Publications.)

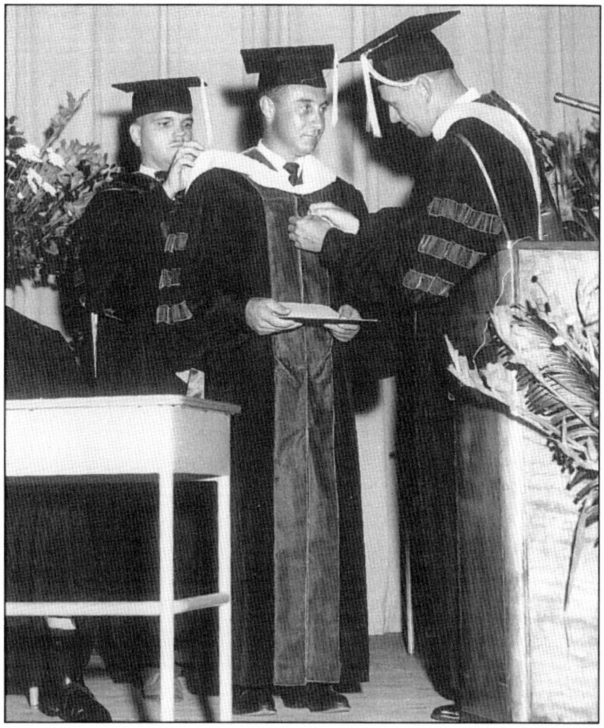

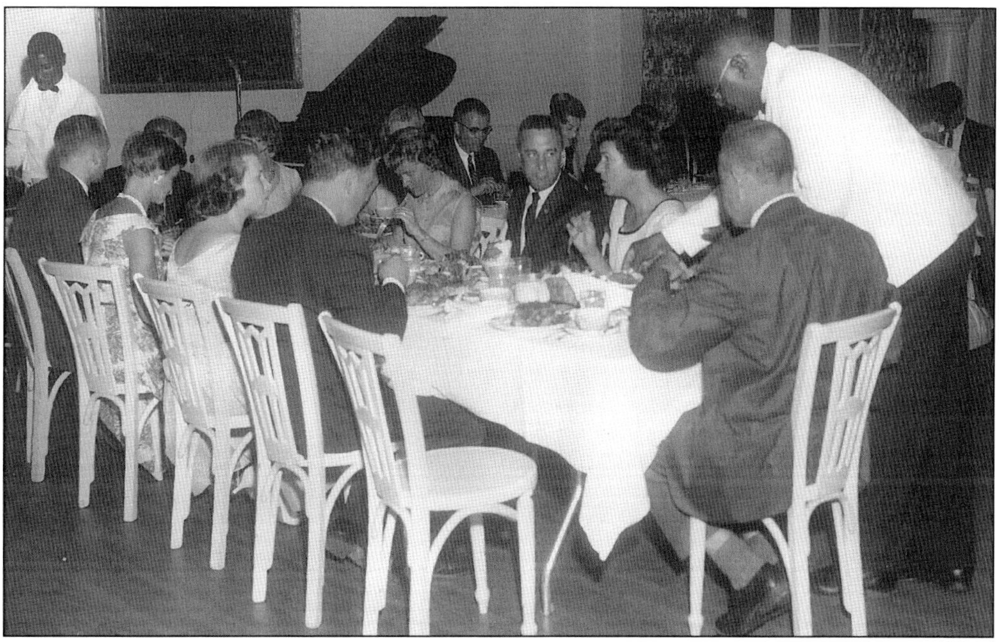

Tom Adams (facing camera in front of the piano) and Gus Grissom (right from Adams) were the guests of honor at the graduation dinner. Adams used his commencement address to rally support for the proposed merger of BEC with the Disciples of Christ and the formation of Florida Christian University at the Country Club Campus. "This is a space age institution in the truest sense," Adams boomed. "It is geared to the future." (Courtesy of University Publications.)

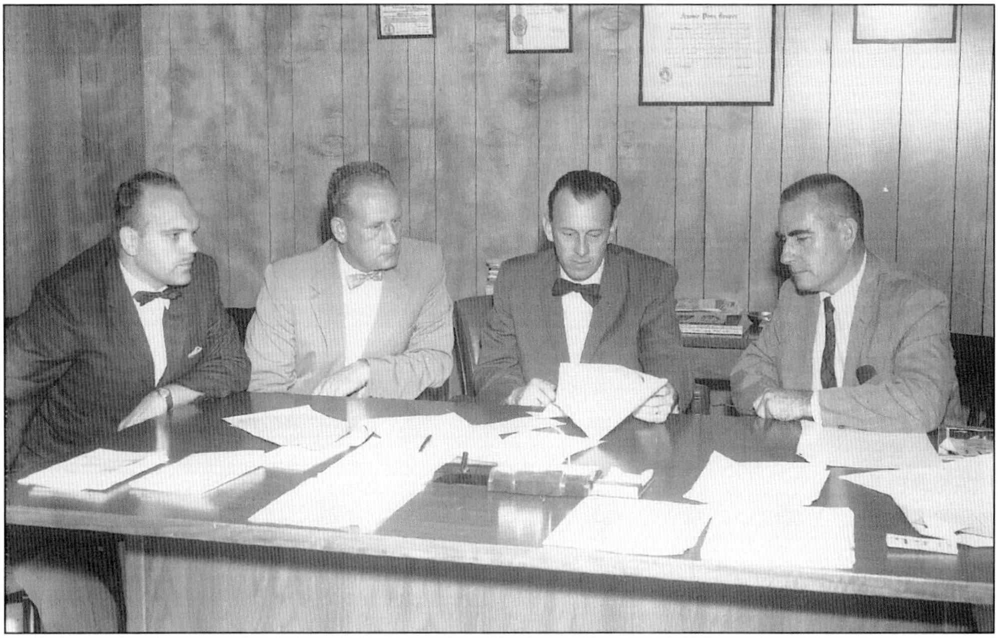

In 1962, BEC launched its first ($250,000) fund-raising campaign in conjunction with the proposed creation of Florida Christian University. Pictured here, from left to right, discussing the capital campaign, are Tom Putnam, university registrar; Ray Work, faculty member and head of the electrical engineering program; Jerry Keuper, president; and Charles Cummings, dean of the graduate school. (Courtesy of Sterling Photo.)

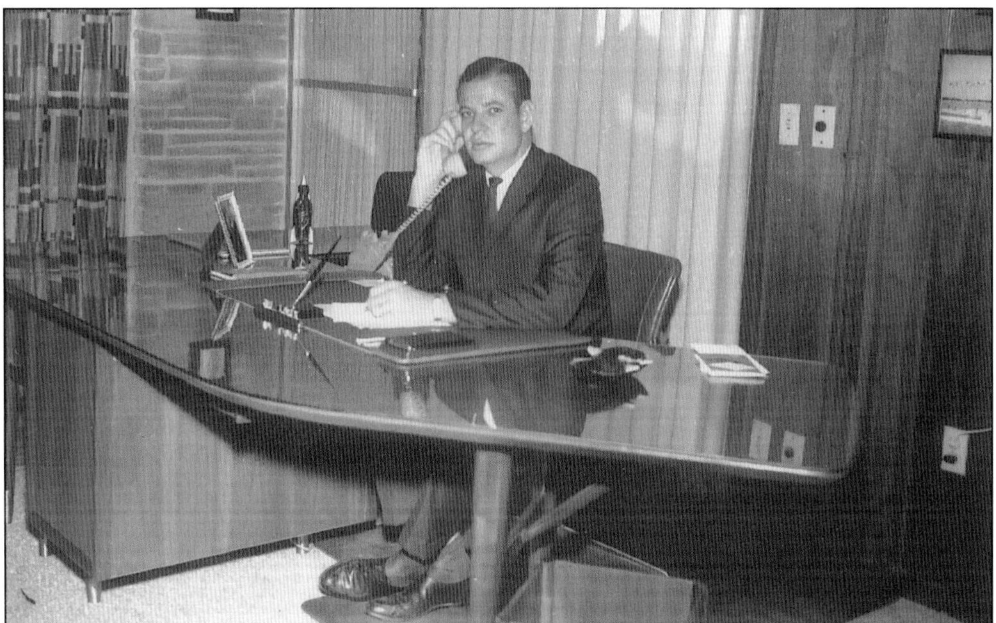

Jim Lyons, manager of Jim Rathmann Chevrolet and president of the Melbourne Chamber of Commerce, rallied support for the BEC in the community. Lyons declared, "This university is the greatest thing we've done since we got that first satellite up." (Courtesy of Sterling Photo.)

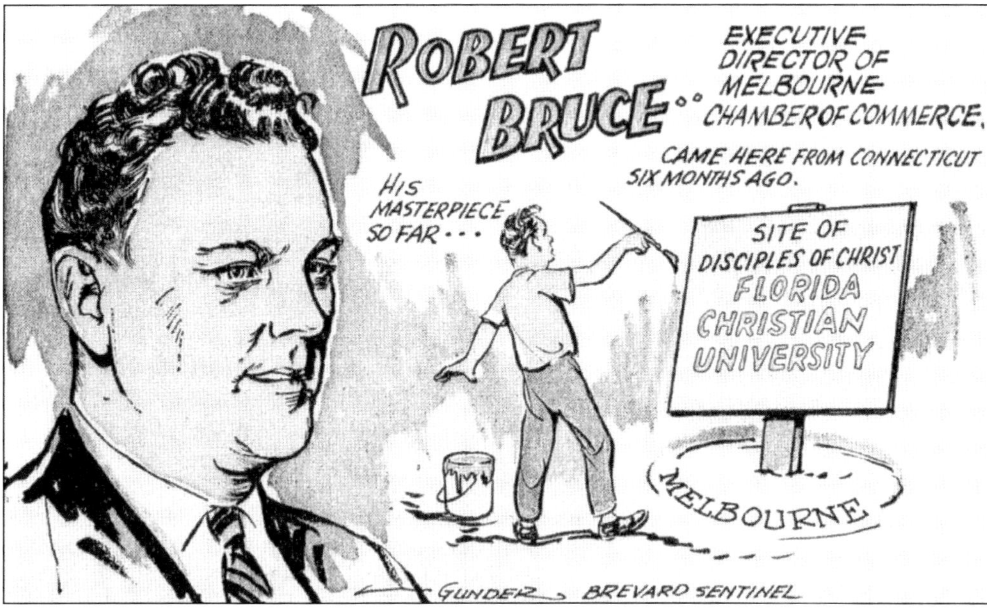

Robert Bruce, executive director of Melbourne's Chamber of Commerce, was instrumental in bringing about a merger agreement between the Disciples of Christ and BEC. Bruce and Keuper envisioned that BEC's engineering and science courses would form the core of the new institution. The new university would include a specialized space institute of technology, a traditional liberal arts college, and a seminary. The plan for the proposed Florida Christian University, however, collapsed in 1963. (Courtesy of *Orlando Sentinel*.)

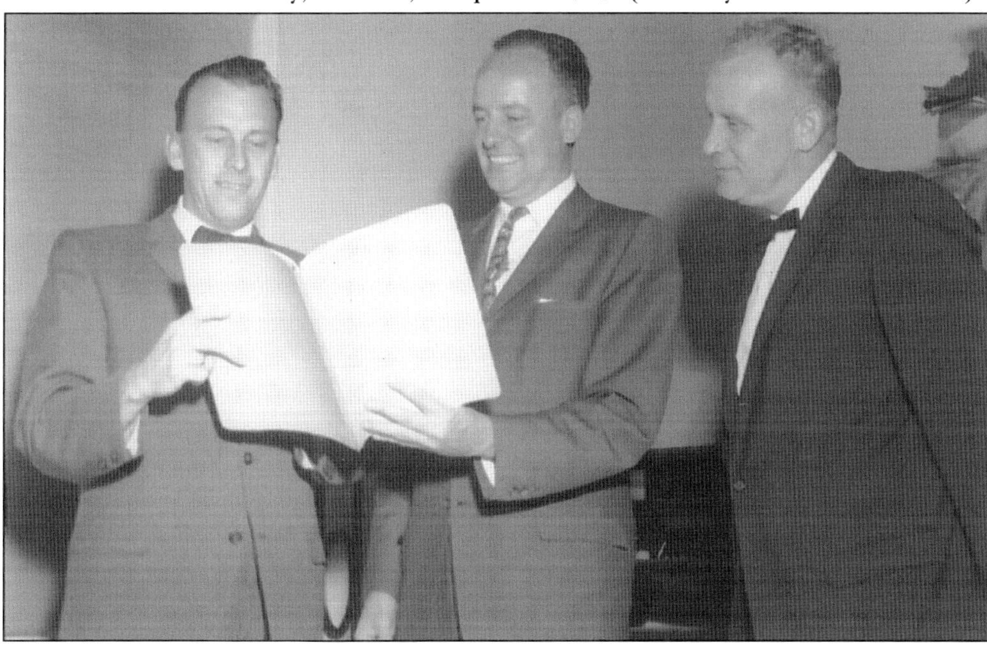

Ben Rogers (center), president of Jacksonville University, is pictured in April 1962 handing Jerry Keuper the documents granting BEC membership in the Independent Colleges and Universities of Florida (ICUF). In the fall of 1962, Keuper resigned his position with RCA and became the college's full-time president. (Courtesy of Sterling Photo.)

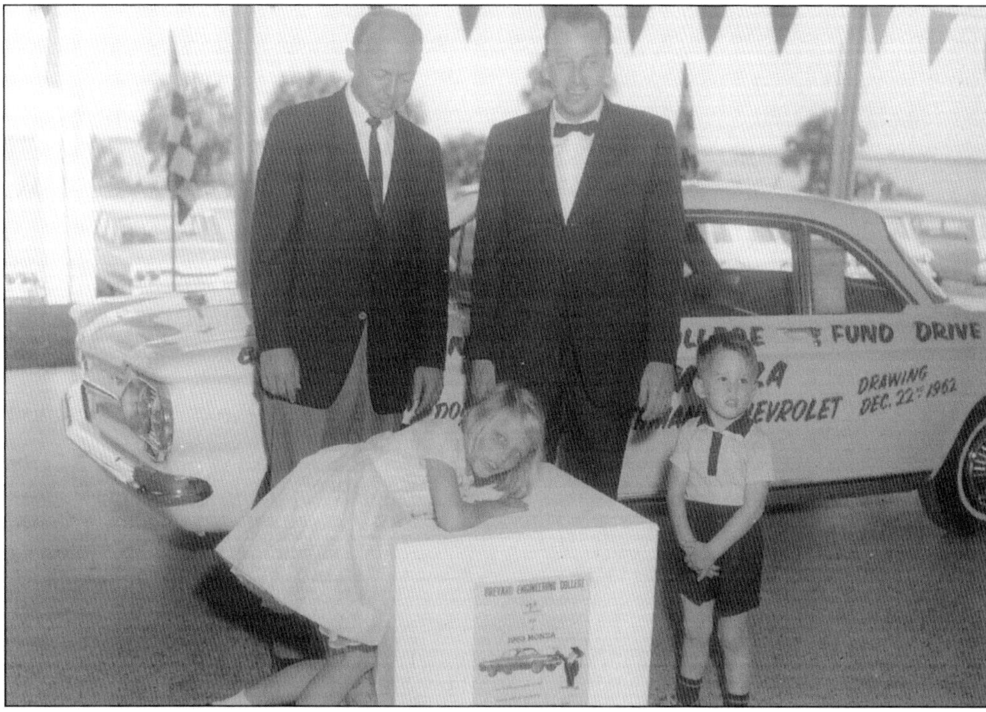

Jim Rathmann, Indianapolis 500 winner and Melbourne businessman, donated a 1963 Monza to the college. The car was raffled off to raise money for the college's first fund-raising drive. All donations were used to improve student facilities. Keuper's daughter, Melanie, is drawing the winning ticket with her brother Philip. (Courtesy of Jerry Keuper.)

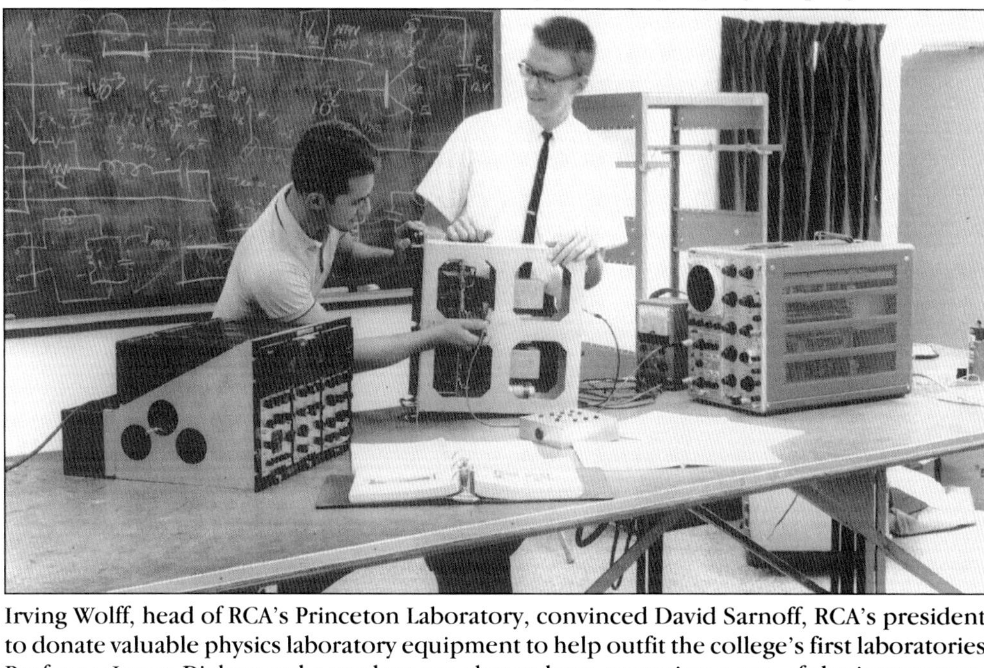

Irving Wolff, head of RCA's Princeton Laboratory, convinced David Sarnoff, RCA's president, to donate valuable physics laboratory equipment to help outfit the college's first laboratories. Professor James Biglow and a student are shown here preparing some of the instruments. (Courtesy of Evans Library.)

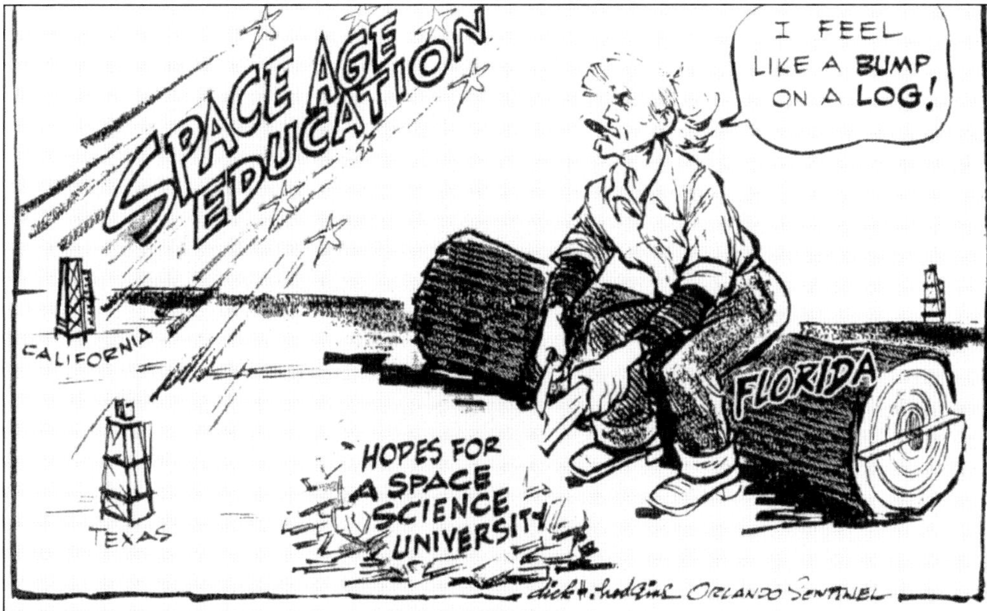

"Let's Stop Whittling"

In 1962–1963, there was a heated debate over the future of the state's role in post-secondary education. Tom Adams, Florida's secretary of state, championed the cause of private education. Others called for the creation of a publicly funded "space university." The *Orlando Sentinel's* Brevard edition chronicled the debate in its editorial cartoons. This 1963 cartoon expresses the *Sentinel's* frustration at the character of the debate. Tom Adams, ever BEC's advocate, maintained that the state should not waste money on second-rate programs. BEC, he declared, "is truly an institution with its feet planted firmly in the ground and its eyes riveted on the heavens." (Courtesy of *Orlando Sentinel*.)

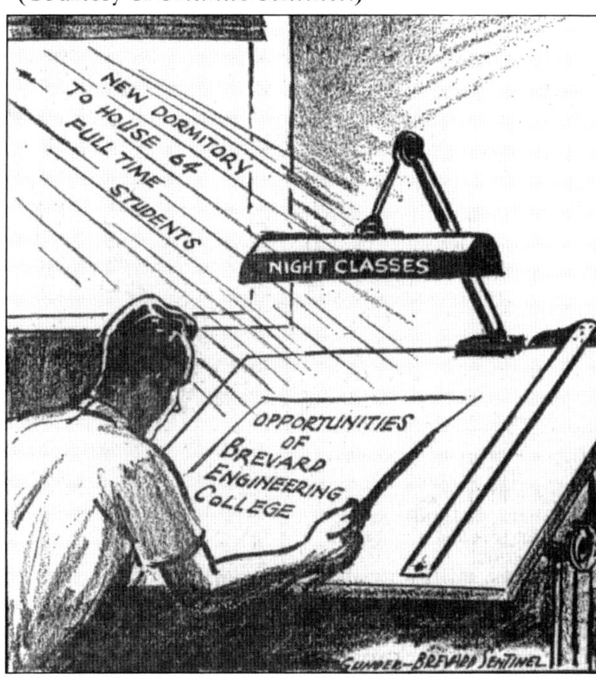

By 1964, politicians had decided to open a publicly financed university in Orlando (Florida Technological University, which eventually became University of Central Florida). While real estate developers argued where the new campus should be located, BEC continued to make great progress. This cartoon depicts some of the notable developments. (Courtesy of *Orlando Sentinel*.)

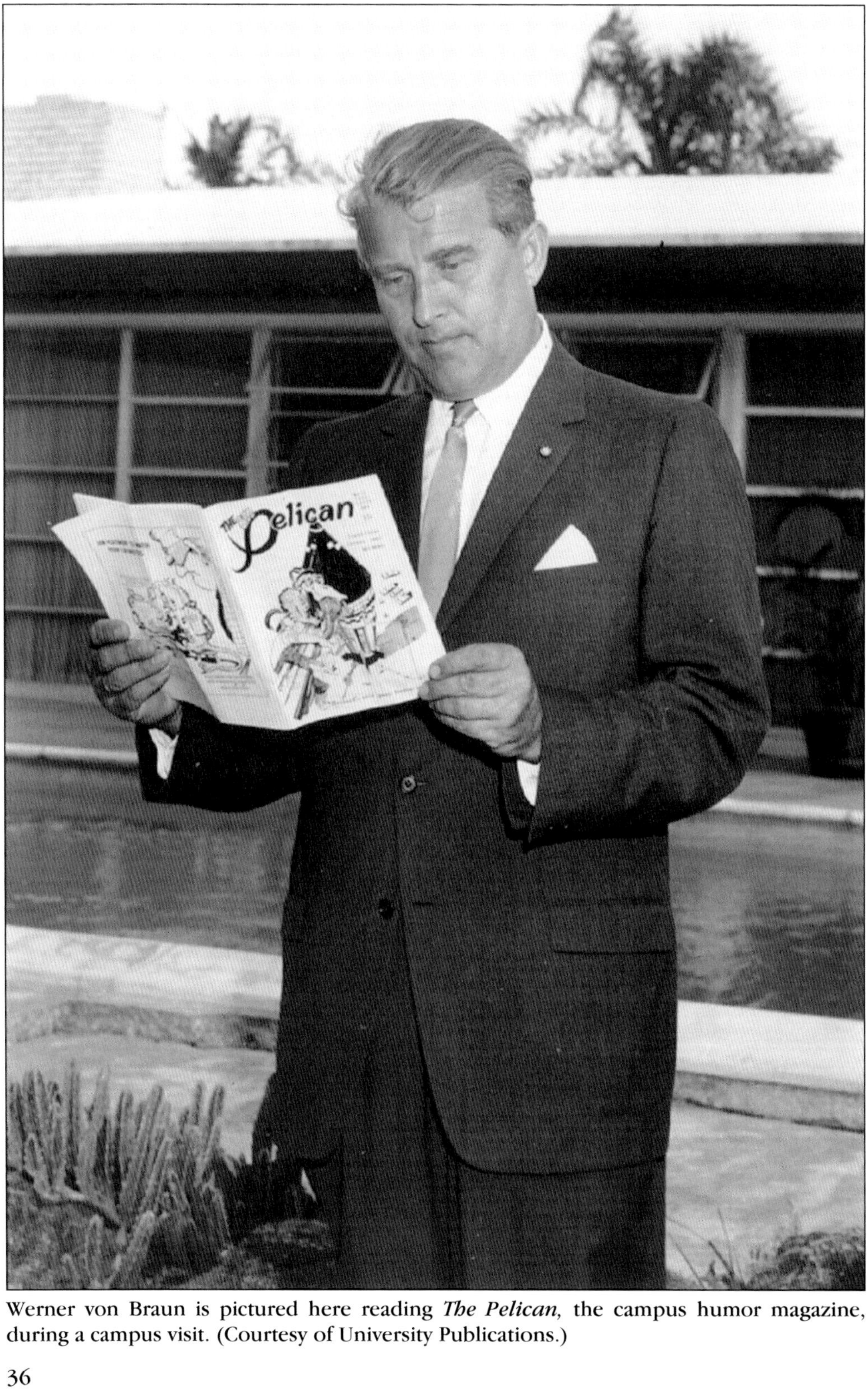

Werner von Braun is pictured here reading *The Pelican,* the campus humor magazine, during a campus visit. (Courtesy of University Publications.)

The Pelican was a student effort to create a magazine that fused *Mad Magazine*, *Playboy*, and *Esquire*. Student editor Dave Crepeau explained that the humor was technical but "we hope that the day will come when missile workers encountering difficulty will kiss it off as 'we have another pelican!'" (Courtesy of Eugene Fetner.)

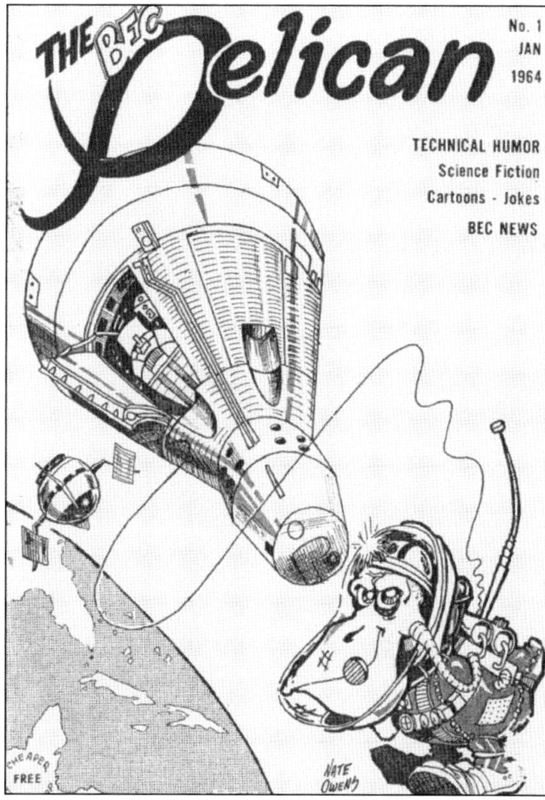

From left to right, Tom Adams, Werner von Braun, and Jerry Keuper are pictured here at a barbecue held in June 1964 before commencement. Behind the scenes, Adams used his position as Florida's secretary of state to secure BEC's right to legally change its name to Florida Institute of Space Technology in 1962. The college continued to be known as BEC until 1966. (Courtesy of University Publications.)

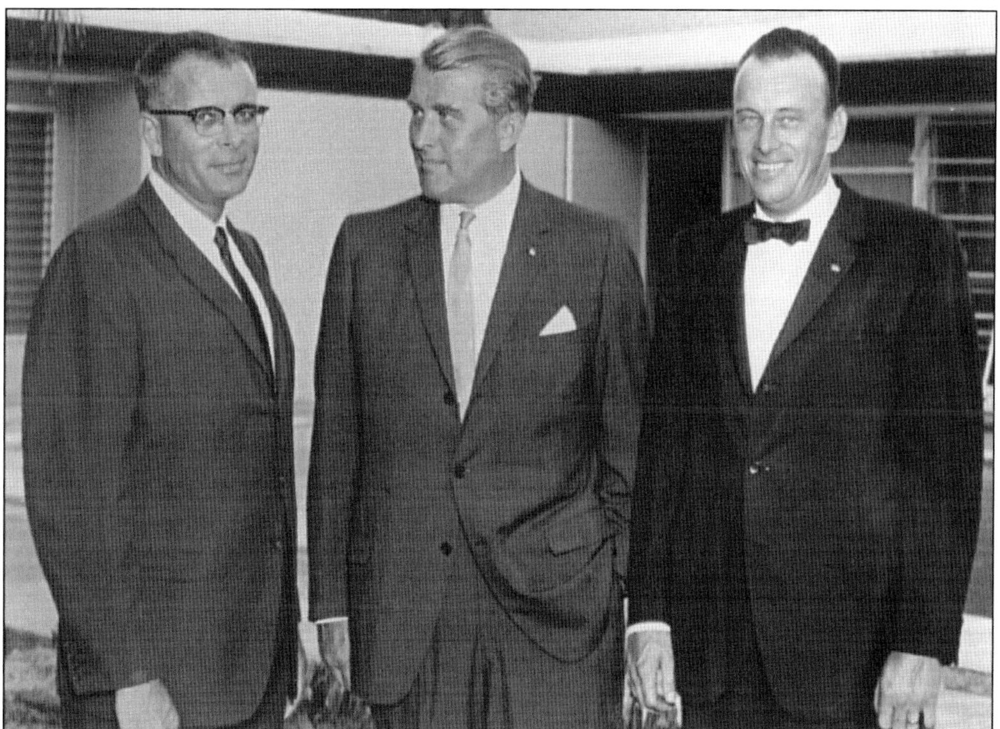

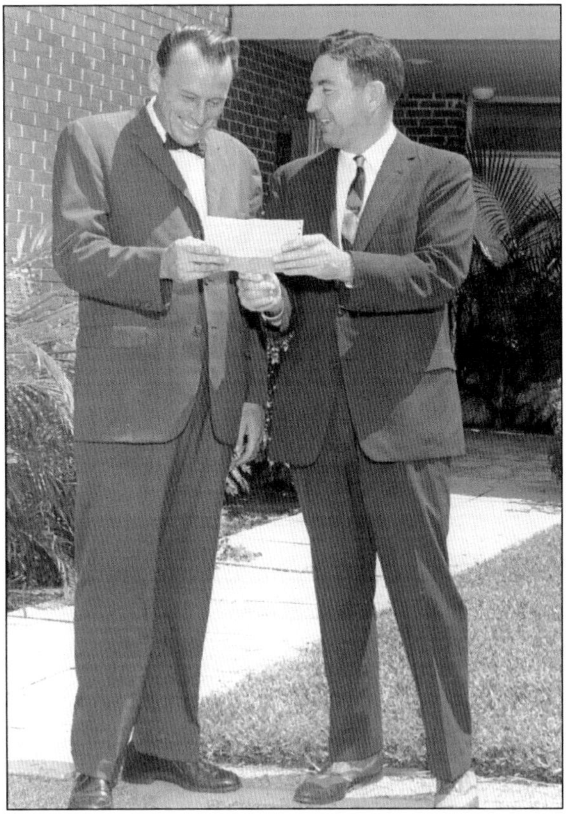

Joe Boyd, an executive with Radiation, Inc., is pictured here in October 1964 presenting Jerry Keuper with an installment on Radiation's pledge to the college. In March 1964, Radiation committed 1% of the company's before-tax-income to BEC. (Courtesy of University Publications.)

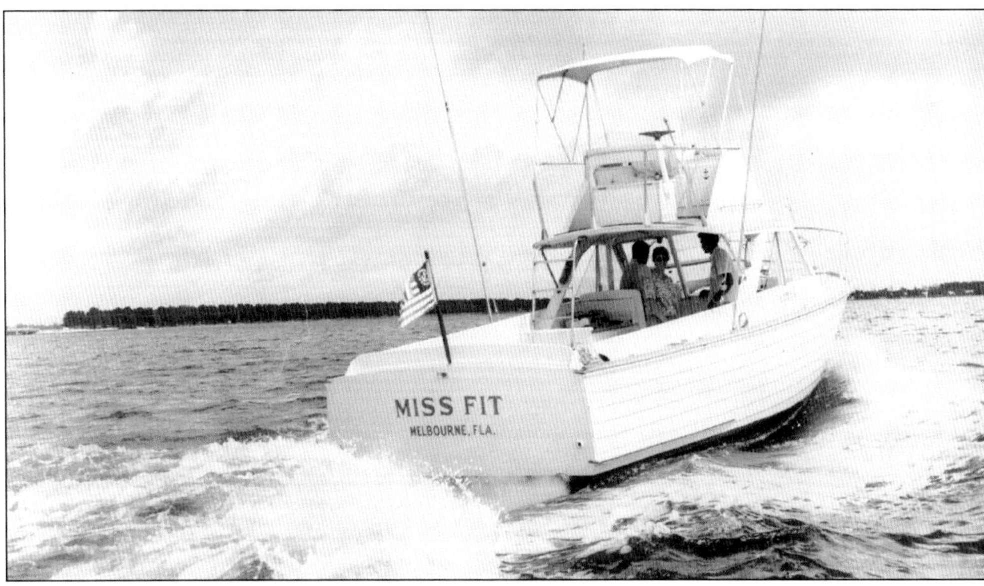

In August 1966, Joe Boyd, who later became president of Harris Corporation (Radiation's successor), donated his personal cruiser to the college. The 39-foot boat became the university's first research vessel. It was named *Miss FIT* to commemorate the board of trustees' decision to change the name of the college to Florida Institute of Technology. (Courtesy of University Publications.)

BEC won full accreditation from the Commission on Colleges Southern Association of Colleges and Secondary Schools (SACS) in December 1964. The accreditation team characterized BEC's 800 students and faculty as possessing an "immediate and pressing motivation" for their courses of study. The report warned, however, that given "the frontier nature of the curriculum" administrators must work constantly to improve communications and create a "coherent pattern" of courses in the humanities. (Courtesy of *Orlando Sentinel*.)

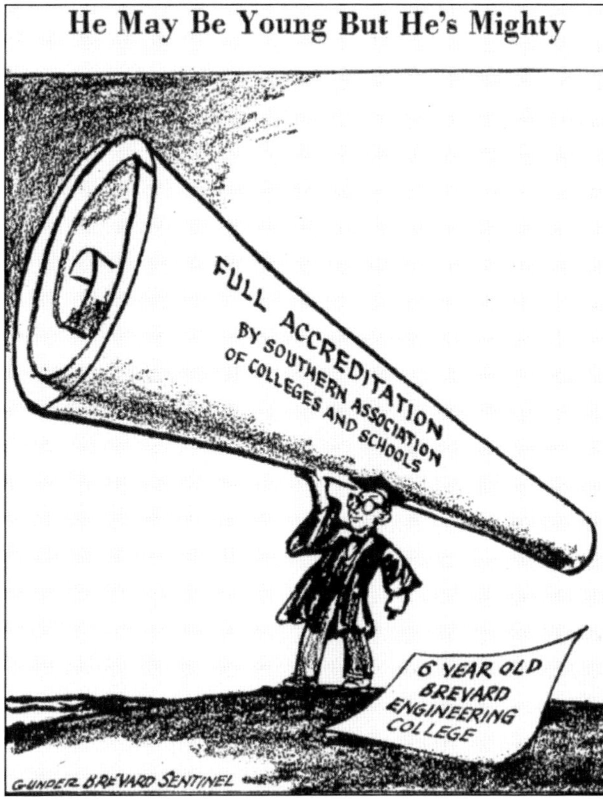

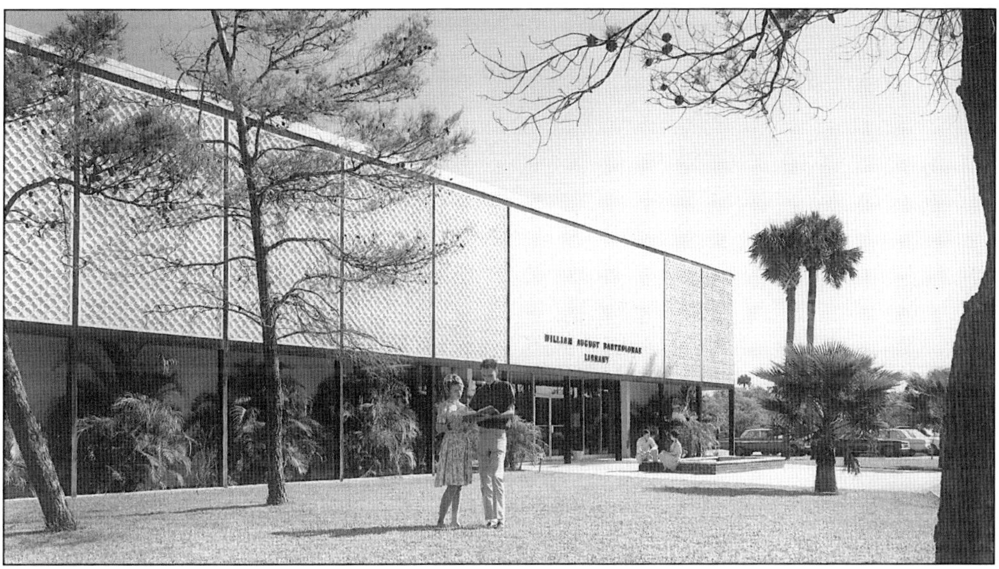

Formal dedication ceremonies for BEC's new library were held on January 23, 1965. Unofficially, the library received its christening in December 1964 when BEC's student government organized a dance to celebrate the college's accreditation. Initially, the library was named in honor of William August Bartholomae. This name was dropped when the Bartholomae family reneged on its pledge to the college. (Courtesy of University Publications.)

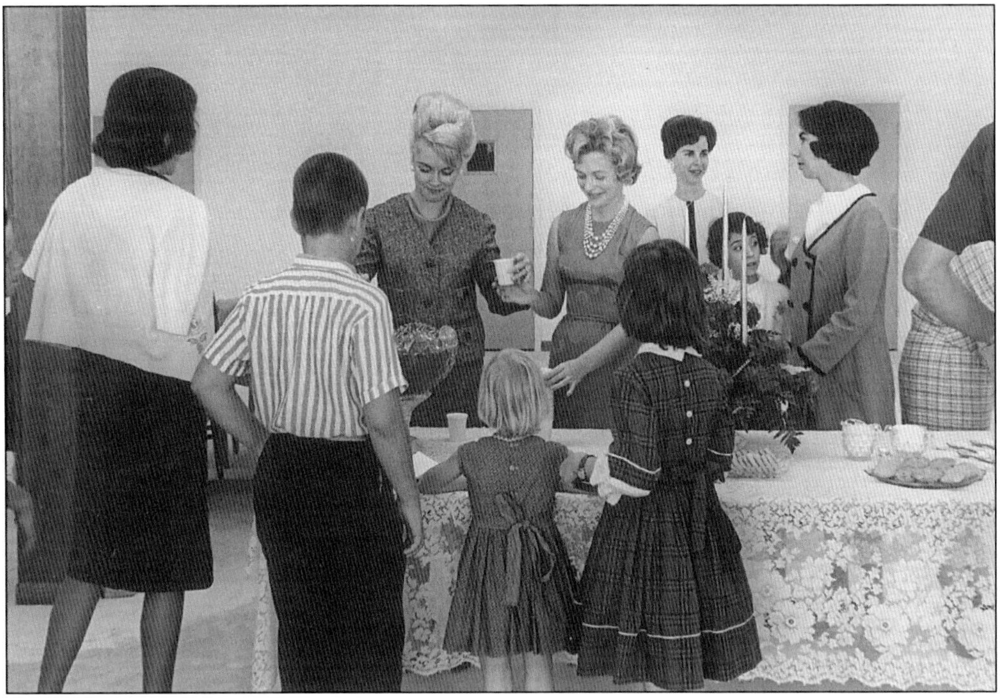

The Melbourne Junior Women's Club deserves much of the credit for making the library a reality. In December 1963, they promised to raise a "substantial sum" for the new library. Members of the Melbourne Junior Women's Club are shown here hosting the reception following the library's official dedication in January 1965. (Courtesy of University Publications.)

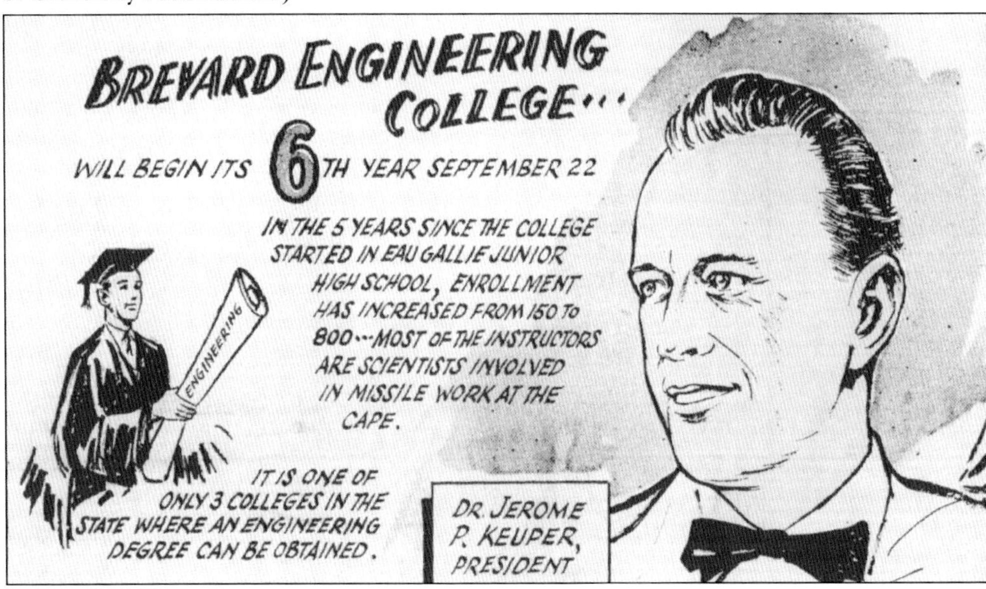

This 1965 cartoon celebrated BEC's accomplishments in its six-year history. Big changes were in store for the college. BEC officials committed the college to an active research program. Work was nearing completion on the college's first dormitory. (Courtesy of *Orlando Sentinel*.)

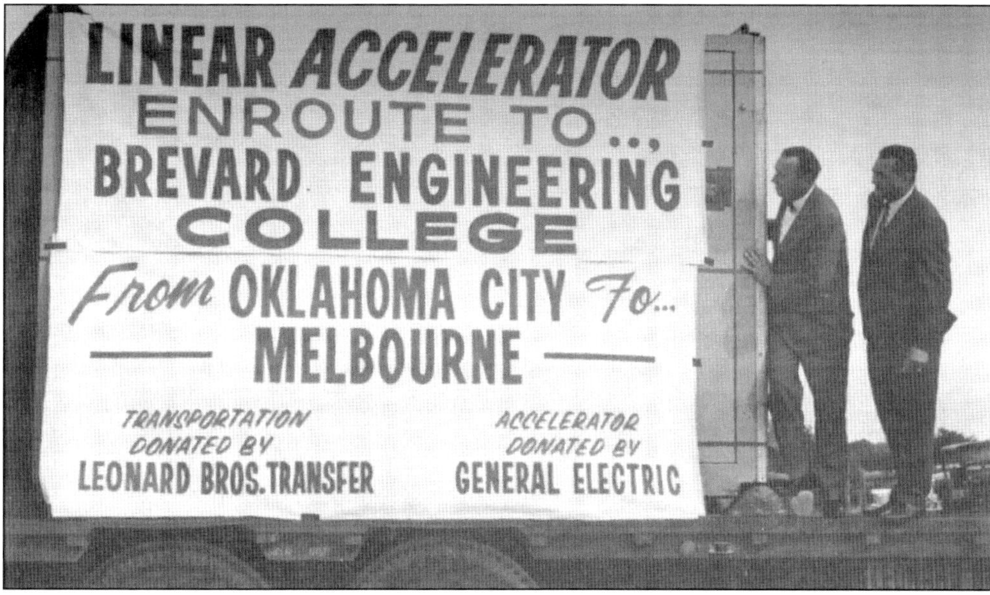

General Electric's donation of a $150,000 linear accelerator gave a boost to the BEC's research program in September 1965. Pictured here is the accelerator's arrival on campus. Jerry Keuper, left, and an unidentified GE official, right, are preparing to unload the accelerator. (Courtesy of University Publications.)

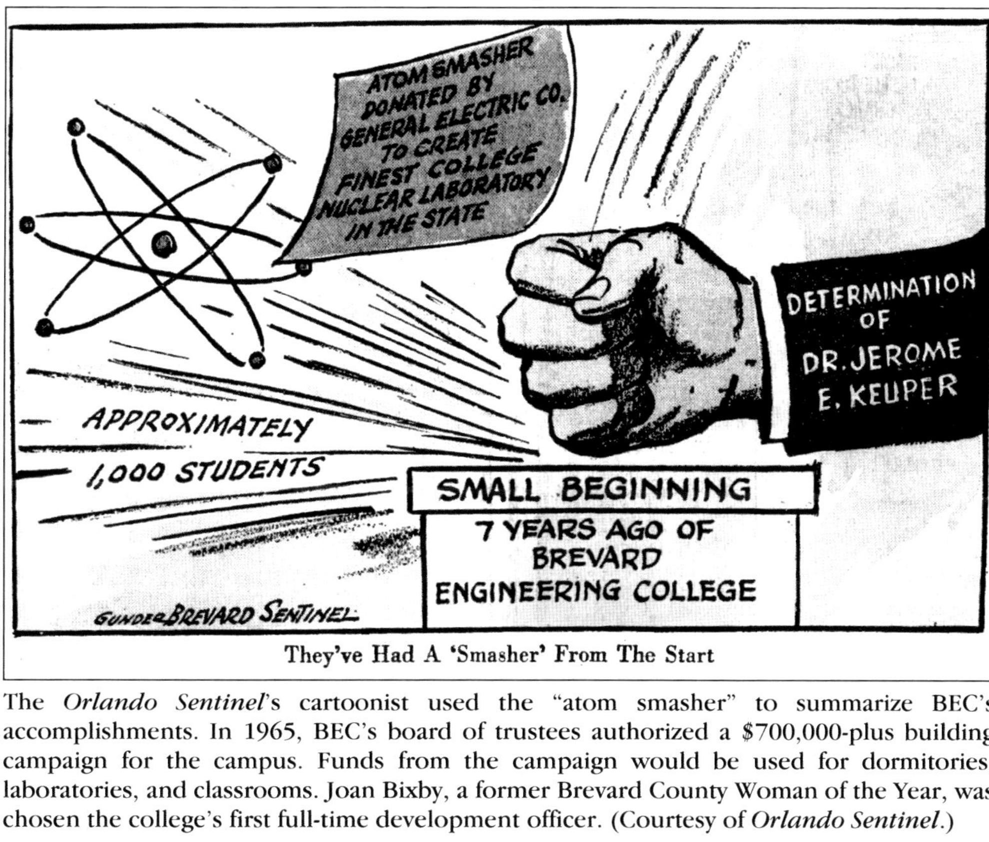

They've Had A 'Smasher' From The Start

The *Orlando Sentinel*'s cartoonist used the "atom smasher" to summarize BEC's accomplishments. In 1965, BEC's board of trustees authorized a $700,000-plus building campaign for the campus. Funds from the campaign would be used for dormitories, laboratories, and classrooms. Joan Bixby, a former Brevard County Woman of the Year, was chosen the college's first full-time development officer. (Courtesy of *Orlando Sentinel*.)

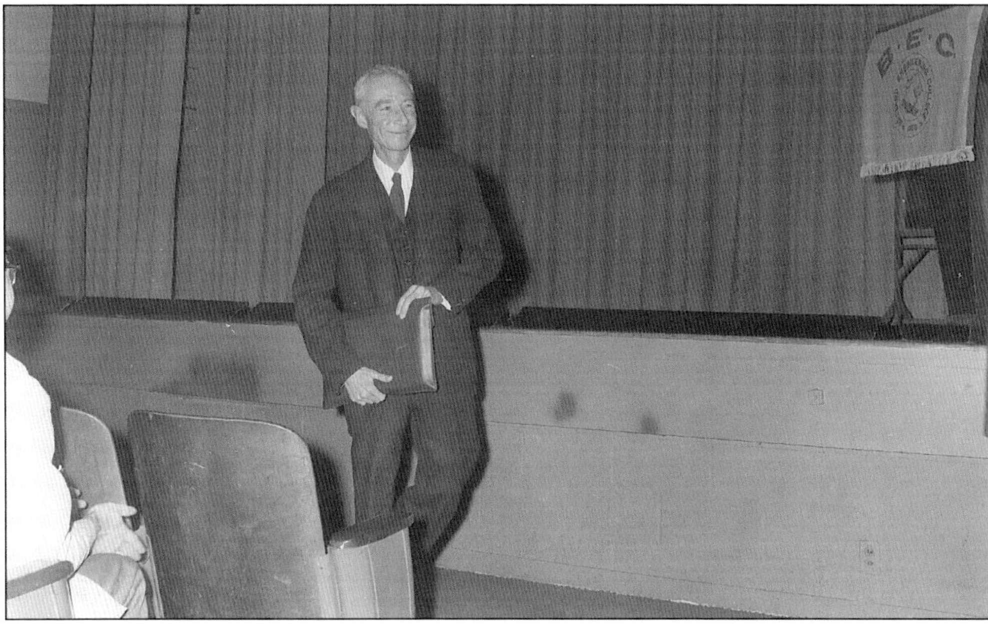

J. Robert Oppenheimer, director of the Institute of Advanced Studies at Princeton, is pictured here concluding his 1965 lecture on Niels Bohr. Oppenheimer was one of a number of distinguished scientists who took part in the BEC Science Seminar. (Courtesy of University Publications.)

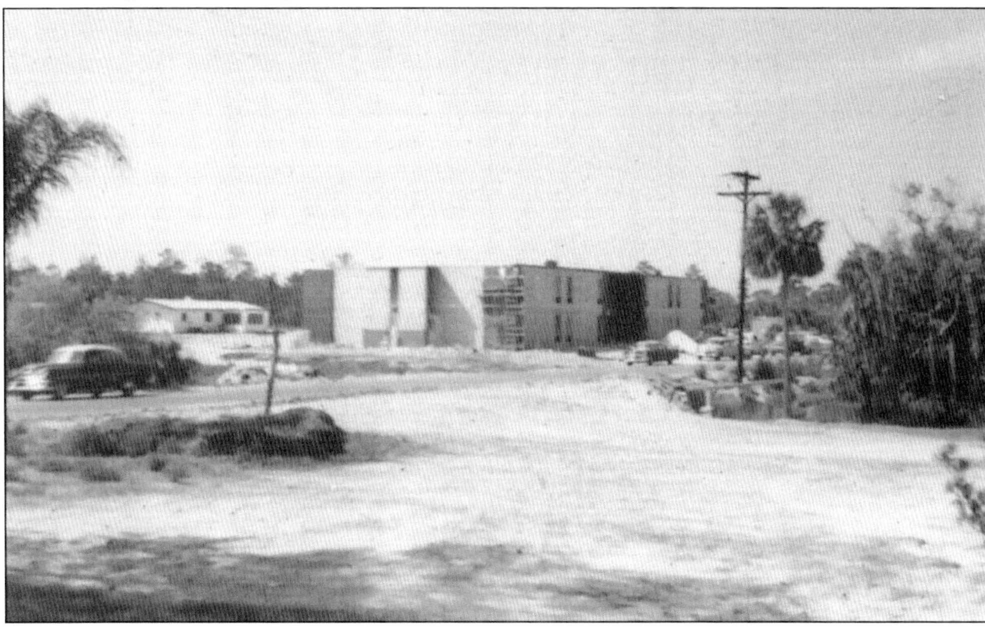

Construction of BEC's first dormitory was completed in July 1965. The dormitory served as home for 65 of the 100 full-time students in the entering freshman class. The other 35 freshmen joined 95 full-time upperclassmen who were housed throughout the community as the college rushed completion of a second dormitory. The second dormitory was named in honor of George Shaw. Total enrollment exceeded 1,000 students in September 1965. (Courtesy of Evans Library.)

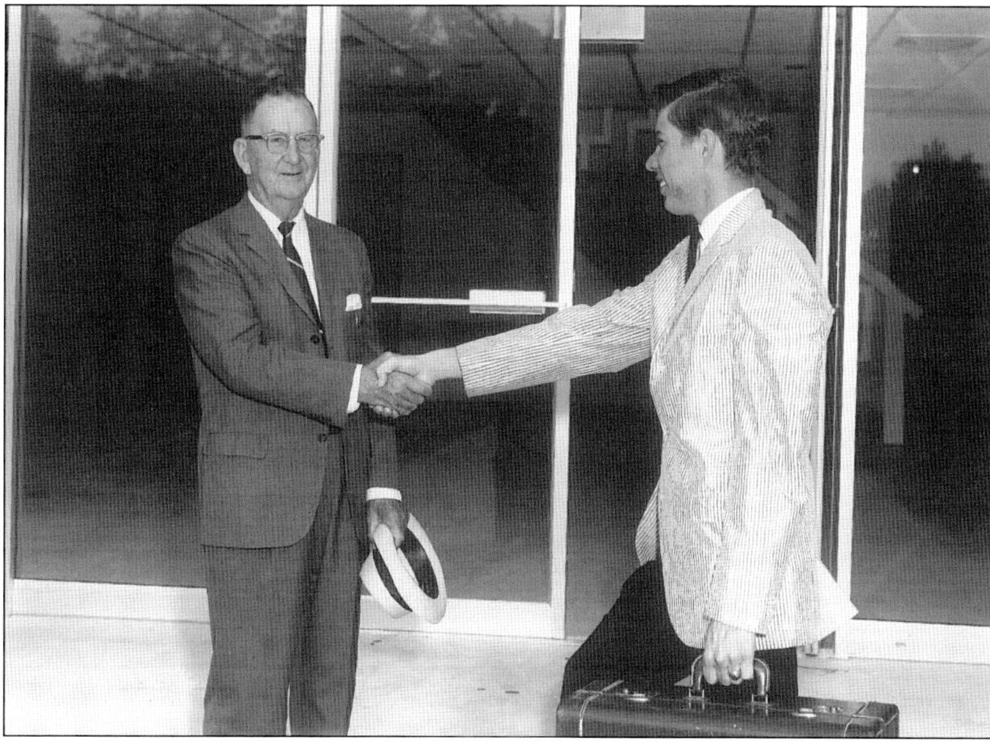

Pictured here is V.C. Brownlie welcoming Allen Green to Brownlie Hall. BEC's first dormitory was named in honor of Brownlie because of the Melbourne businessman's contributions to the college. (Courtesy of University Publications.)

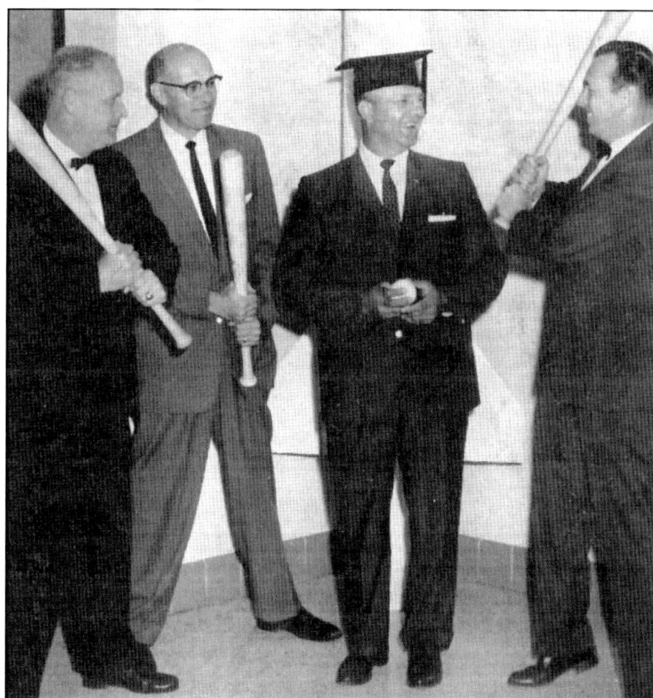

BEC's decision to become a full-time residential college necessitated a number of changes. In 1964, students approached Ray Work and asked his support in organizing the college's first basketball team. In February 1965, veteran Philadelphia major-leaguer Andy Seminick became the college's first athletic director. Dr. Joseph Dollar, a Melbourne podiatrist, served as assistant director. Pictured here, from left to right, are Ray Work, Joseph Dollar, Andy Seminick, and Jerry Keuper. (Courtesy of *Melbourne Times*.)

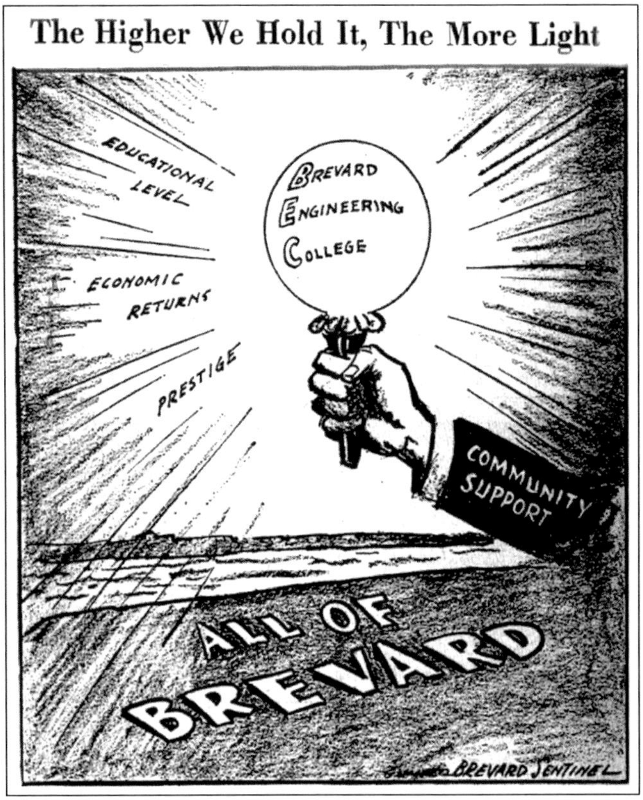

When this cartoon appeared in the *Orlando Sentinel* late in 1965, BEC was well on the way to becoming a full-time residential college. In November, students organized the college's first fraternity, Phi Kappa Alpha. A month later, college officials announced a new degree program in computer science. (Courtesy of *Orlando Sentinel*.)

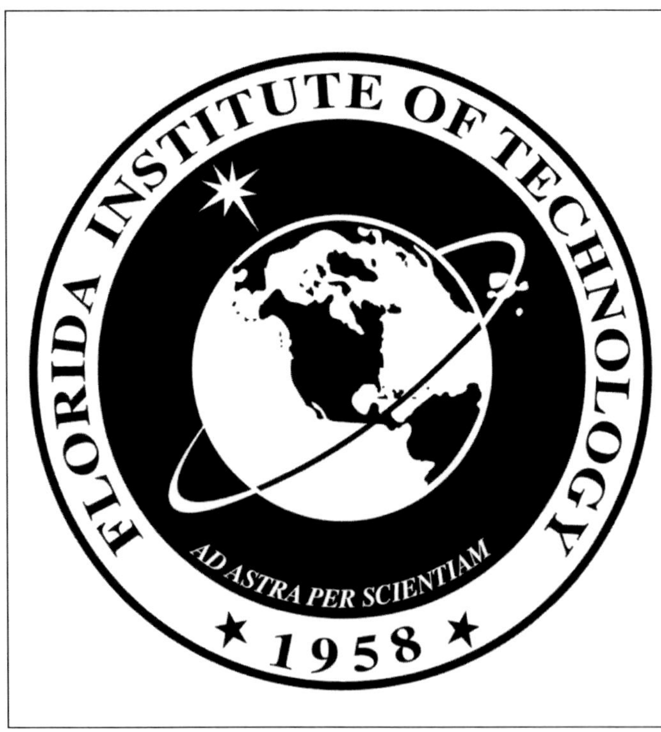

In June 1966, Tom Adams, Florida's secretary of state and BEC trustee, granted BEC exclusive use of the name Florida Institute of Technology. The school adopted the new name officially at its August board of trustees meeting. Keuper instructed the manager of the new "FIT Bookstore" to raise the price on the old "BEC tee-shirts" because they were now collectors' items. The college's new seal is pictured here. (Courtesy of University Publications.)

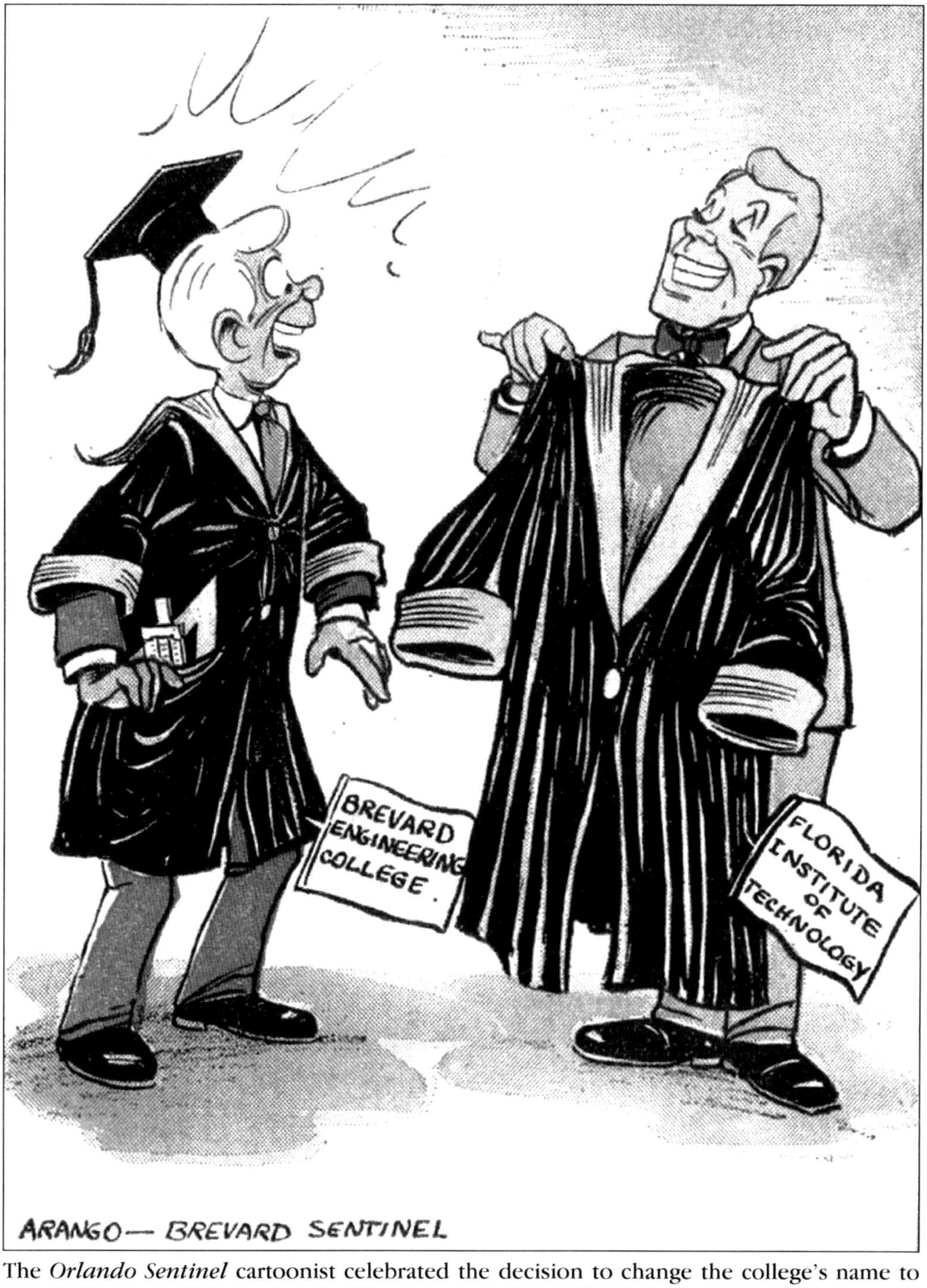

The *Orlando Sentinel* cartoonist celebrated the decision to change the college's name to Florida Institute of Technology in this cartoon. College officials believed that the new name reflected the school's growing national stature. (Courtesy of *Orlando Sentinel*.)

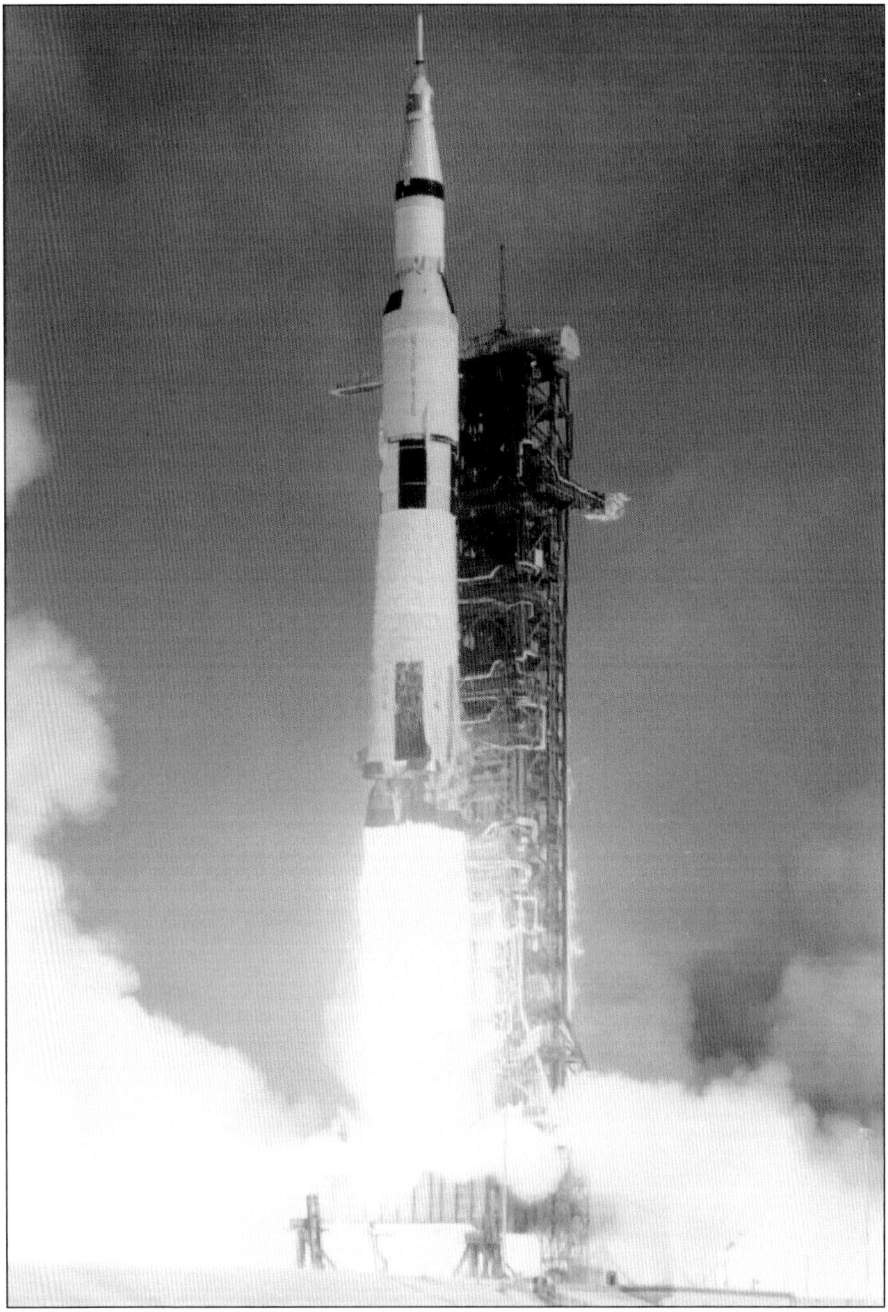

Pictured here is the launch of Apollo 11. Ironically, the success of the Apollo moon project ushered in a period of drastic reductions in NASA's budget. The cutbacks in the space program, the war in Vietnam, and growing domestic unrest transformed America in the period between 1966 and 1975. During these years, Florida Institute of Technology redefined its mission and institutional character. Leadership of the university passed from the "missilemen" to a new generation of academicians. Programs in oceanography (1966), aeronautics (1967), science education (1970), and biology (1971) were introduced. (Courtesy of Air Force Space and Missile Museum.)

Three

Charting the Course: 1967–1974

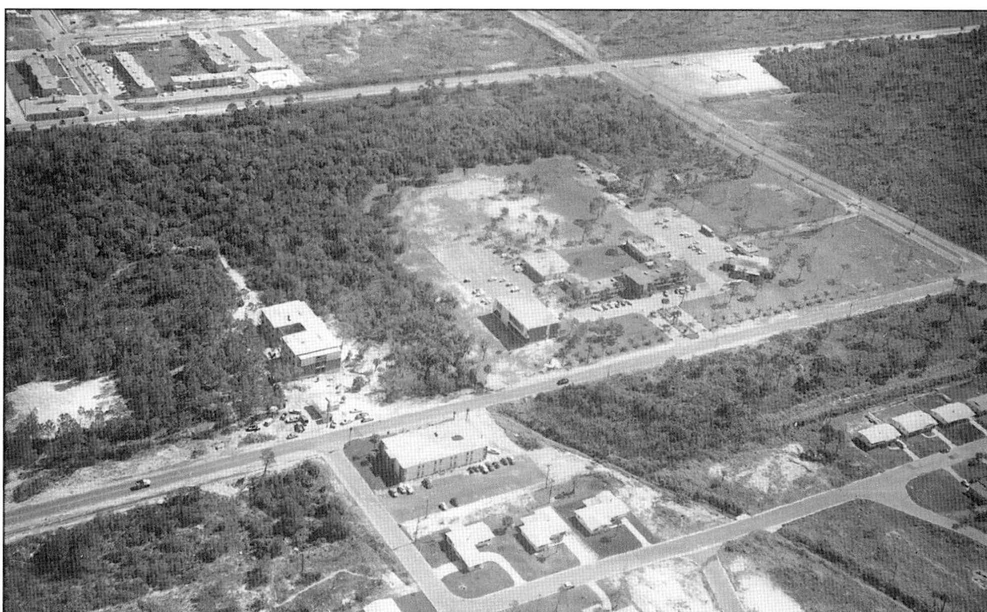

In September 1966, 1,492 students enrolled in FIT's undergraduate and graduate programs. Tuition for the 516 full-time undergraduates was $760. "We offer," Jerry Keuper observed, "Florida's biggest bargain in education." This aerial photograph shows the campus in January 1966. Brownlie Hall (foreground) and Shaw Hall were completed. Two additional dormitories (East and West Halls) were added later in the year. In 1967, East Hall was renamed in honor of Gus Grissom after the tragic fire on Apollo 1. (Courtesy of Sterling Photo.)

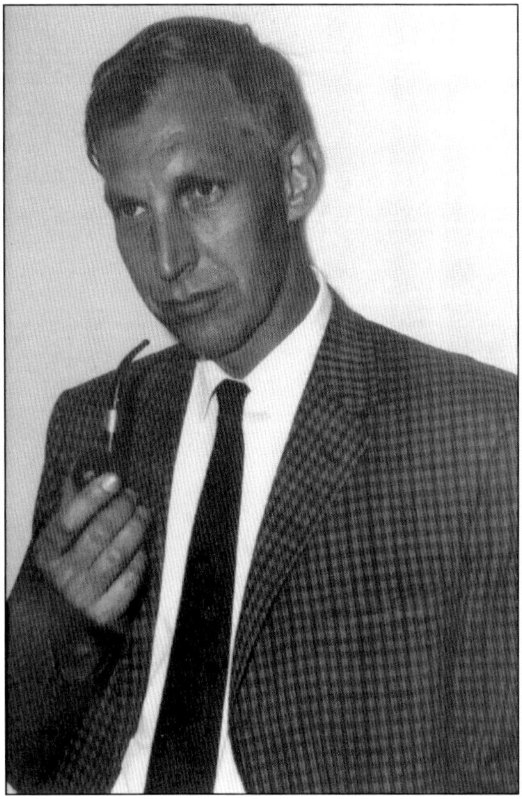

In September 1966, John E. Miller took charge of FIT's faculty and academic programs. Miller earned his Ph.D. at the University of Virginia where he and Jerry Keuper were classmates. Between 1952 and 1966, Miller served as Distinguished Alumni Professor of Physics at Clemson University. Keuper charged Miller with strengthening FIT's undergraduate curriculum and introducing a Ph.D. program in the college's graduate school. (Courtesy of *Ad Astra*.)

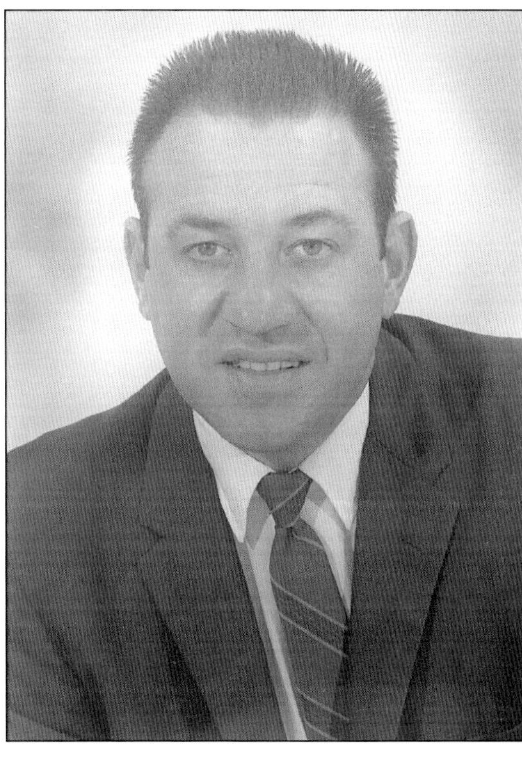

John Miller initiated a series of administrative changes. Miller chose Harry Weber (pictured here) in 1966 to revamp the college's engineering and science curriculum. Under Miller and Weber's leadership, FIT strengthened its academic programs. Miller convinced Dr. James Potter, Ph.D. (Yale) to leave Texas A & M to lead FIT's physics department. (Courtesy of Evans Library.)

In 1967, Harry Weber persuaded Andy Revay (shown here) to join FIT's electrical engineering program. Revay and Weber had shared an office at the University of Pittsburgh. "We are one of the few universities in the country," Weber explained, "which permit undergraduates to do independent research." FIT's electrical engineering program won professional accreditation in 1970. (Courtesy of *Ad Astra*.)

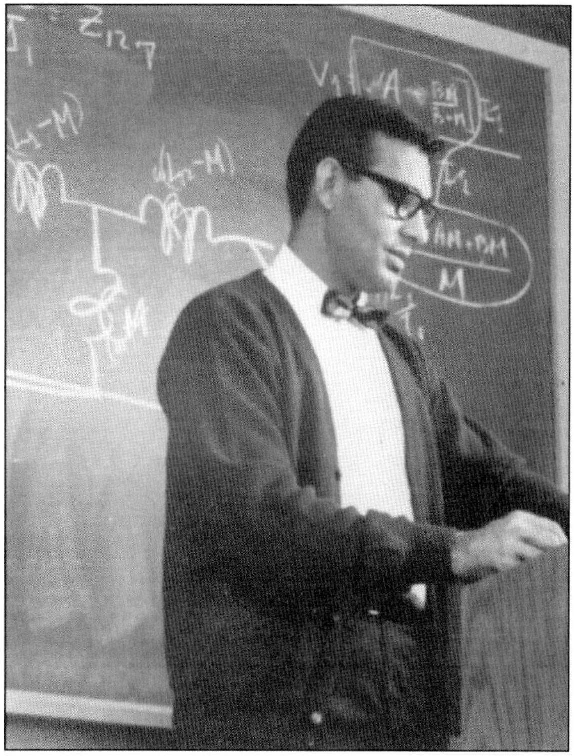

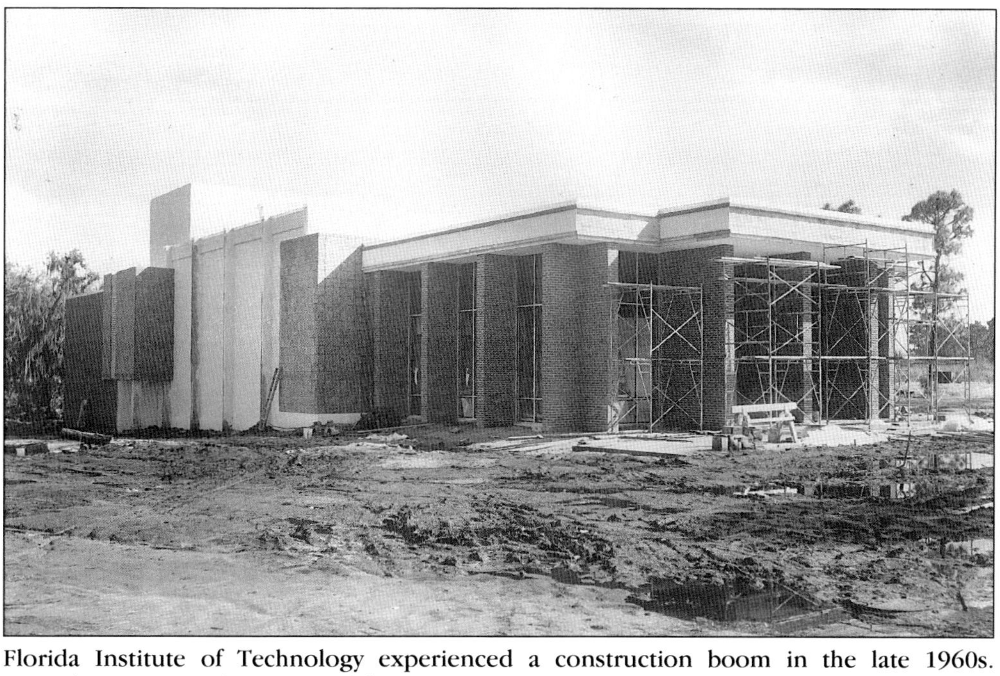

Florida Institute of Technology experienced a construction boom in the late 1960s. New dormitories, classrooms, laboratories, auditoriums, and arenas were added to the campus. Work on Gleason Auditorium (pictured above) began in May 1966. Named for W. Lansing Gleason, the 510-seat auditorium cost $310,000 to construct. (Courtesy of University Publications.)

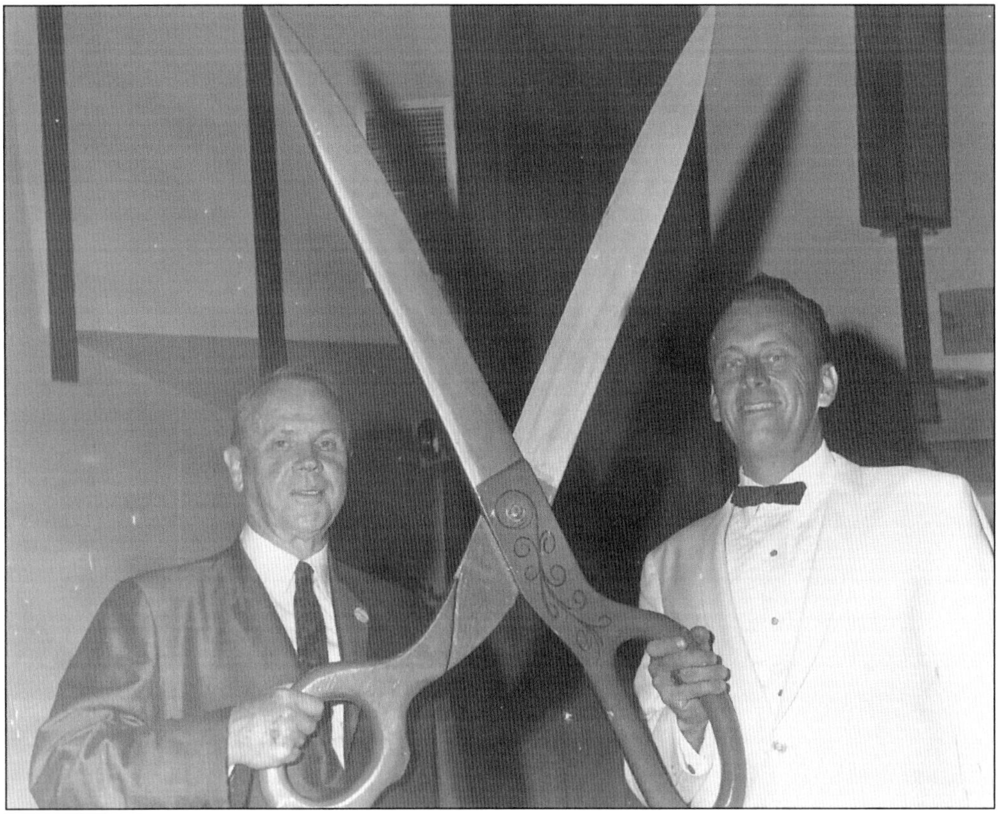

Gleason Auditorium was officially dedicated on October 15, 1967. Pictured here, from left to right, are W. Lansing Gleason and Jerry Keuper at the auditorium's grand opening. The Gleason family has shown its commitment to FIT through generous gifts and Carrie Gleason's service on the college's board of trustees. (Courtesy of University Publications.)

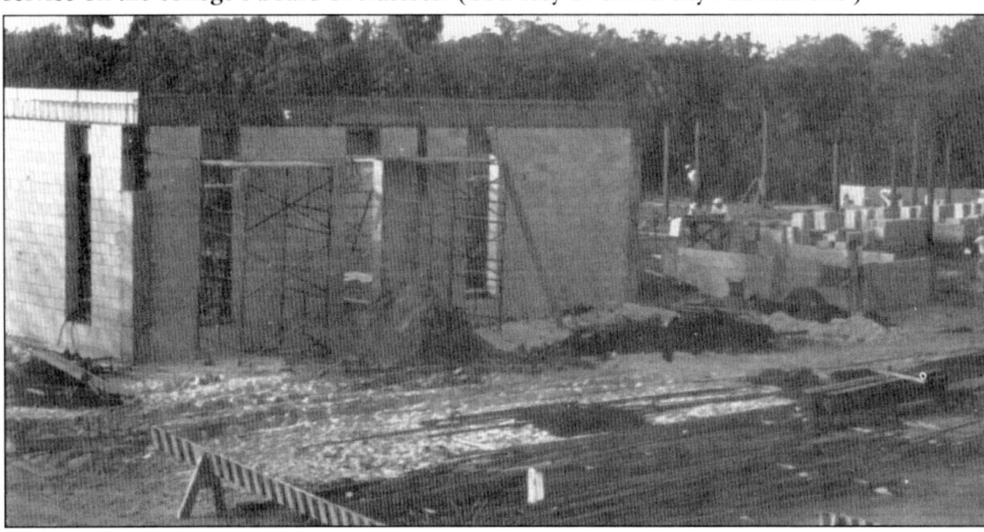

Ground was broken in August 1967 on the school's $500,000 student union. Named in honor of Homer Denius, the Denius Student Center quickly became the focus of student activities when it opened in 1968. (Courtesy of *Ad Astra*.)

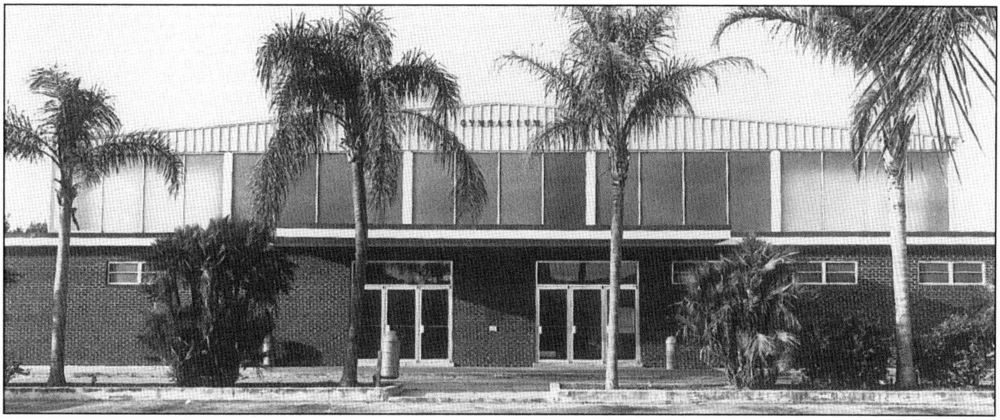

In July 1968, work started on a $130,000 gymnasium. The gymnasium led to intercollegiate athletic programs in crew, volleyball, soccer, and golf. In 1986, the gymnasium was named in honor of Percy Hedgecock (trustee and founder of Satellite Beach). In February 2000, ground was broken on the site of Hedgecock Gymnasium for the $6.6-million Charles and Ruth Clemente Recreation Center. (Courtesy of University Publications.)

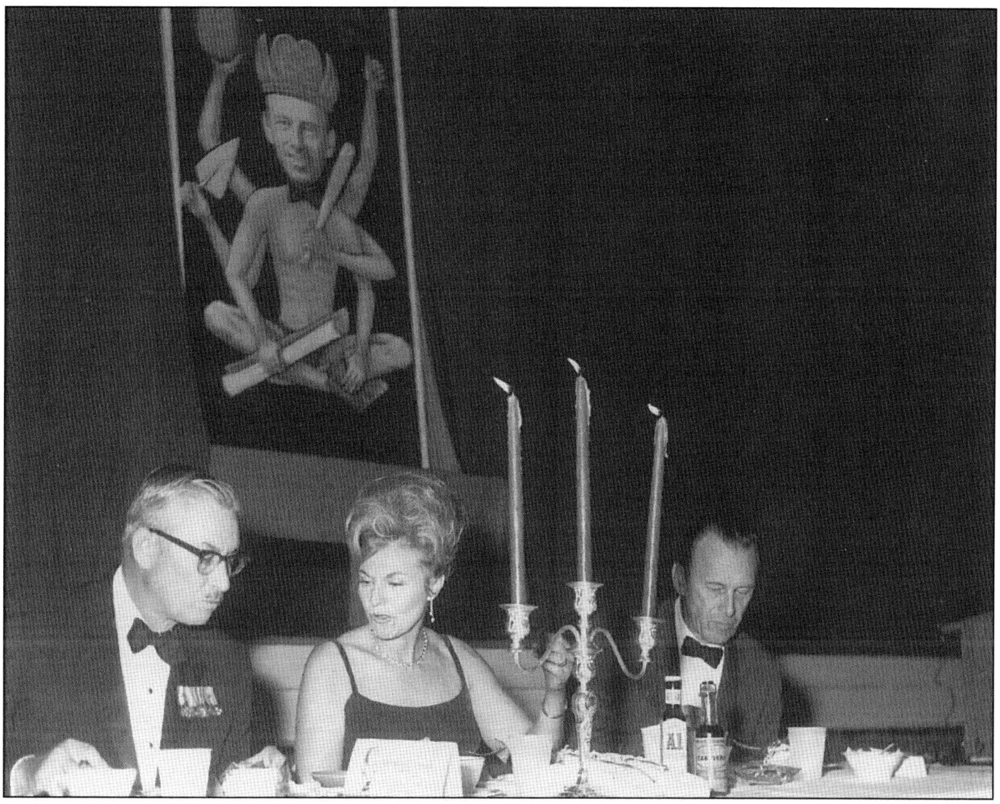

Pictured here, from left to right are retired Gen. John Medaris, Natalie Keuper, and Jerry Keuper celebrating FIT's tenth anniversary. The multi-armed caricature in the background was a birthday gift from TRW, Inc. Dubbed "Big Daddy" by a maintenance worker, the picture depicts a semi-nude, six-armed Keuper seated in a Yoga position holding blueprints, a trowel, a basketball, a palm tree, a baseball bat, and a wad of money in each hand. (Courtesy of University Publications.)

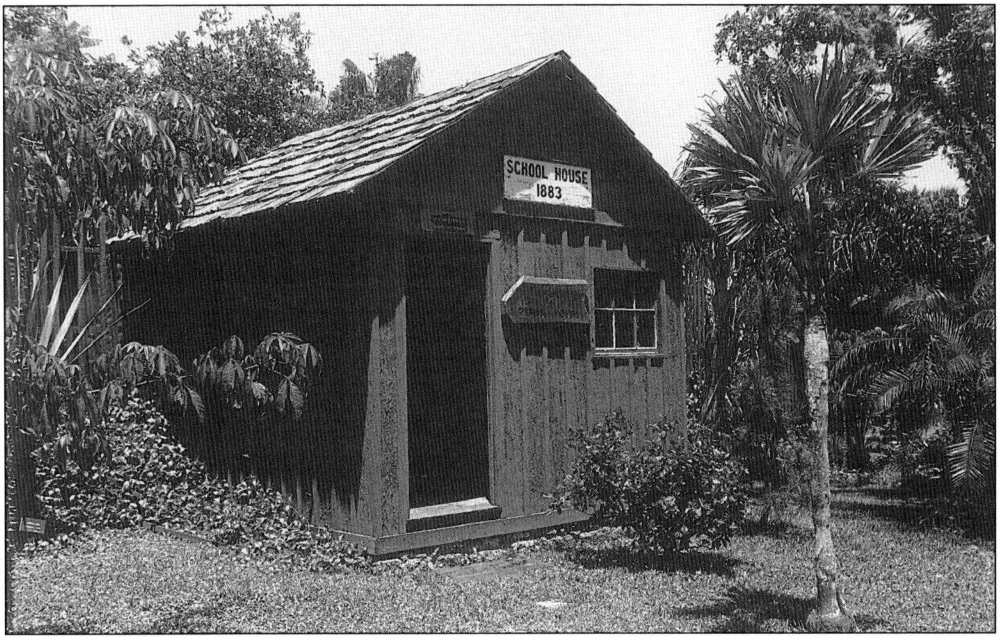

Melbourne's first schoolhouse (1883) found a new home at the edge of the college's botanical garden in 1970. The 9-foot-by-12-foot schoolhouse's first class of students consisted of both African Americans and whites (meeting in separate sessions). Members of the Inter-Fraternity Council joined with the South Brevard Historical Society in relocating the schoolhouse. (Courtesy of University Publications.)

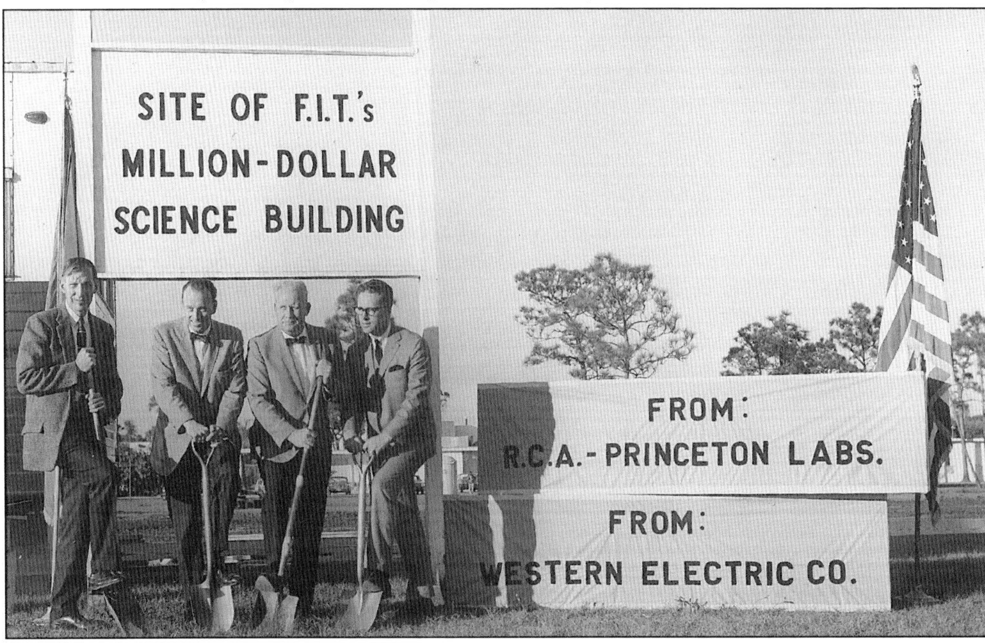

Construction on the Crawford Science Building began in December 1968. Named for Fred Crawford, a distinguished engineer and industrialist, the seven-story building cost $1,250,000. Pictured here, from left to right, are John Miller, Jerry Keuper, Ray Work, and an unidentified individual. (Courtesy of University Publications.)

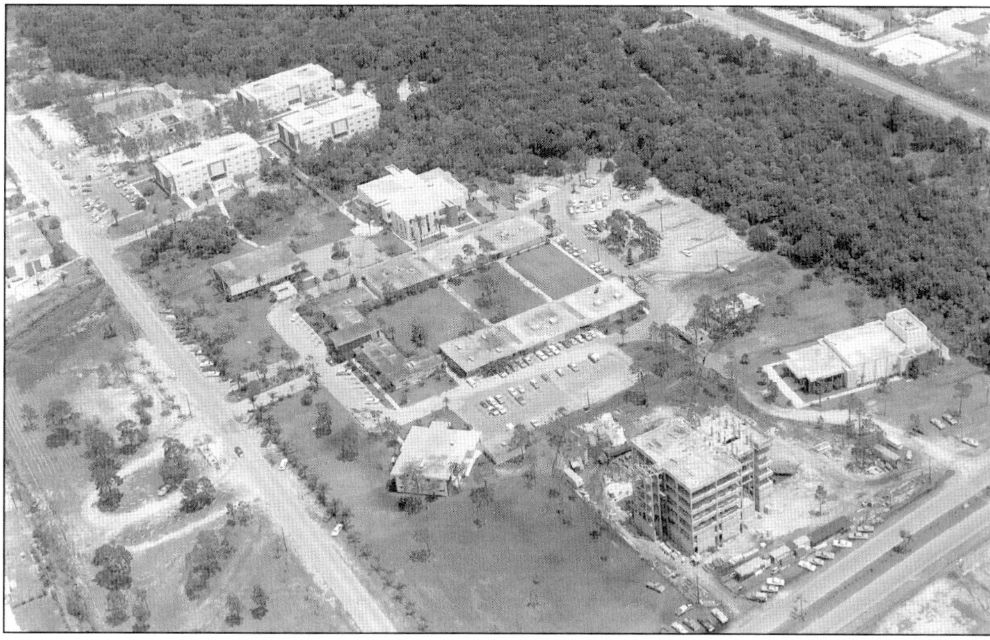

This aerial photograph (August 1969) shows the progress on the construction of the Science Building (foreground). Gleason Auditorium is immediately to the right of the Science Building. The Quad (center),Library, Denius Student Center, as well as Shaw, Grissom, and Campbell Residence Halls (upper left) can be seen. (Courtesy of Sterling Photo.)

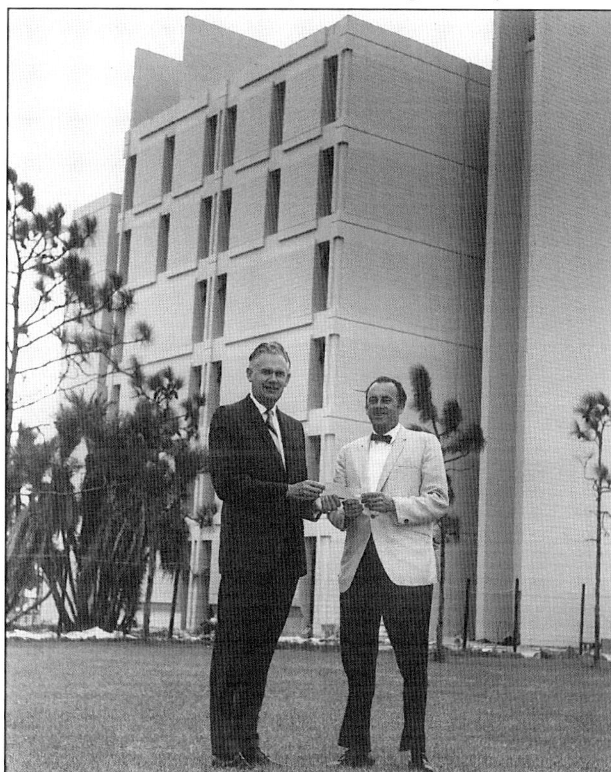

Pictured here is Denton Clark, head of RCA at the Cape and later president of RCA Canada, presenting Jerry Keuper with RCA's contribution to the nearly complete Crawford Science Building (background). Clark served as chairman of FIT's board of trustees in 1970. Tuition for full-time undergraduates was $1,260. (Courtesy of University Publications.)

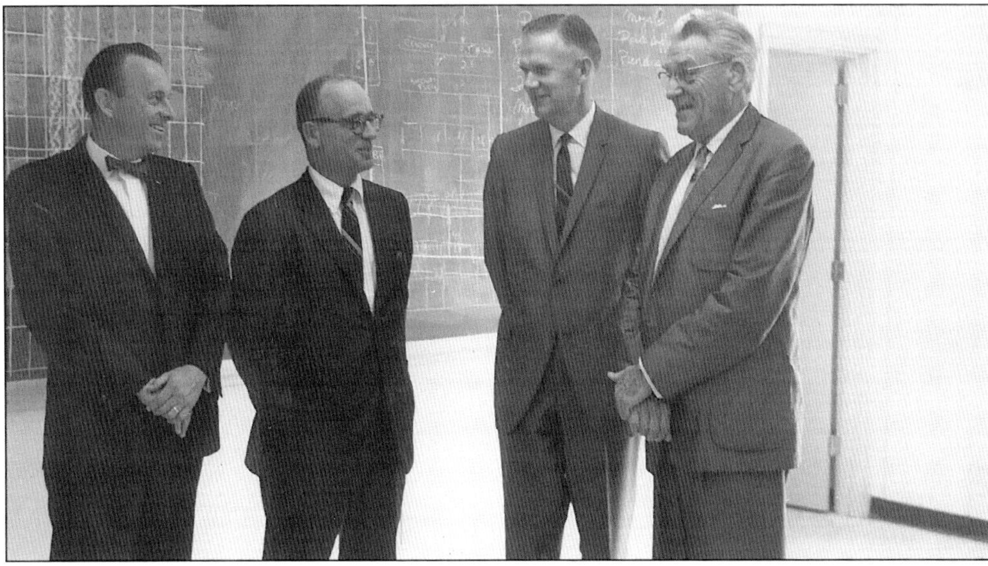

New dormitories were needed for the growing number of full-time students. Jerry Keuper, an unidentified individual, Denton Clark, and Fred Roberts, pictured from left to right, are shown here discussing plans for a proposed multi-story residence hall in the late 1960s. Fred Roberts, a trustee and benefactor of the college, was instrumental in making the new dormitory, Roberts Hall, a reality. (Courtesy of University Publications.)

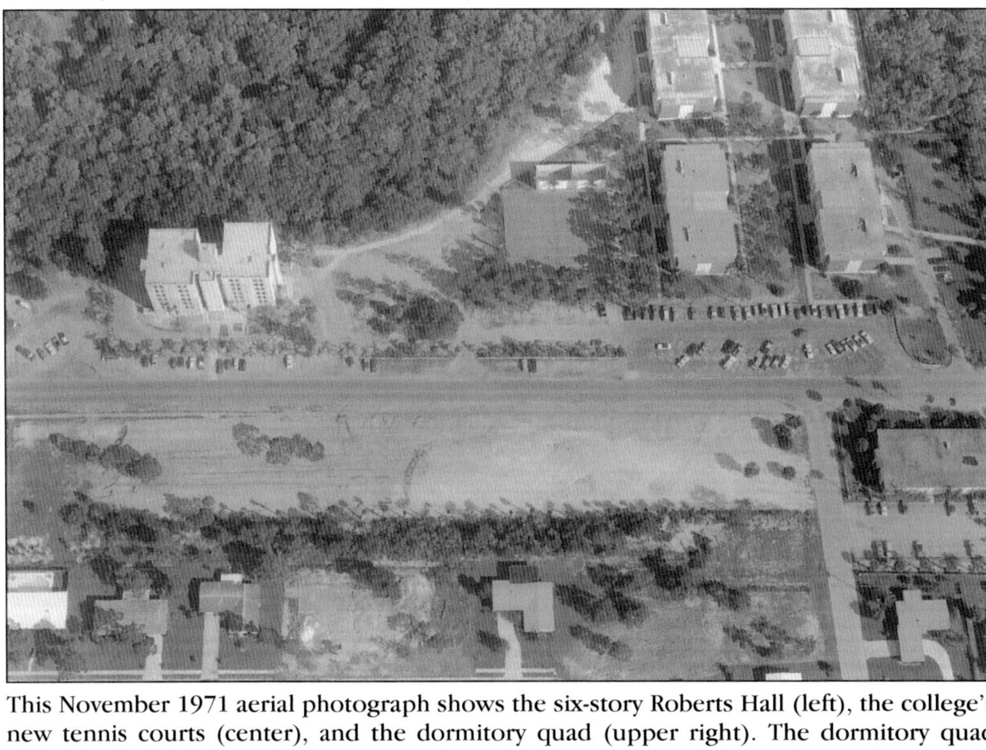

This November 1971 aerial photograph shows the six-story Roberts Hall (left), the college's new tennis courts (center), and the dormitory quad (upper right). The dormitory quad consisted of Wood and Shaw Halls (left to right, nearest the parking lot) and Campbell and Grissom Hall (left to right). Wood Hall (1970) was named in honor of Virginia Wood, founder of the University of Melbourne. (Courtesy of Sterling Photo.)

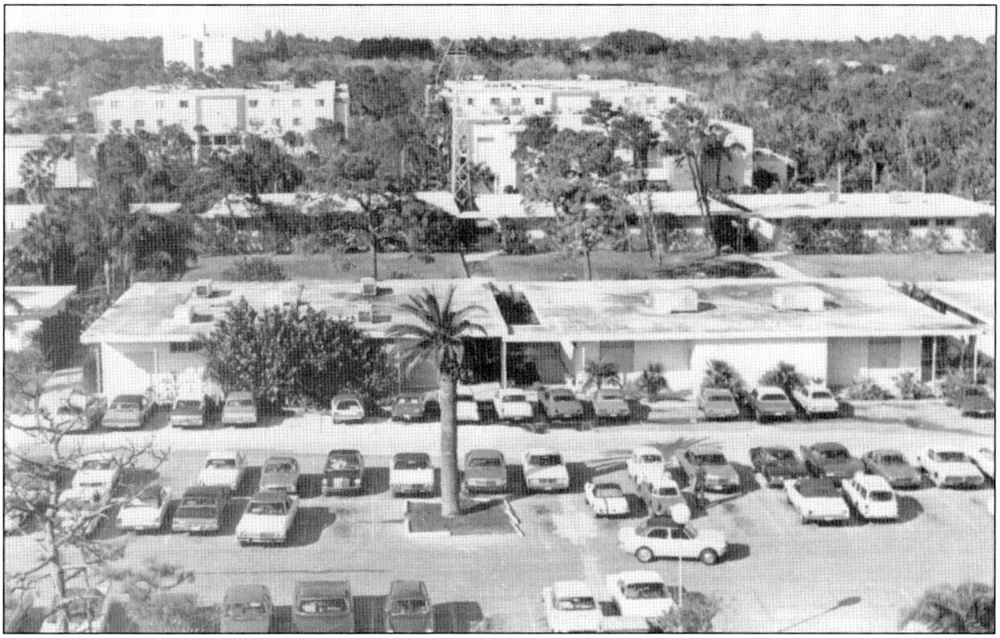

As this 1971 picture of the Melbourne campus shows, finding a parking place was already a problem. Students used the antenna (center) for their ham radio club. Denius Student Center, the dormitory quad, and Roberts Hall can be seen in the background. (Courtesy of *Ad Astra*.)

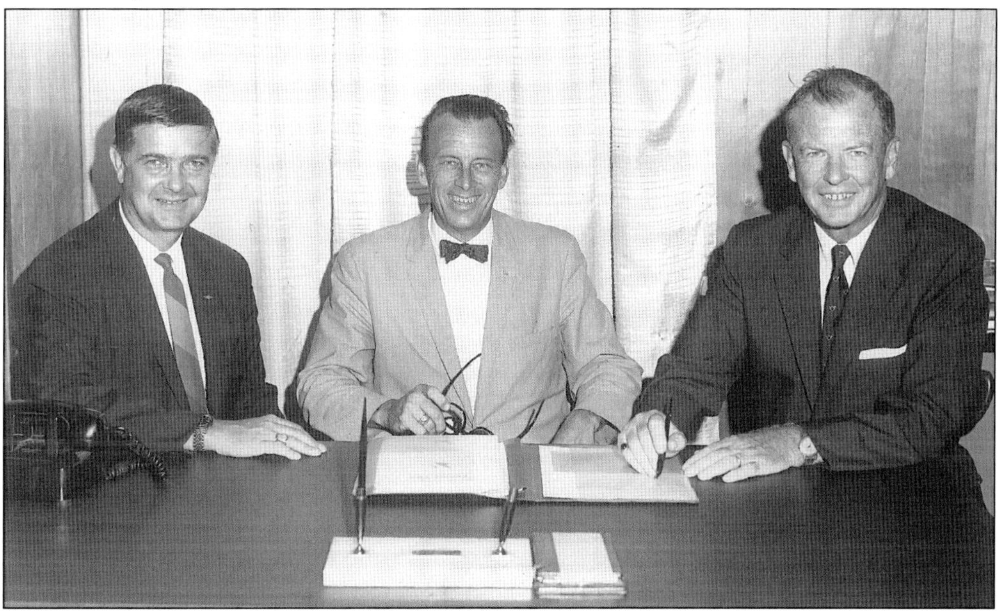

In 1967, John Miller recruited Jerry Lauderbaugh to organize the college's Aerospace Technical Institute (ATI). Working out of an office in the basement of Grissom Hall, Lauderbaugh oversaw the college's acquisition of Campbell Aviation. In 1972, ATI became FIT's School of Aeronautics. Pictured here in July 1968, from left to right, are Jerry Lauderbaugh, Jerry Keuper, and Stuart Campbell. Campbell Hall was named in honor of Stuart Campbell. (Courtesy of University Publications.)

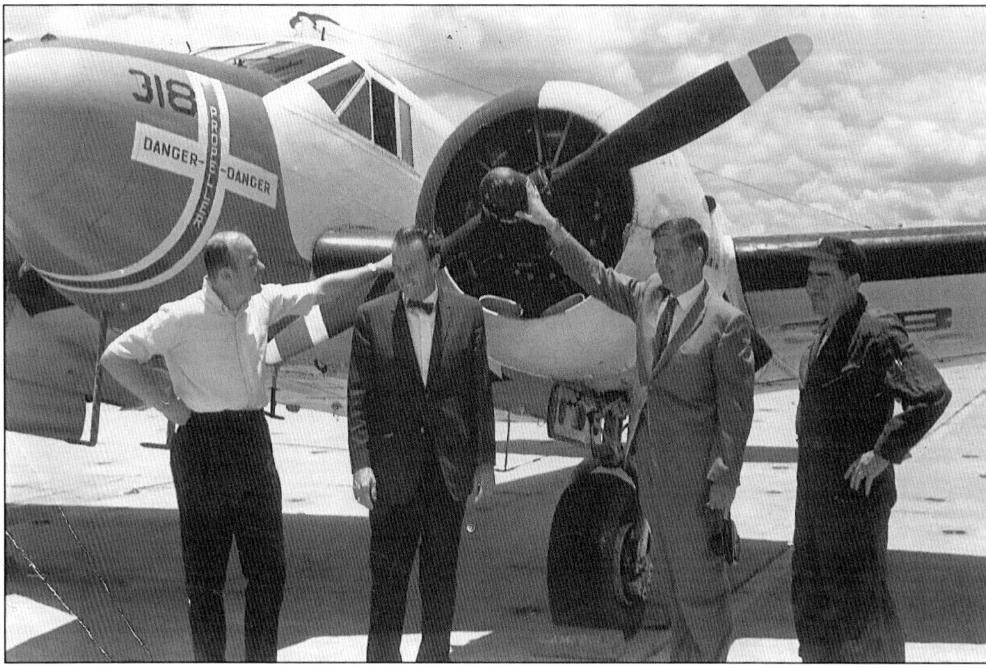

Jerry Keuper, center left, and Jerry Lauderbaugh, center right, hand on propeller, are inspecting a twin-engine Beechcraft in this 1968 photo taken at the college's Melbourne Airport facilities. Student enrollment in the aviation program grew rapidly. As a stopgap, the college leased the Cape Kennedy (Melbourne) Airport Motel to house students. In August 1969, FIT purchased the Trade Winds Hotel in Indialantic to serve as a dormitory. (Courtesy of University Publications.)

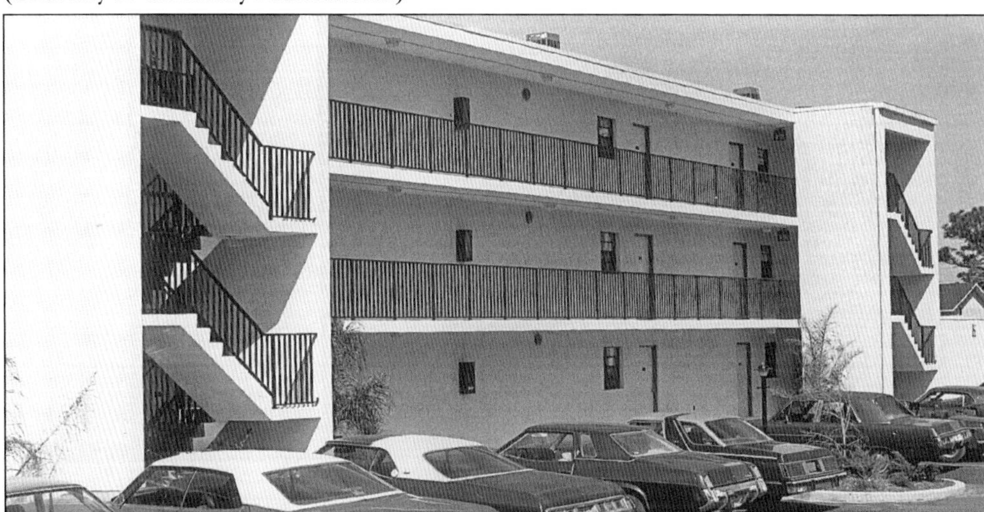

City officials in Indialantic blocked the continued use of the Trade Winds as a dormitory in 1974. FIT purchased the Southgate Apartment complex on Babcock Street to serve both as the administrative offices (Southgate A Building) for the School of Aeronautics and student housing. Pictured here are the Southgate dormitories in the late 1970s. (Courtesy of University Publications.)

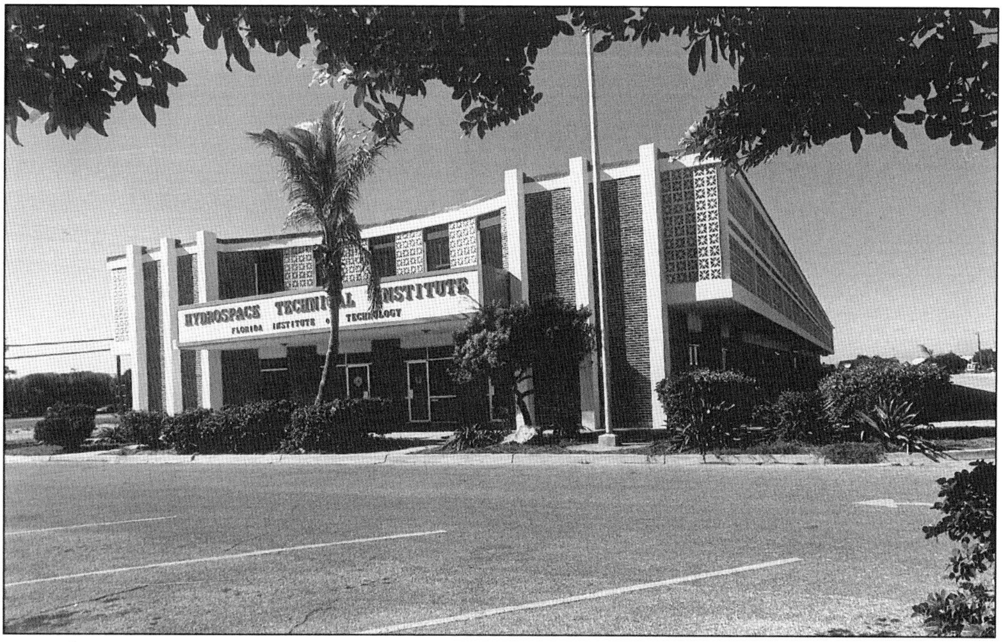

In 1968, FIT chartered the Hydrospace Technical Institute (HTI) as a non-profit technical training institute. The Bertil Malmquist family donated the 30,000-square-foot Canaveral Administrative Complex building in Cocoa Beach to the college in 1969. Ernest (Tim) Tealey headed HTI's programs in oceanographic technology. In 1972, HTI was reorganized as the School of Marine and Environmental Technology (SOMET) and relocated in Jensen Beach. (Courtesy of University Publications.)

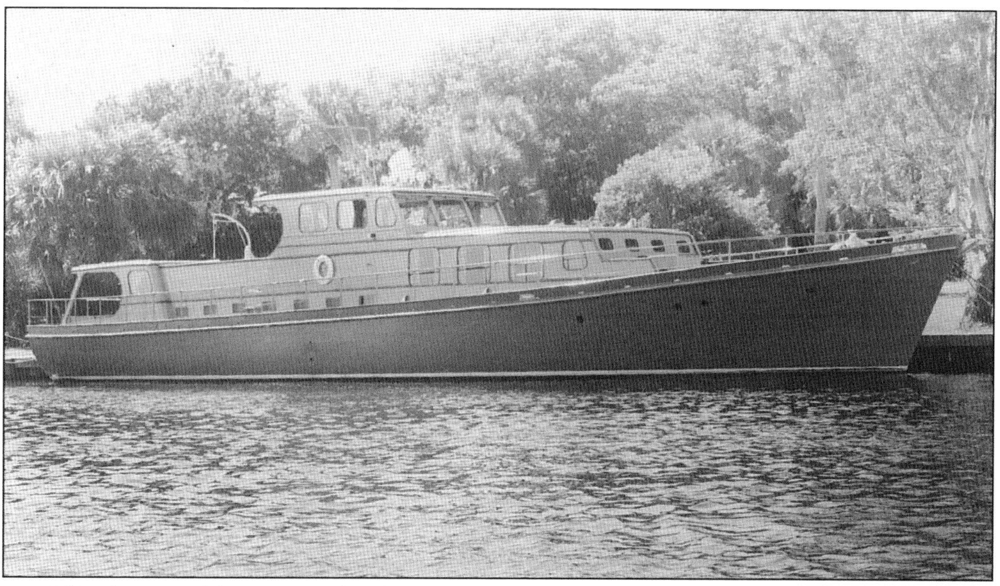

In 1968, the Republican Party held its National Convention in Miami. It was rumored that Richard Nixon was considering Claude Kirk for his running mate. Jerry Keuper used his Republican friends at the convention to rally support for FIT. Keuper persuaded New York's governor, Nelson Rockefeller, to donate his yacht the *Dragon Lady* (pictured above) to the college. (Courtesy of University Publications.)

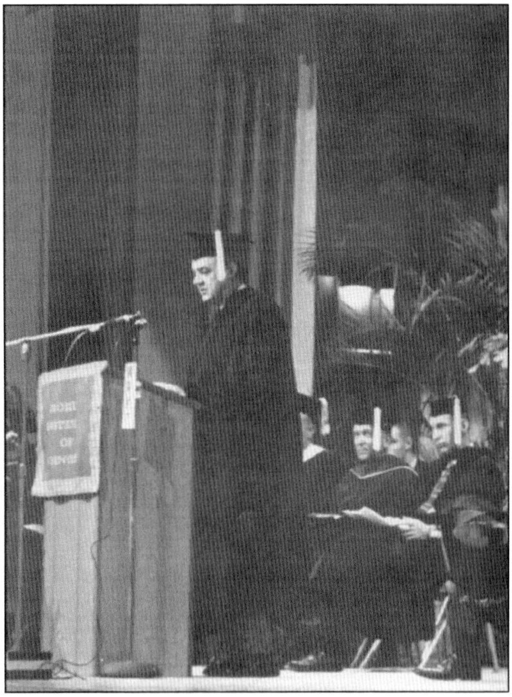

Claude Kirk is shown here speaking at FIT's 1968 commencement exercises at the Melbourne Civic Auditorium. Kirk was the first Republican to be elected Florida's governor since Reconstruction. Pictured here are Claude Kirk (speaking) and John Miller (far right). (Courtesy of *Ad Astra*.)

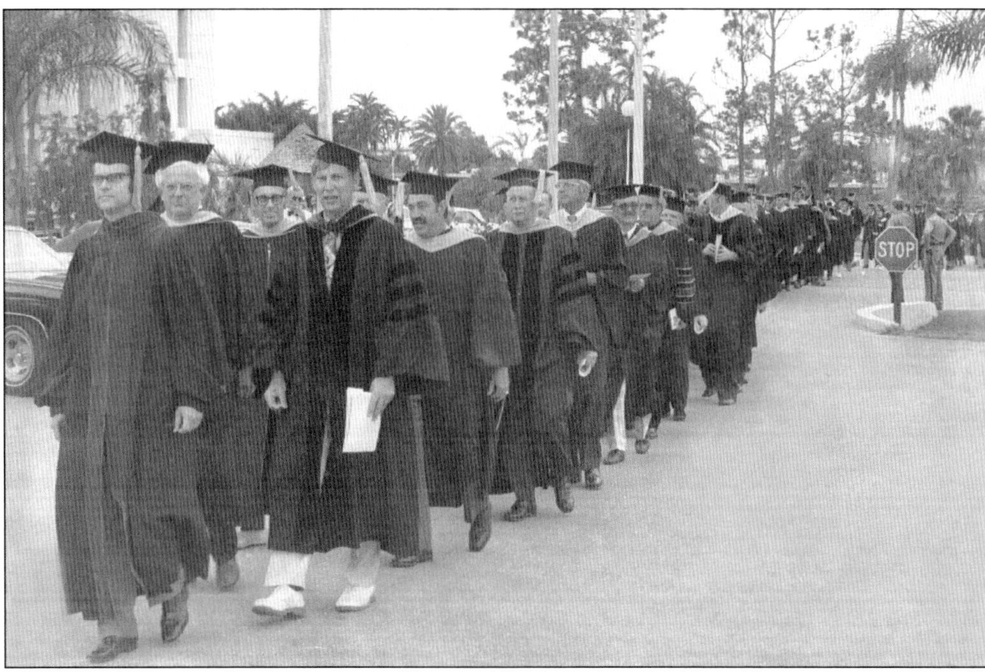

Pictured here is the 1976 commencement party proceeding to the gymnasium. Pieter S. Dubbeldam (front left) is followed by Arthur Burns (chairman of the Federal Reserve and commencement speaker) and John Miller. Burns told the 297 graduates that inflation was a "dangerous disease . . . the economic equivalent of high blood pressure." By 1975, FIT's tuition had risen to $1,944 per year ($648 flat rate for 12 or more hours per quarter.) (Courtesy of University Publications.)

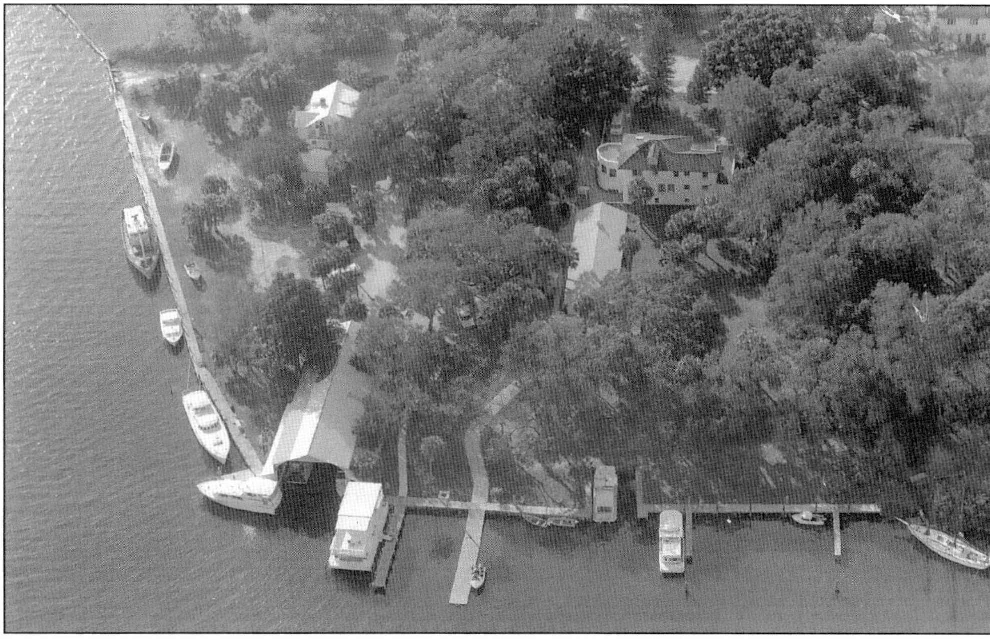

This aerial photograph shows Melbourne Harbor in early 1972. Fred Roberts, trustee, donated the boathouse and anchorage to the college. The *Dragon Lady* was at sea when this photograph was taken. The houseboat (right of boathouse) served as FIT's VIP guest quarters until the late 1980s. (Courtesy of Sterling Photo.)

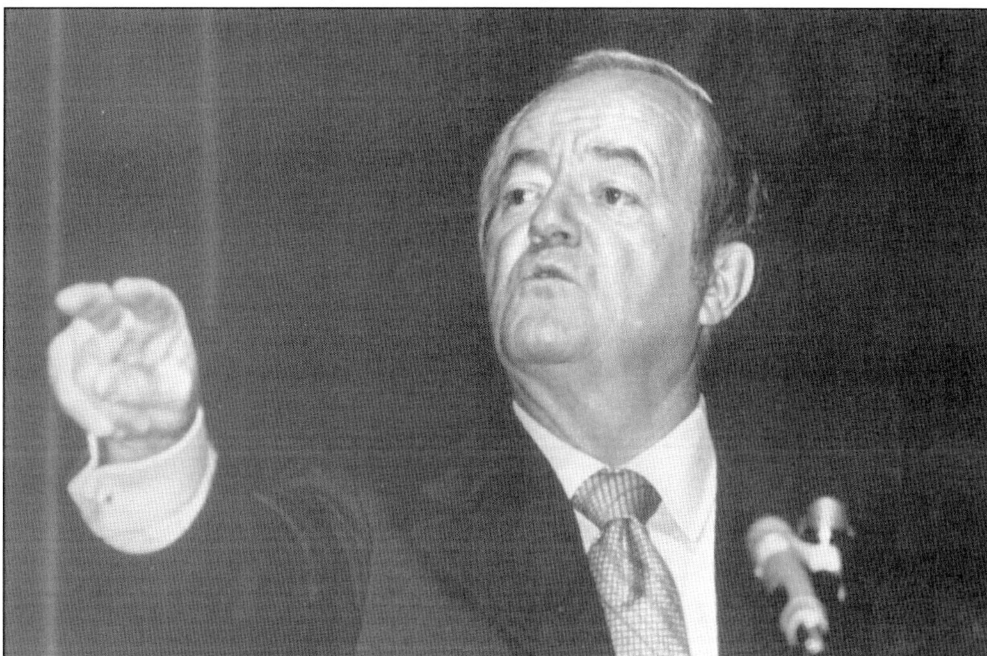

Republicans were not the only politicians interested in Florida Tech. Pictured here is Vice President Hubert Humphrey addressing students and faculty members in the midst of his 1968 presidential campaign. (Courtesy of *Ad Astra.)*

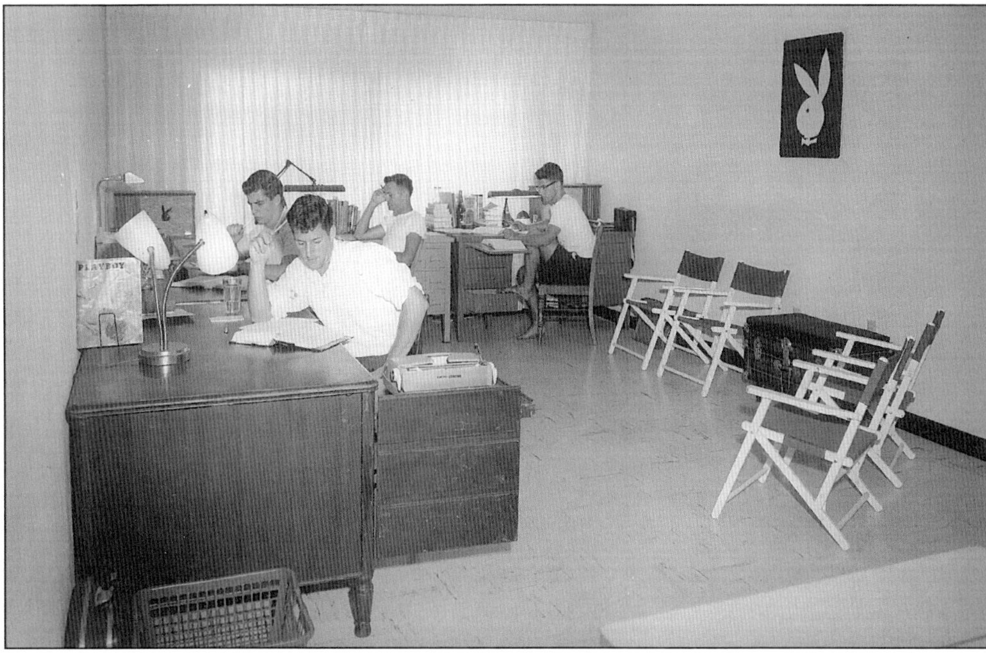

FIT administrators required students to follow a stringent dress code. The 1968 *Student Handbook* explained that "College dress is a matter of good taste . . . Shorts, slacks, and pedal pushers are considered inappropriate for campus wear . . . Male students should shave daily . . . Beards and 'beatnik' hairdos are not acceptable at FIT." Pictured here is a dormitory study area. (Courtesy of University Publications.)

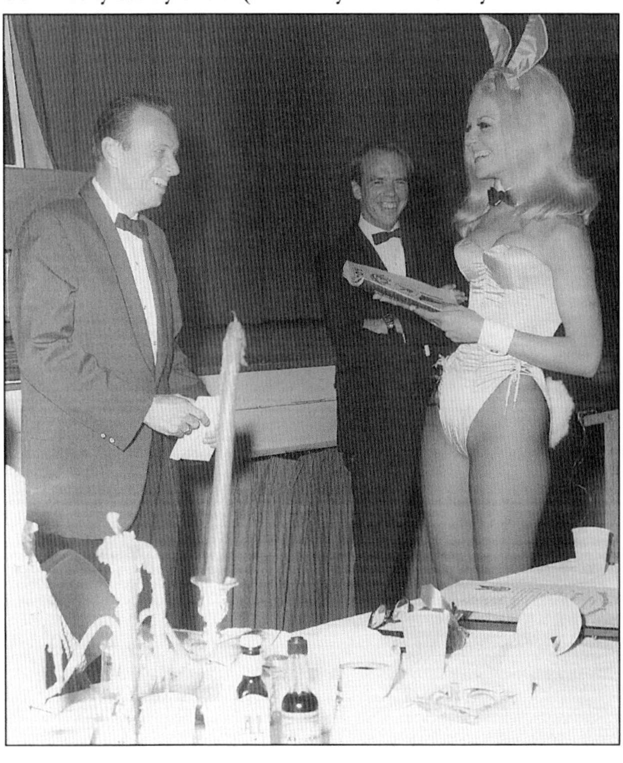

Florida Tech's student body president (center), D. Wayne Rardon ('69 electrical engineering), looks on gleefully as Playboy Bunny Kathy Kennedy presents Jerry Keuper with a lifetime subscription to *Playboy Magazine* at the November 1968 commemoration of the tenth anniversary of the college's founding. Speaking of the larger significance of the occasion, General John Medaris observed, "What has happened at FIT is very little short of a miracle." (Courtesy of University Publications.)

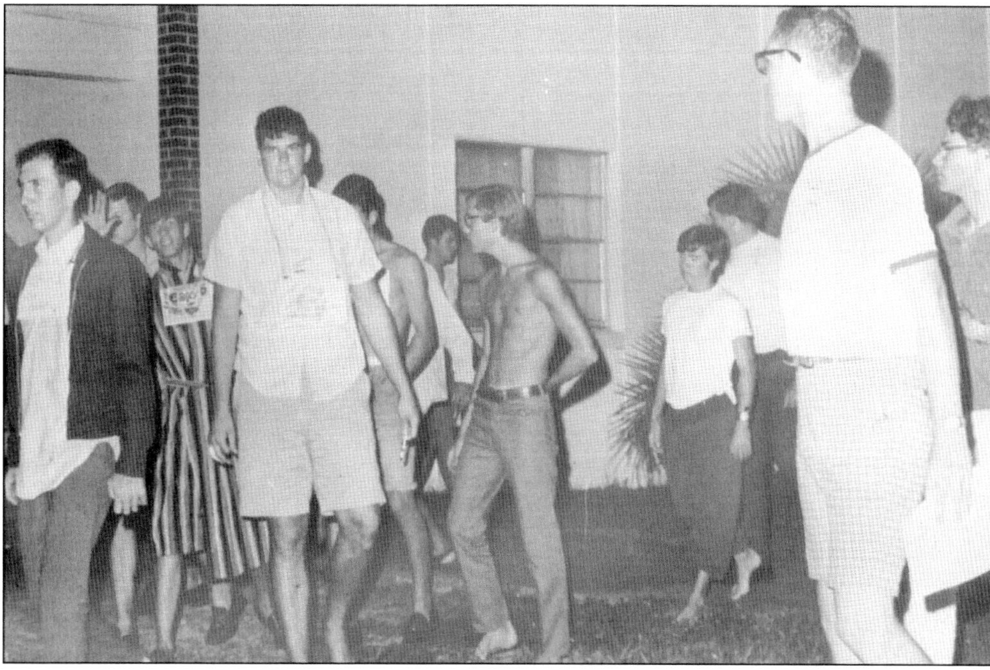

Pictured here are students standing in the dorm quad during a 2 a.m. fire drill during freshman orientation in 1968. Entering freshman received "Beanies" when they arrived on campus. At the beginning of fall quarter, incoming freshmen were dubbed "Frogs." This tradition continued through the mid-1970s. (Courtesy of Evans Library.)

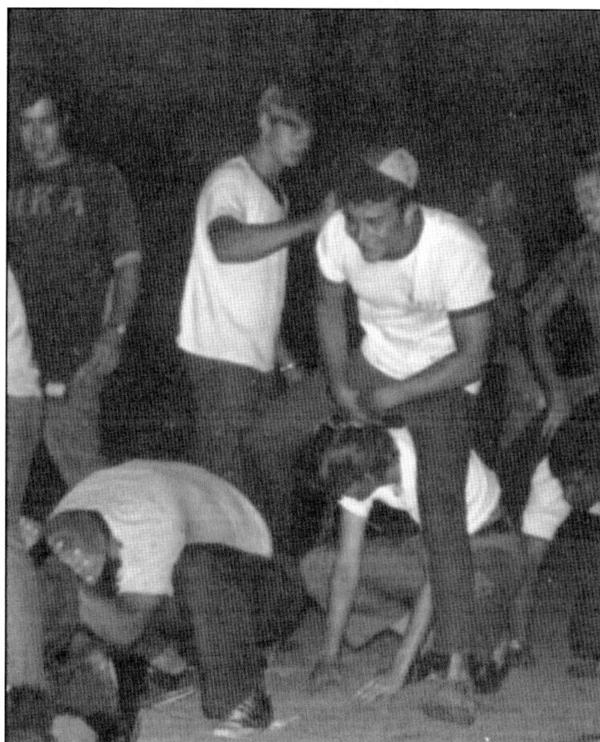

Pictured here is a group of "Frogs" hopping down Country Club Road in 1970. All freshmen recited the "Frog Pledge": "I, Frog (name), . . . realize my poor state. I am lower than the belly of the lowest earthworm that crawls and squirms beneath the hallowed surface of FIT . . . Although I may never become the best Frog, I pledge to uphold FIT's tradition of tip-top-toads." (Courtesy of *Ad Astra*.)

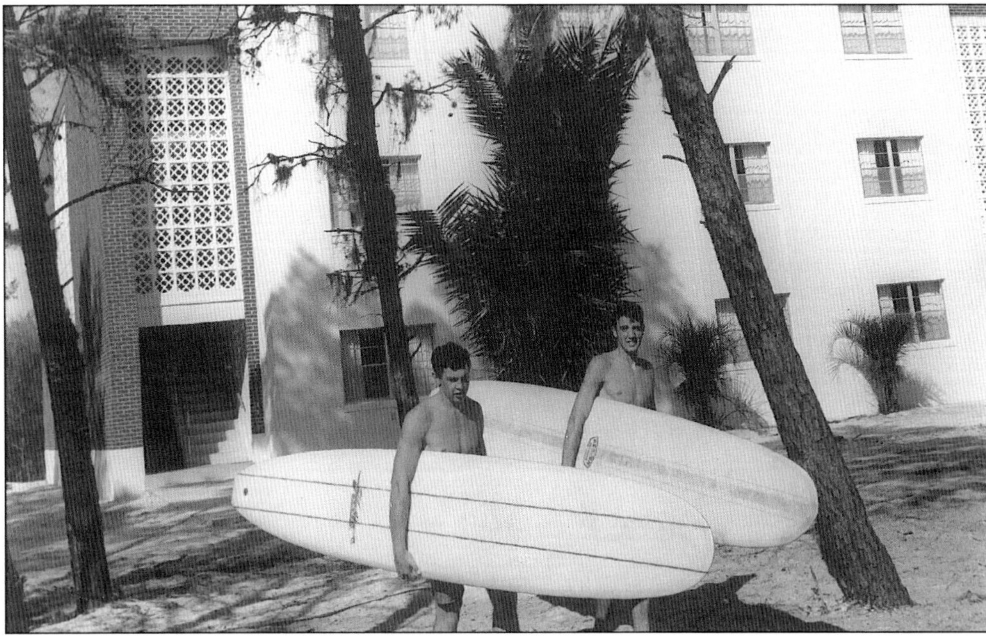

Under FIT's dress code even student surfers were required to maintain clean-cut appearances. Pictured here are two students leaving Shaw Hall in 1967–1968. (Courtesy of University Publications.)

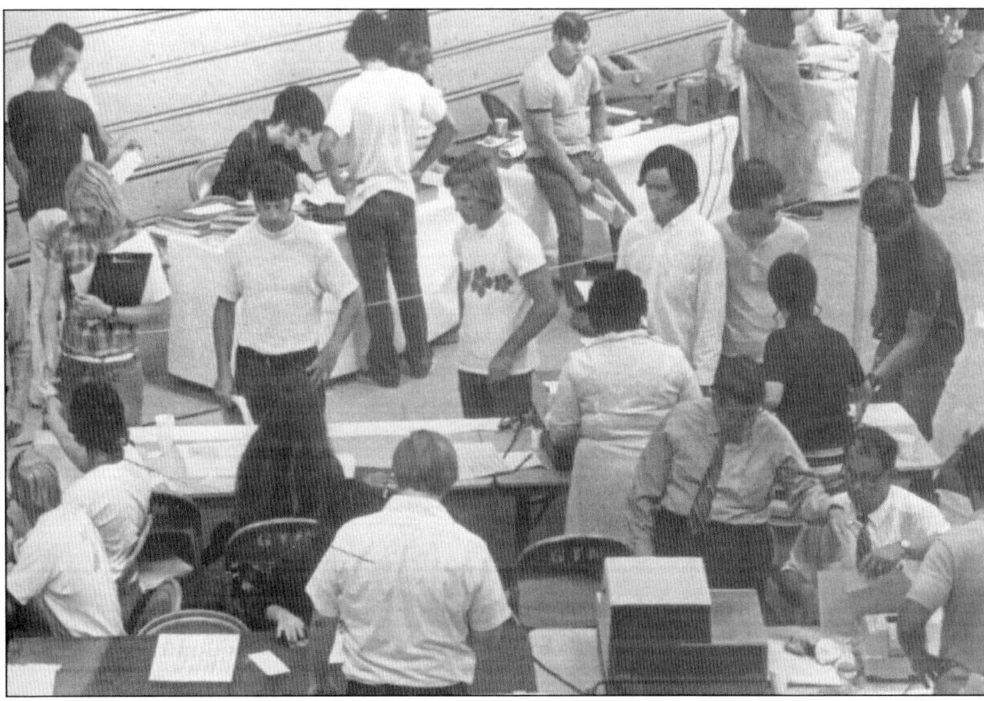

FIT's official dress code ban on long hair and beards collapsed in the late 1960s. By 1972, students had organized protests against the war in Vietnam, tuition increases, and campus food service. Pictured here is 1972 registration for new students held in the gymnasium. (Courtesy of *Ad Astra*.)

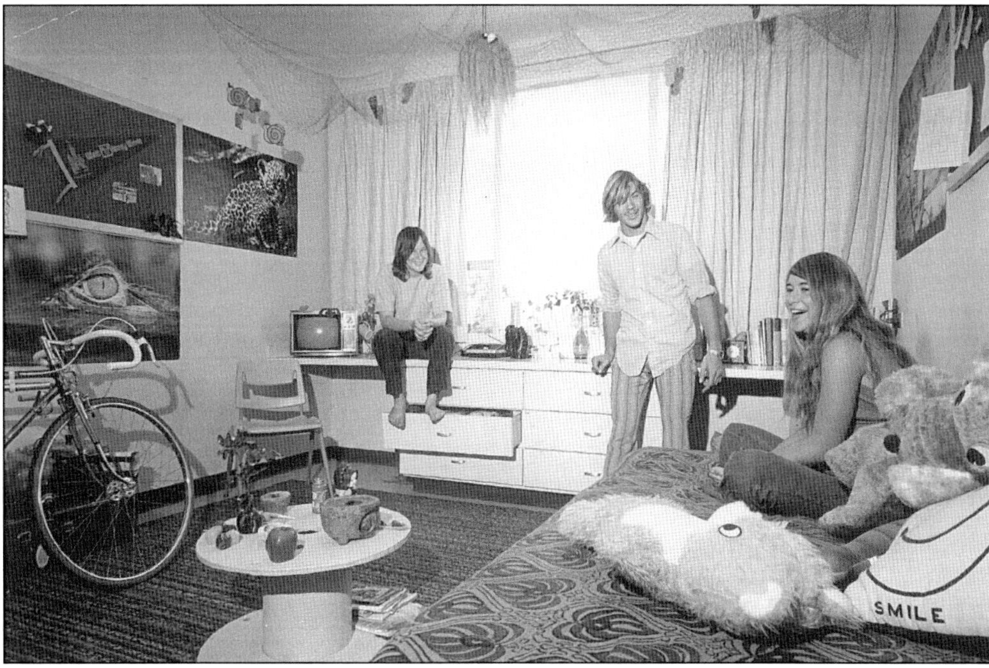

Dormitory life took on a different character in the 1970s. Male and female students were allowed to visit one another. The Rathskeller, located in the basement of Evans Hall in 1973, provided students with a place to meet after class. The dormitory was named in honor of Florence Evans, the college's first woman trustee. (Courtesy of University Publications.)

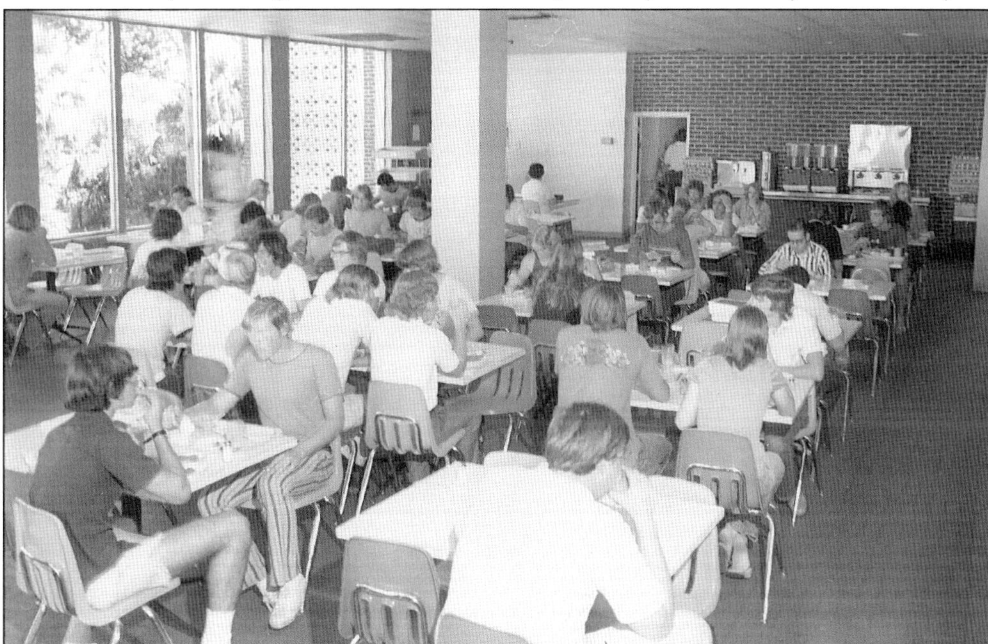

Until 1973, the SUB cafeteria, located in the Denius Student Center, served as the principal dining facility. In 1973, a new cafeteria (above) opened in Evans Hall. (Courtesy of University Publications.)

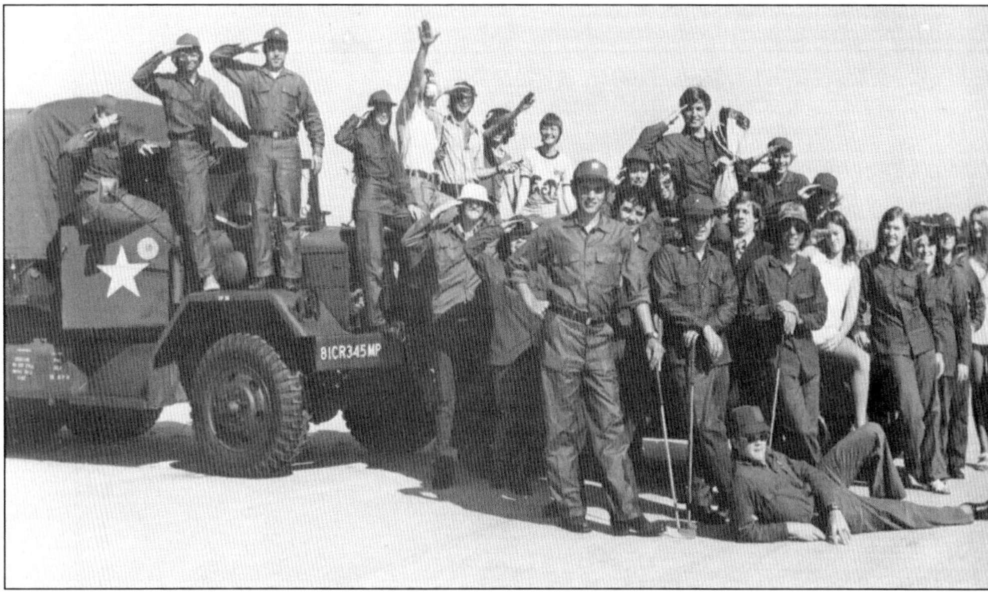

Students sought new outlets for their creative energies in the late 1960s. In 1969, the College Players, FIT's drama society, formed. The Players' first production, *If a Man Answers*, premiered in May 1969. Pictured here is the cast of College Players' 1974 production of *MASH*. (Courtesy of *Ad Astra*.)

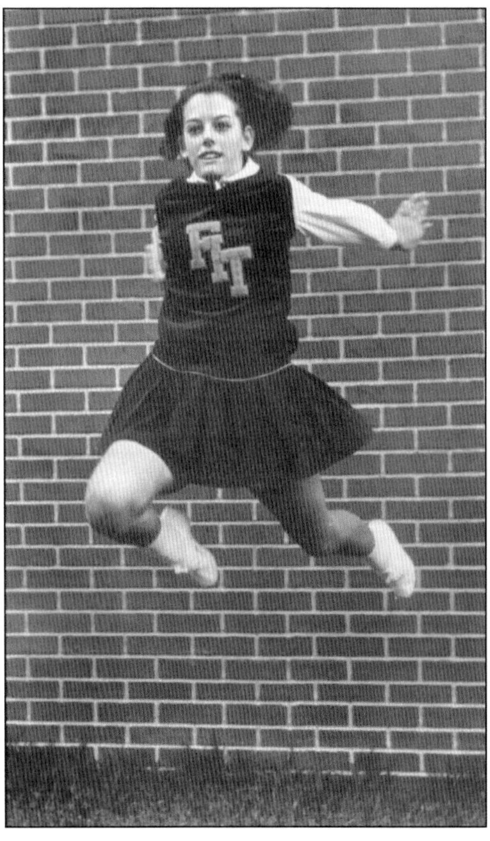

In 1970, basketball coach Leonard "Bing" Yandle told reporters that he wanted his team to be called "Florida Tech" in newspaper articles. "We've got Florida Tech striped down the side of our new uniforms," the coach explained, "and we feel the name better explains where we're from." Here cheerleader Gale Rohde rallies support for Florida Tech in 1969. (Courtesy of *Ad Astra*.)

Florida Tech's basketball program was launched in 1964. After three losing basketball seasons, the Engineers defeated Stetson University (80-77) in January 1967. Pictured here is Florida Tech's Don Gabbard rising above an MIT defensive player in a 1974 cliffhanger. The Engineers lost the game in overtime 77-69. (Courtesy of University Publications.)

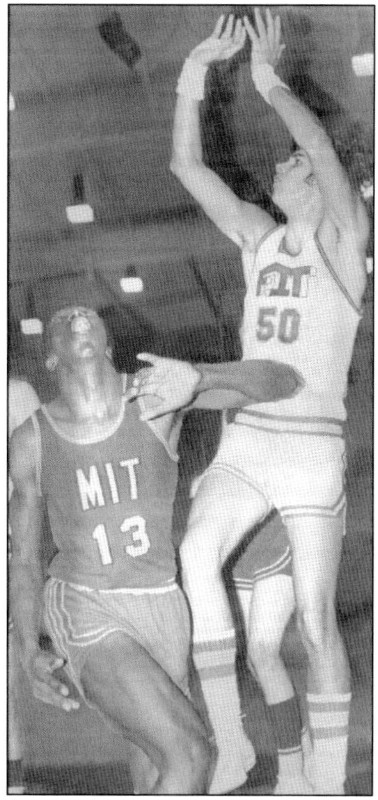

Athletic director and former major league player Andy Seminick had to wait until 1968 for Florida Tech's first win in baseball. Shown here are members of the winning team, which defeated St. Joseph's of Fort Lauderdale, 11-1, in April 1968. (Courtesy of *Ad Astra*.)

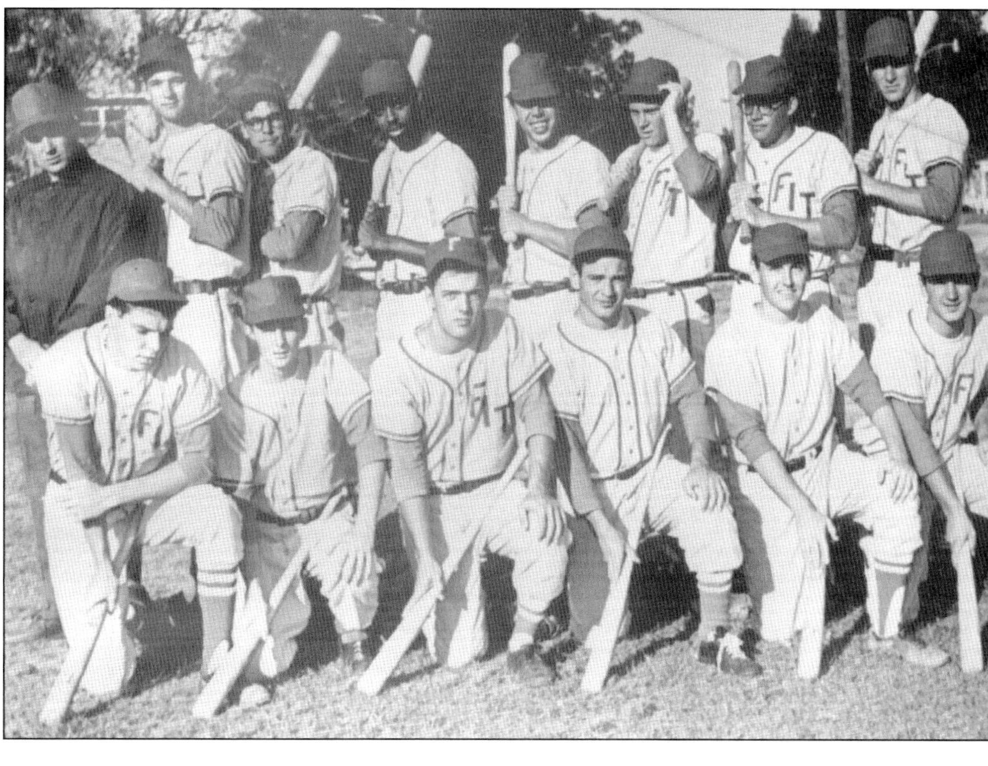

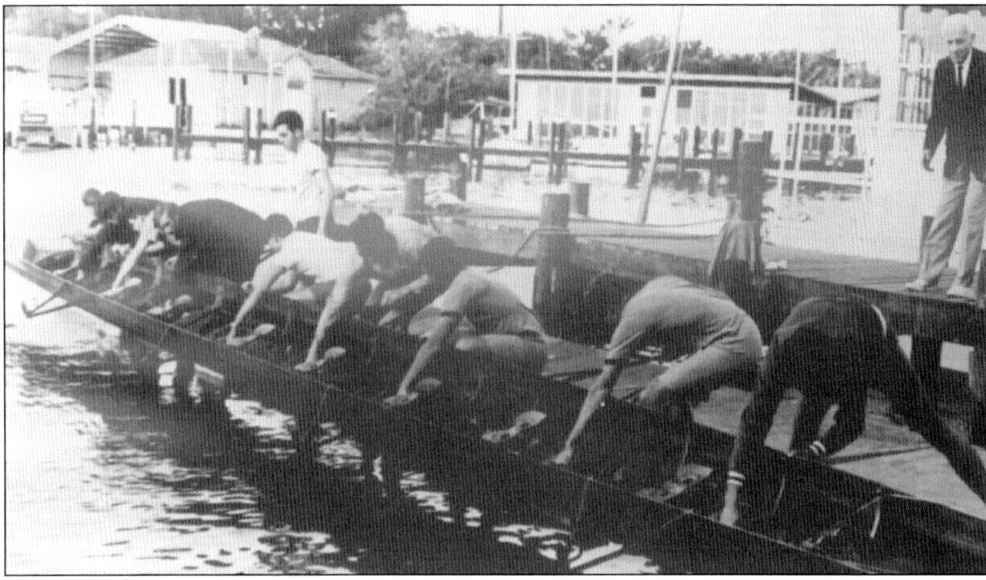

Bob Dunlap (standing) was responsible for launching Florida Tech's crew program. In 1968, Dunlap organized the college's first crew team. Fred Roberts, Florida Tech trustee, provided the team with an anchorage at Melbourne harbor. (Courtesy of *Ad Astra*.)

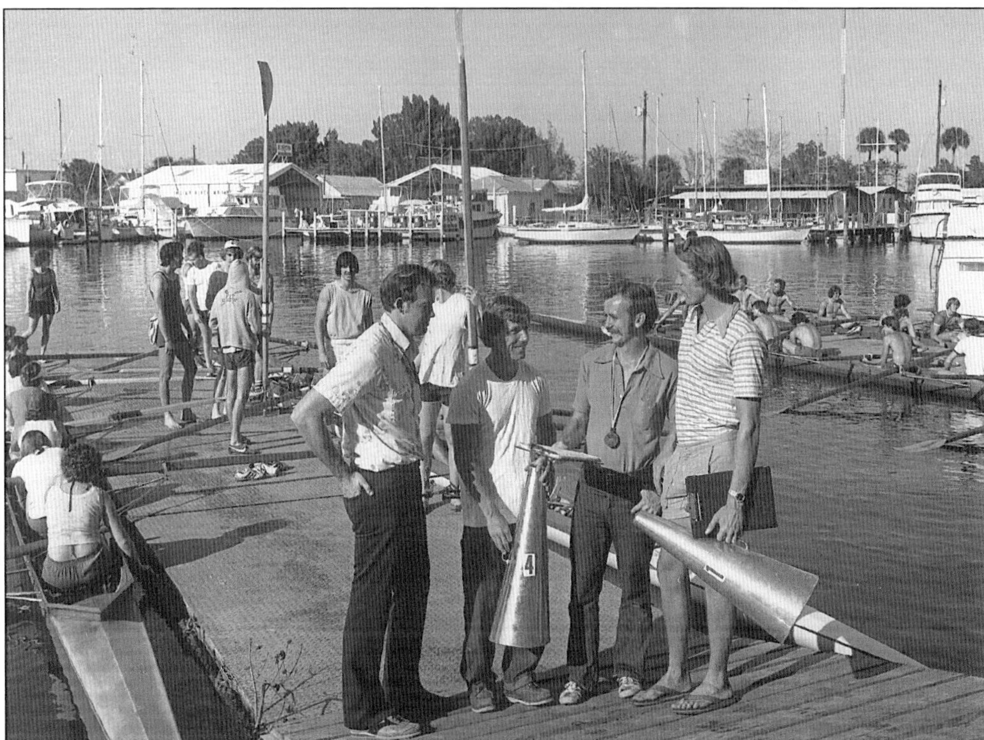

In 1969, Bob Dunlap recruited Bill Jurgens to coach Florida Tech's crew team. Pictured here in 1977, from left to right, are Bill Jurgens, Matt Stoudt, Steve Wagner, and Casey Baker preparing for a training session. In 1982, Florida Tech's men's varsity 8 crew team won its first national championship in the Dad Vail Regatta. (Courtesy of University Publications.)

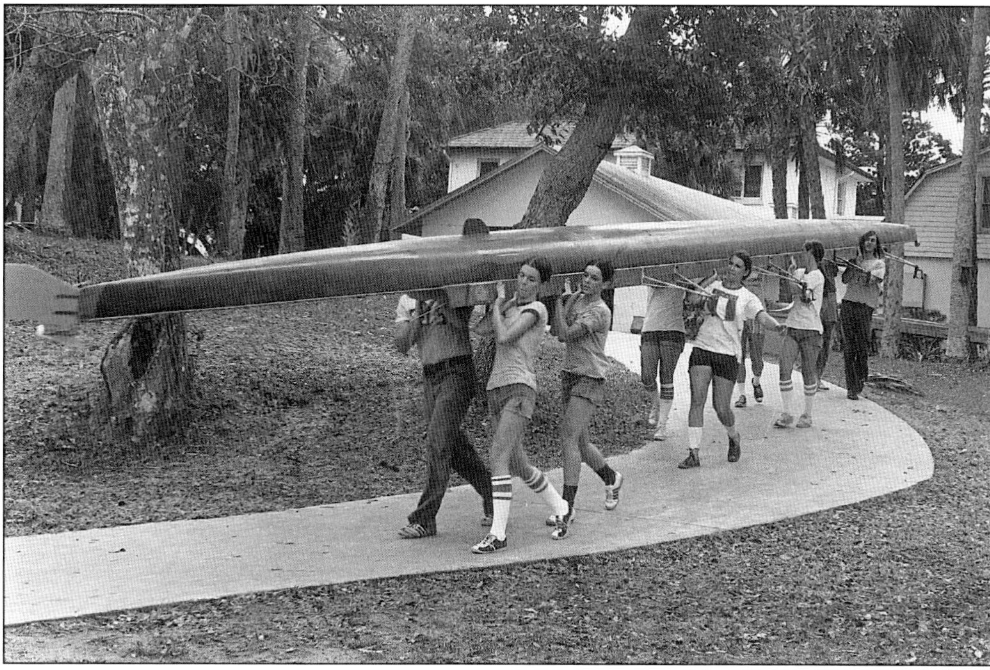

By 1975, Florida Tech's women's crew team was winning national attention. Jeanne Flanagan ('79 oceanography) was the first Florida Tech graduate to win a gold medal (at the 1984 Olympic Games). Pictured here is the 1974 women's crew team returning from practice. (Courtesy of University Publications.)

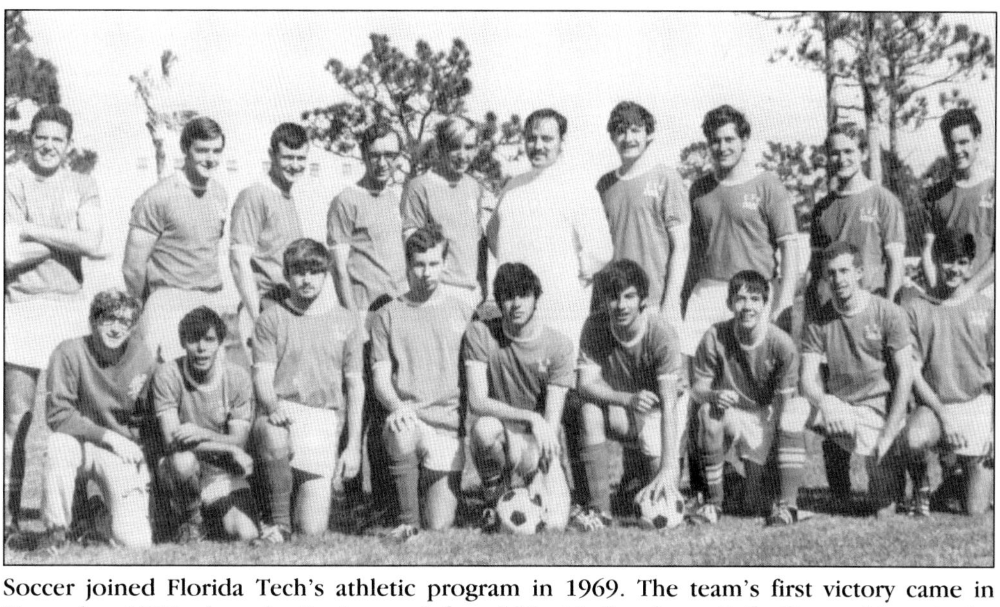

Soccer joined Florida Tech's athletic program in 1969. The team's first victory came in November 1970 when the Engineers defeated Florida Southern (1-0). Pictured here is the 1969–1970 team. (Courtesy of *Ad Astra*.)

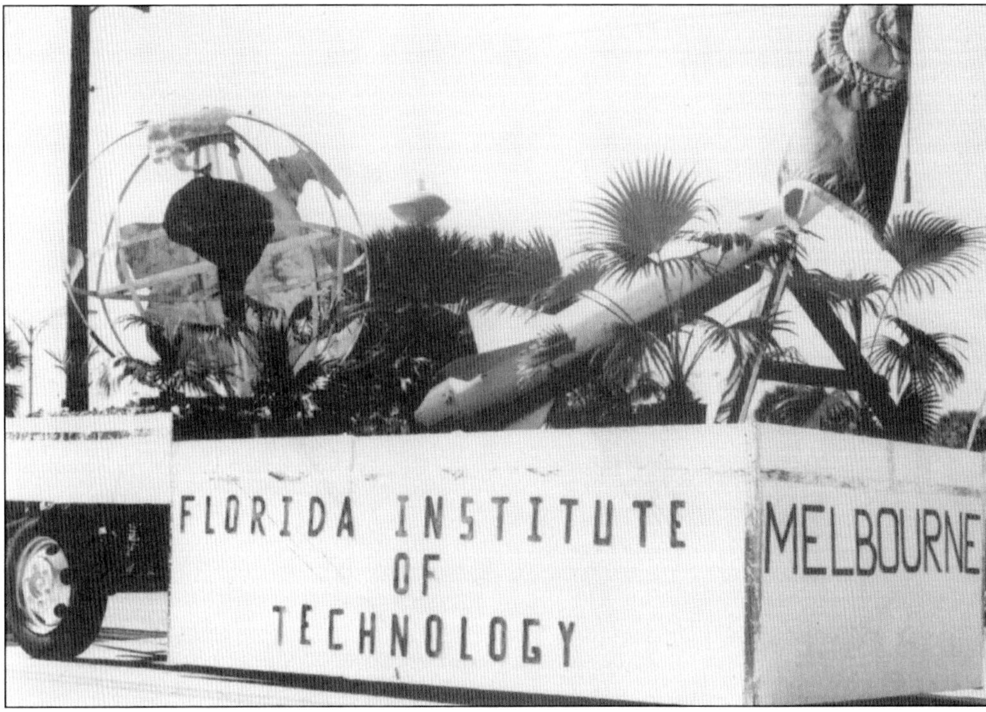

Florida Tech celebrated its first official homecoming in 1972. Pictured here is an early float celebrating the college's close connection with the space program. (Courtesy of University Publications.)

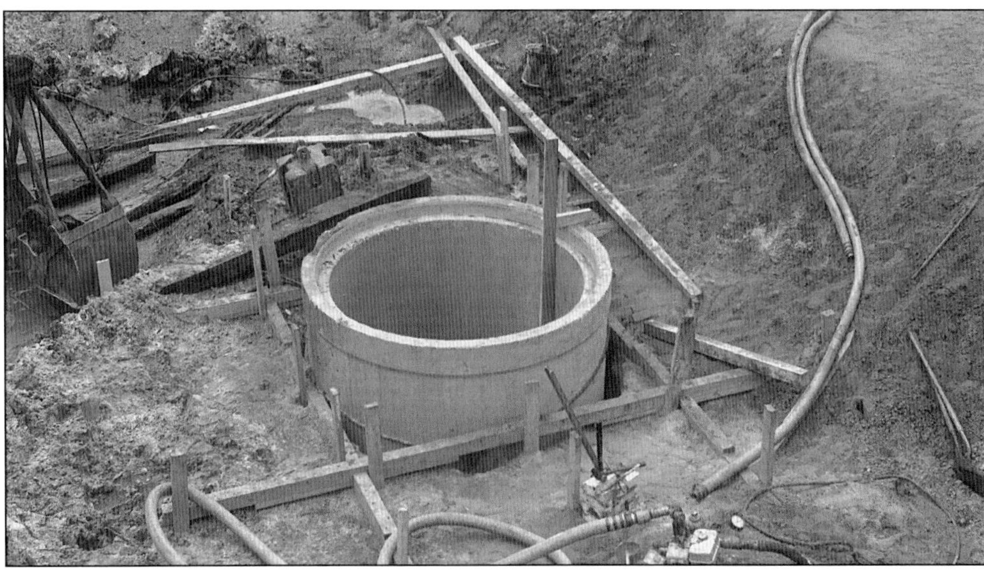

David Woodbridge, Florida Tech's first research director, won national attention in July 1970 when *Time Magazine* published an article describing Woodbridge's efforts to use radioactive cobalt-60 to purify water. Using an underground facility next to the Crawford Science Building (pictured here under construction), Woodbridge conducted a series of experiments in what students irreverently named the "atomic toilet." (Courtesy of Evans Library.)

In March 1974, Florida Tech's students demonstrated that the college's stringent dress code was a thing of the past. More than 500 students chanting "We're Number One" streaked across campus in what was reputed to be the largest college streak. (Courtesy of *Ad Astra*.)

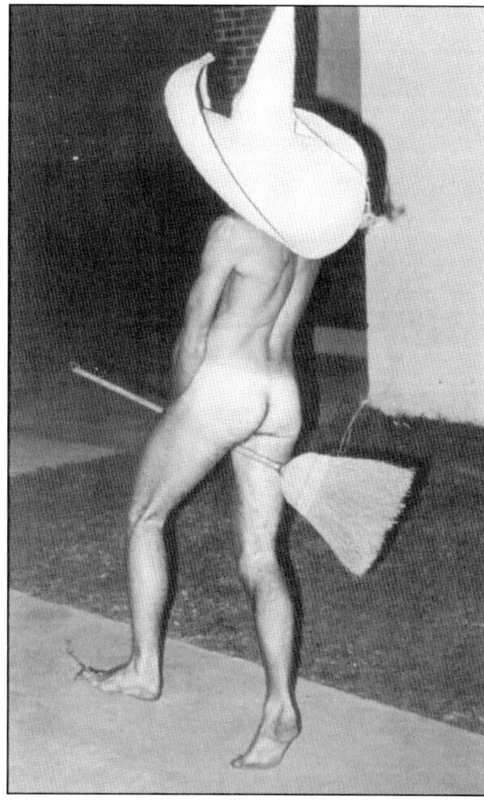

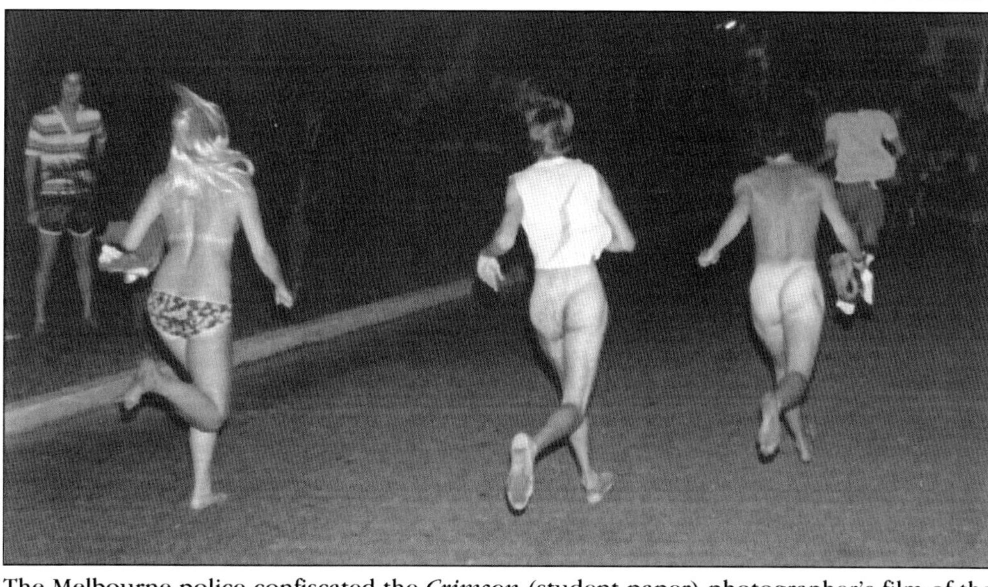

The Melbourne police confiscated the *Crimson* (student paper) photographer's film of the mass streak. Biology Professor Kerry Clark won the film's return. Others worried about the decline in student morals. The *Melbourne Times* reported that Reverend Edward D. Thompson called for "a short time for prayer on Sunday for the purpose of healing our city and community after the lamentable happenings at the Florida Institute of Technology." (Courtesy of Bryan Walus, '74 computer science.)

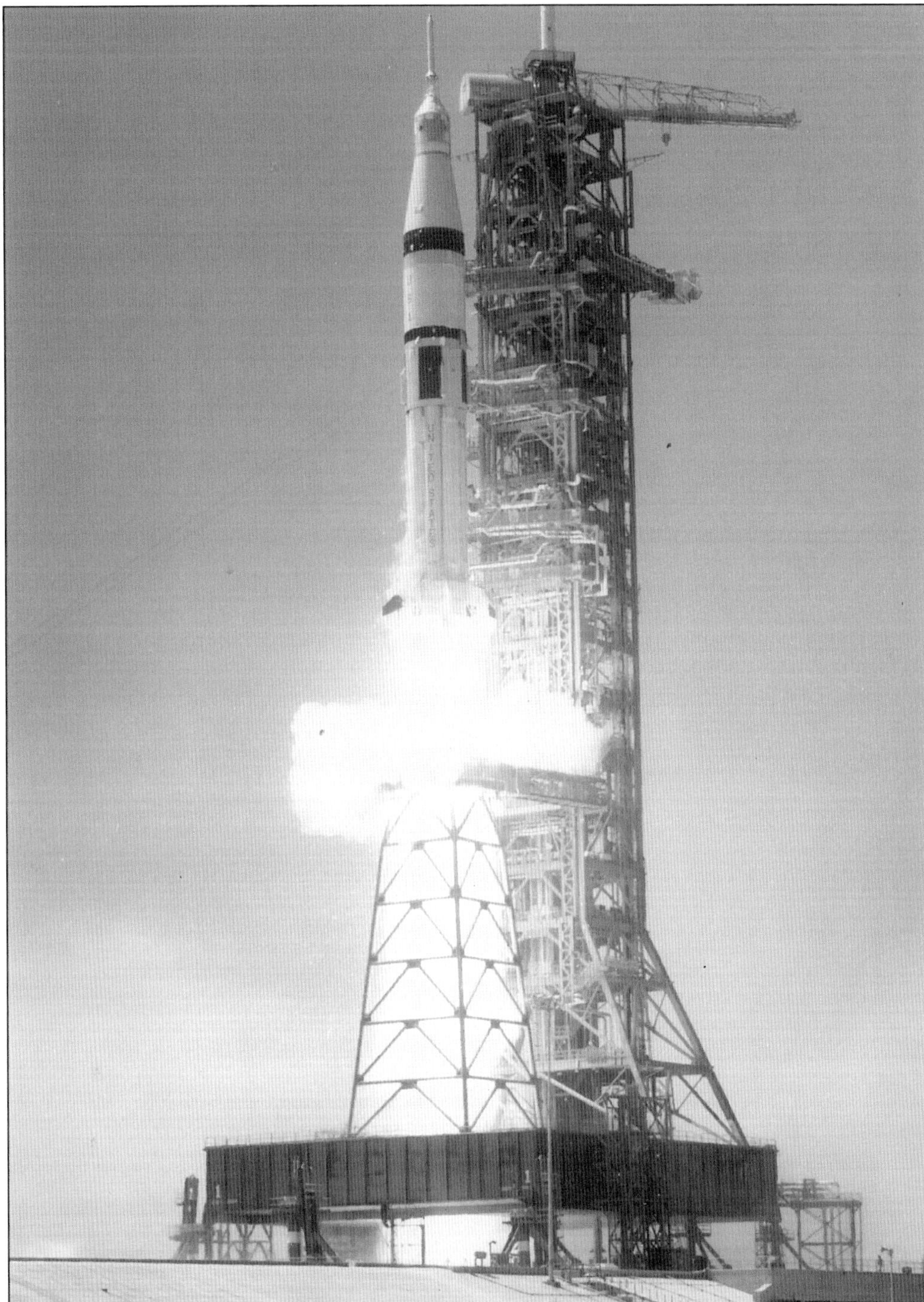

The Apollo Soyuz Saturn 1B launch vehicle is shown here lifting off from Launch Complex 39B at Kennedy Space Center on July 15, 1975. The mission marked the end of one phase in the U.S. space program. The giant Saturn launch vehicles were replaced in the next decade by the Space Shuttle.(Courtesy of Air Force Missile and Space Museum.)

Four

Challenges and Opportunities: 1975–1987

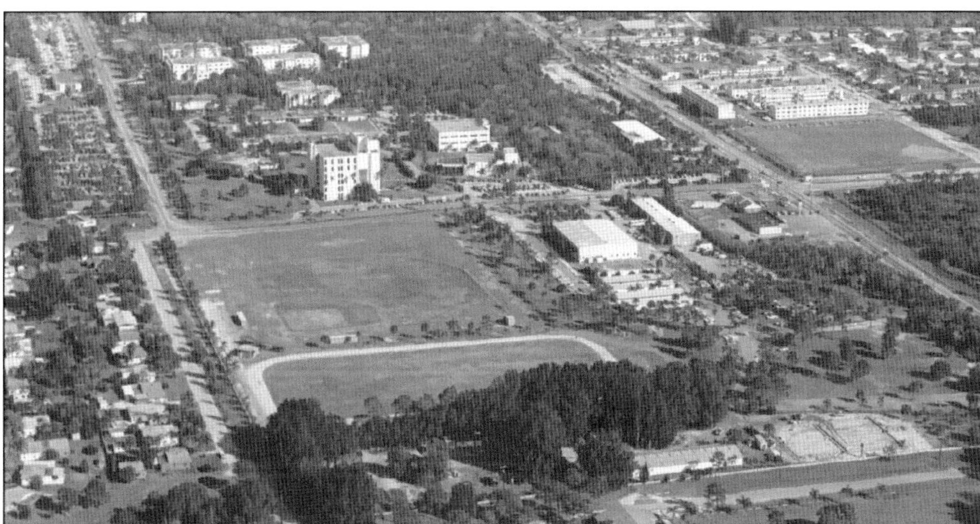

Florida Tech underwent profound changes between 1975 and 1987. Enrollment soared in Melbourne. The burden imposed by the acquisition of Hawthorne College in 1981 and declining enrollment at Jensen Beach (after 1982) strained the university. Jerry Keuper announced his retirement in 1985. John Miller, Florida Tech's second president (1986–1987) oversaw the closing of the Jensen Beach campus. Pictured here is a 1982 aerial view of the Melbourne campus. (Courtesy of University Publications.)

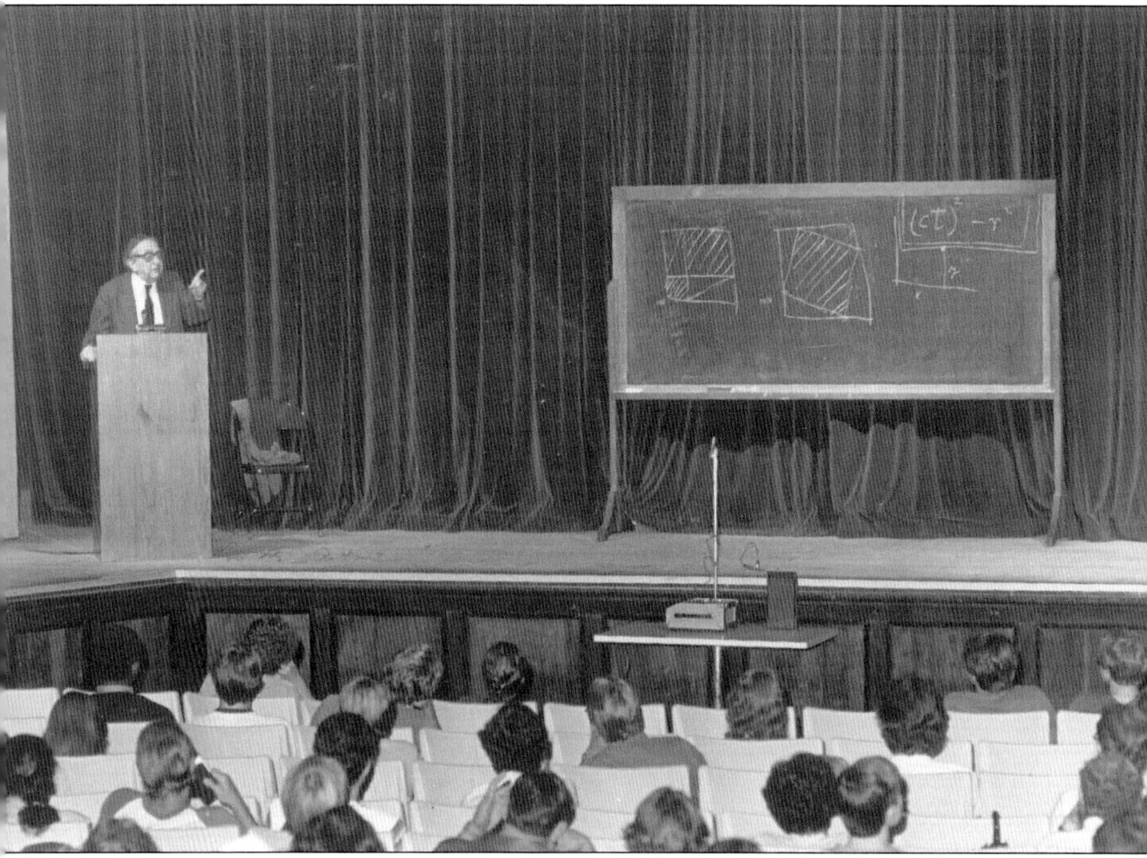

In 1978, Florida Tech commemorated the twentieth anniversary of its founding in a festive "Under the Palms" celebration. Edward Teller, known as the "father of the Hydrogen Bomb" and winner in 1962 of the Enrico Fermi Award, expressed his conviction "Where M.I.T. has failed, F.I.T. can take over." (Courtesy of University Publications.)

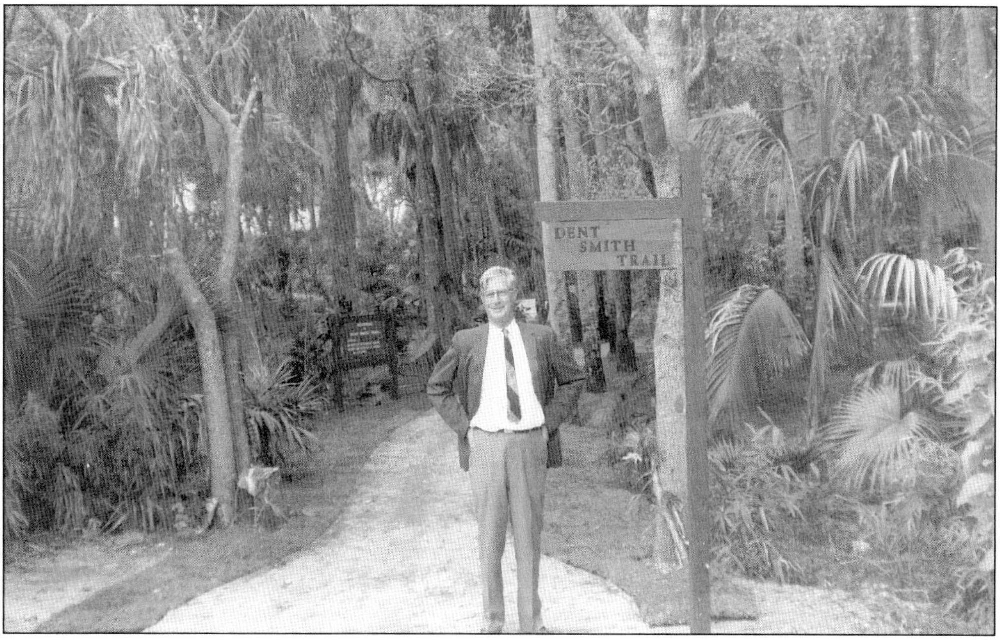

The celebration's "Under the Palms" theme was well chosen. In the early 1960s, Jerry Keuper enlisted the support of Dent Smith (above), a retired Wall Street executive and avid collector of rare palms. Smith contributed to establishing the college's collection of rare palms. The Dent Smith Trail winds through one of the largest collections of exotic palm trees in the continental United States. (Courtesy of University Publications.)

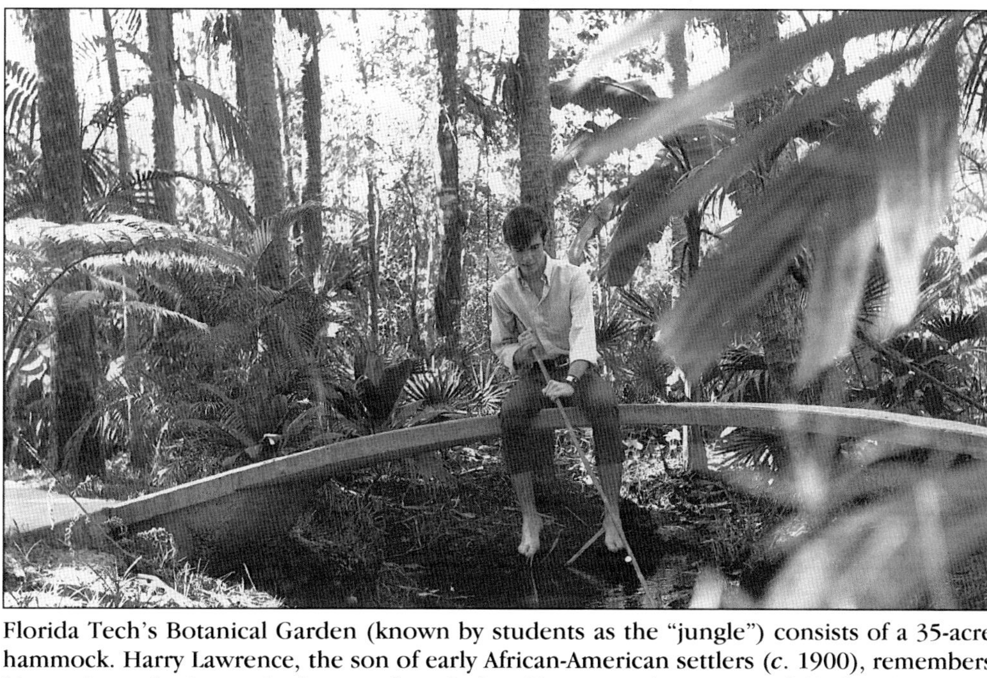

Florida Tech's Botanical Garden (known by students as the "jungle") consists of a 35-acre hammock. Harry Lawrence, the son of early African-American settlers (*c.* 1900), remembers his mother referring to the hammock as Cathead because "the area was full of wild cats and panthers. We would see them peering at us from the trees. But they never harmed anyone." Pictured here is a Florida Tech student. (Courtesy of University Publications.)

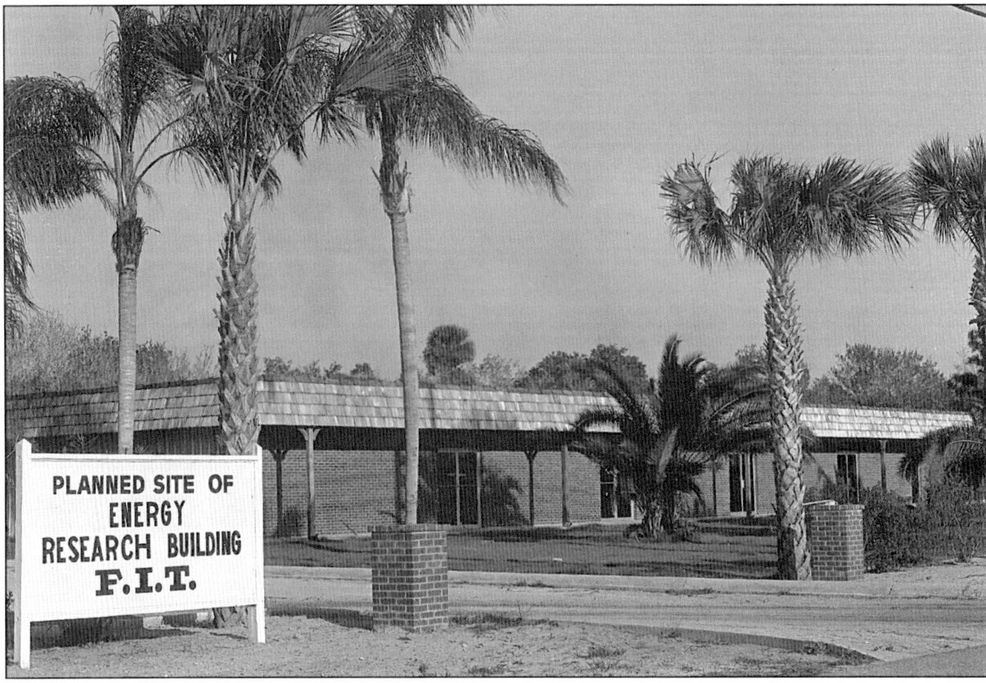

NASA donated the Frueauff Building to the university in 1977. NASA used this building as an early visitor's center. The Frueauff Building housed the university development office and energy laboratories through the 1980s. Later, it served as home for the civil engineering department. (Courtesy of University Publications.)

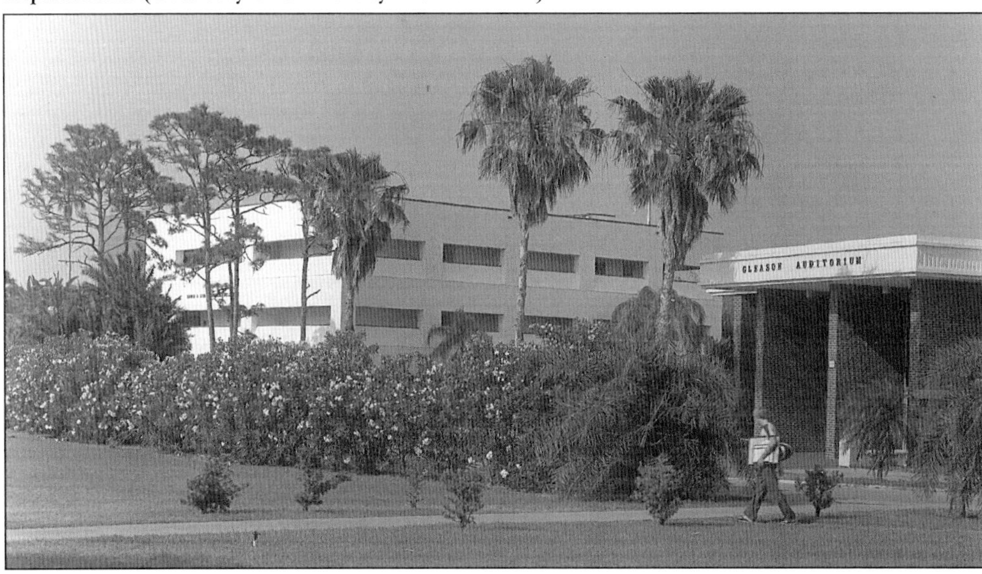

Completed in 1977, the Link Engineering Building was officially dedicated in 1979. Edwin Link, scientist and early friend of the university, devised the first flight simulator and did pioneering research in ocean engineering. John Evans Library's Special Collections contains Edwin Link's papers. The Link Building served as home for the oceanography, ocean engineering, chemical engineering, and biology programs in the 1970s and 1980s. (Courtesy of University Publications.)

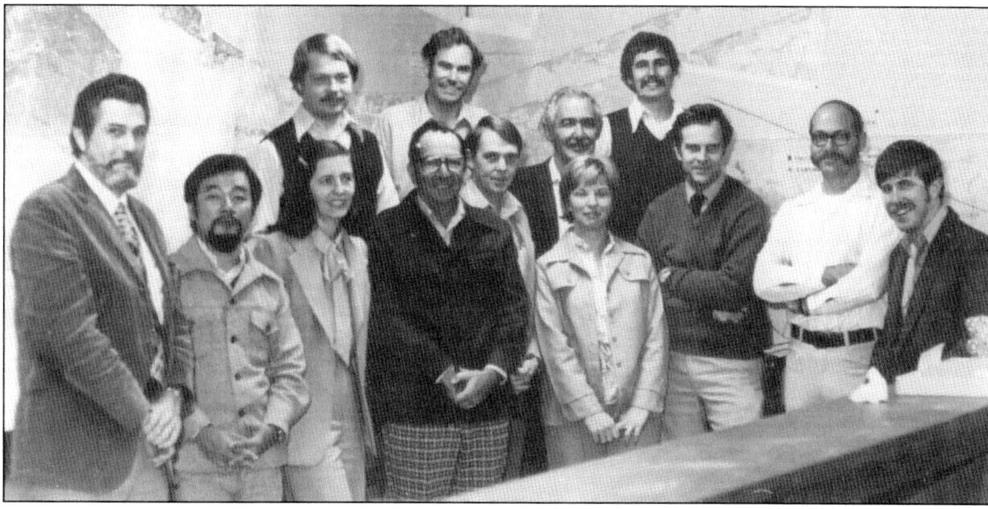

FIT launched its program in oceanography in 1966 and ocean engineering in 1972. Pictured here are members of the oceanography and ocean engineering departments in 1979. From left to right are N.W. O'Hara (head), T. Anzai, D. Barile, J. Trefry, D. Stauble, J. Schwalbe, D. Norris, T. Andrews, A. Kerlo, R. Pierce, P. Dubbleday, J. Roberts, and J. Morton. (Courtesy of *Ad Astra*.)

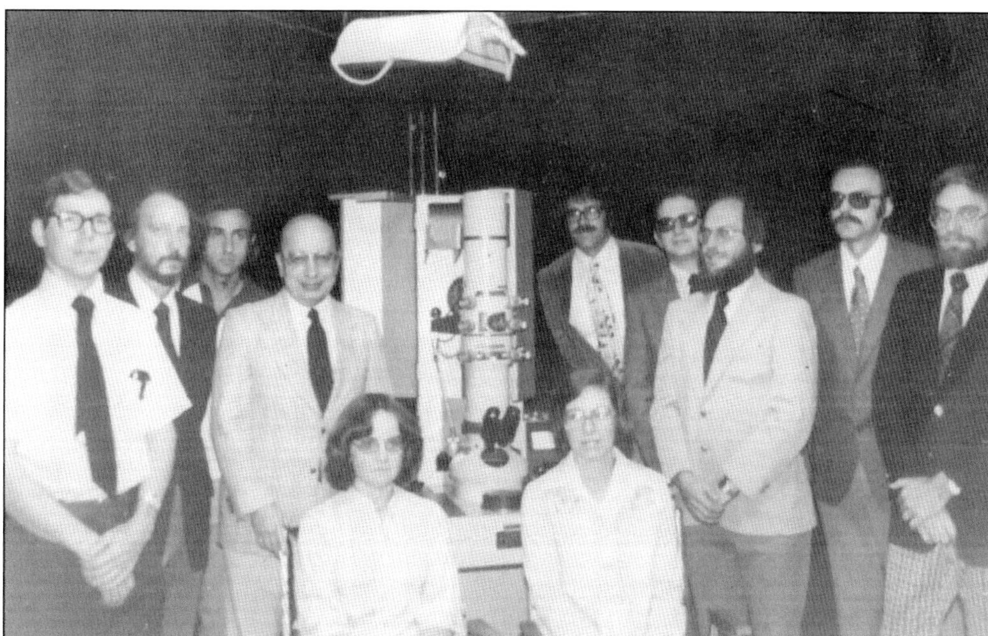

In 1971, John Miller asked NASA biologist George Webster to lead the newly formed biology department. Pictured here in 1979 are, from left to right, R. Turner, J. Morris, W. Alevizon , G. Webster, D. Looney, C. Sorrell, G. Cohen, G. Wells, K. Kasweck, C. Polson, and K. Clark (Courtesy of *Ad Astra*.)

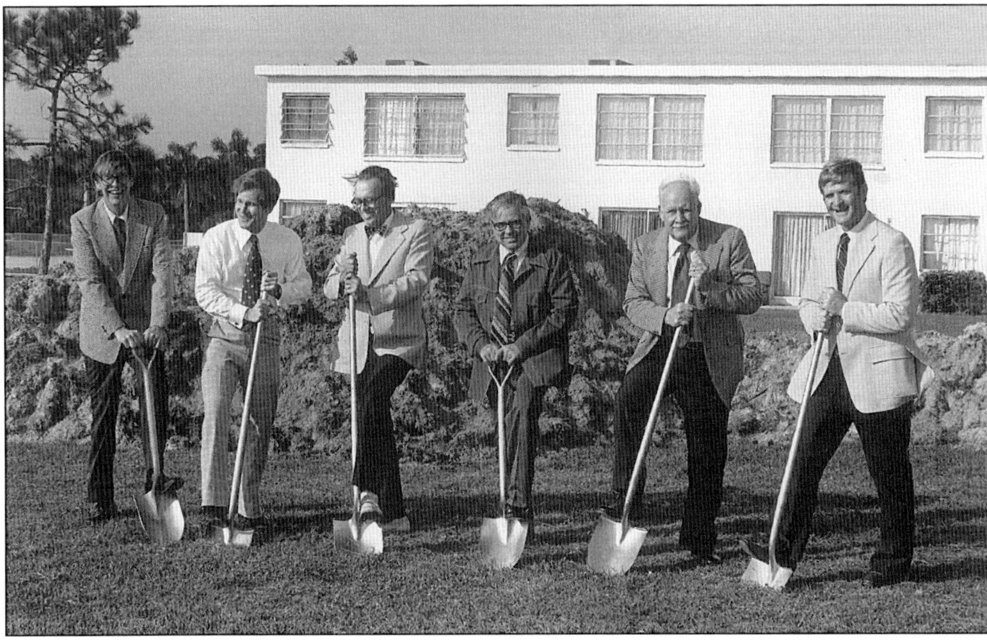

In 1979, construction began on a $1.7-million expansion of the Southgate Apartments. Pictured here, from left to right, are John Miller, executive vice president of academic affairs; Congressman Bill Nelson; Jerry Keuper; John Simmons, vice president of financial affairs; Ray Work, vice president of administrative affairs; and Barry Fullerton, vice president of student affairs. (Courtesy of University Publications.)

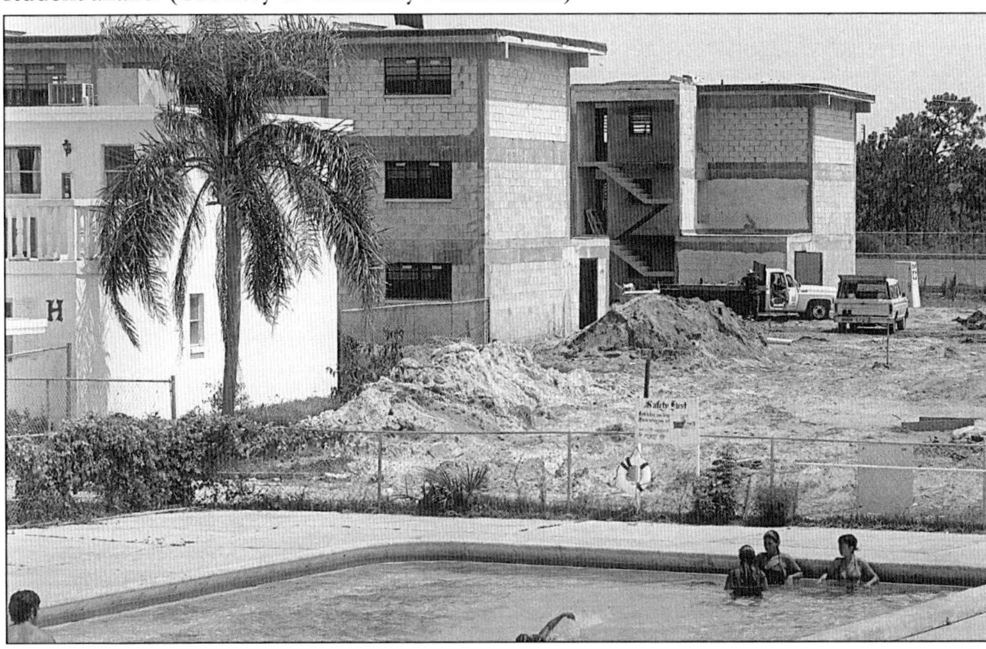

Workers succeeded in finishing the Southgate expansion (pictured here) in time for the beginning of classes in September 1979. Tuition was $57.50 per credit hour. An undergraduate engineering student carrying 15 hours would spend $2,587 for a year's tuition. (Courtesy of University Publications.)

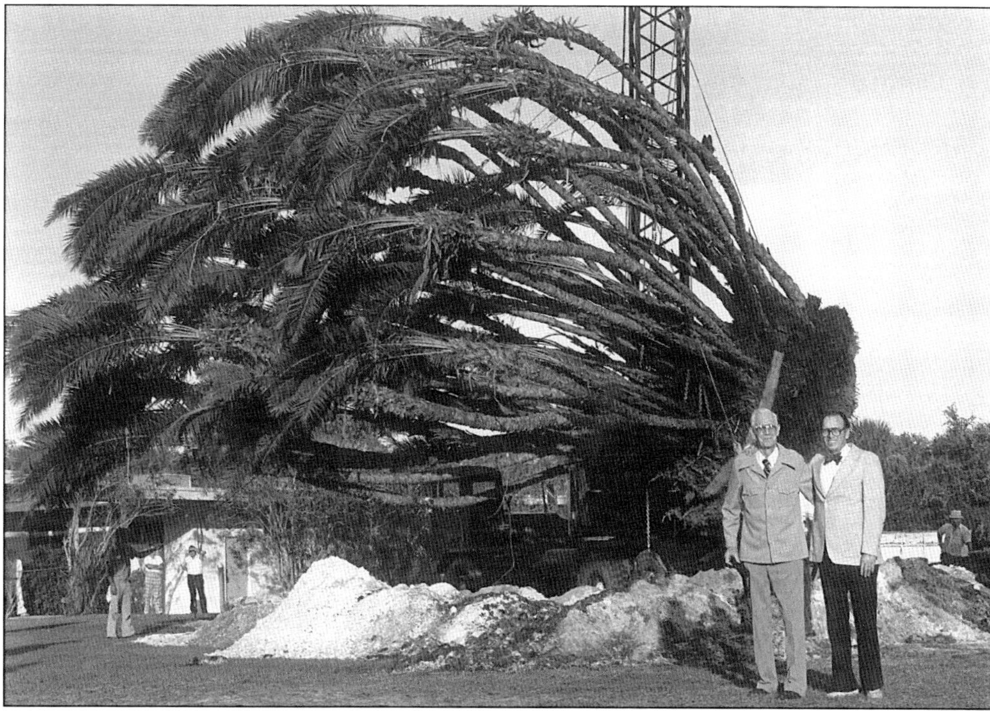

Norman Lund, left, a founding member of the board of trustees, gave the university an early Christmas present when he donated this 64-trunked *Phoenix reclinata* to the campus in December 1979. Florida Tech's groundskeepers required a police escort to get the tree to campus. (Courtesy of University Publications.)

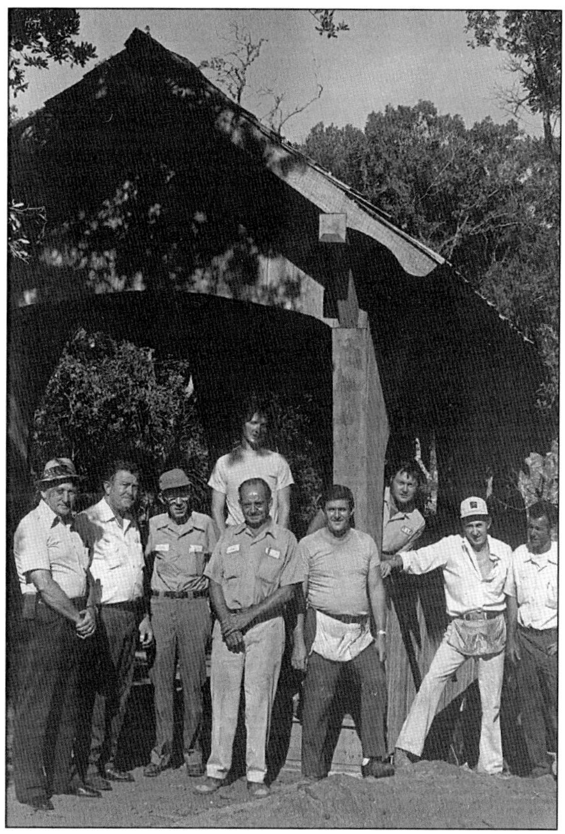

Pictured here are members of Florida Tech's Buildings and Grounds department at the completion of one of the campus's covered bridges. Dale Simcox (foreman) devoted countless hours to landscaping the campus. Simcox Square (across from the School of Business) is named in his honor. Pictured, from left to right, are (front row) D. Simcox, F. Clark, J. Toker, G. Sias, D. Lewis, B. Fleming, and J. Thompson; (back row) T. Pineo and H. Hughes. (Courtesy of University Publications.)

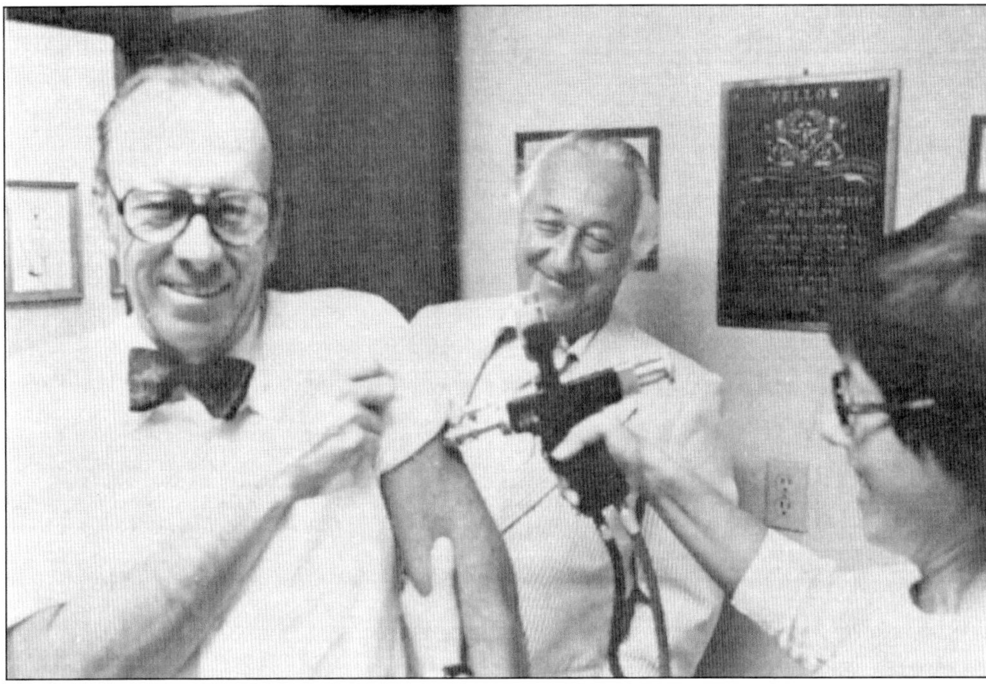

President Keuper is receiving a swine flu shot given by nurse Sue Barge, 1976, while Dr. Oswald Holzer, medical director of Florida Tech's student health center, observes the procedure. (Courtesy of University Publications.)

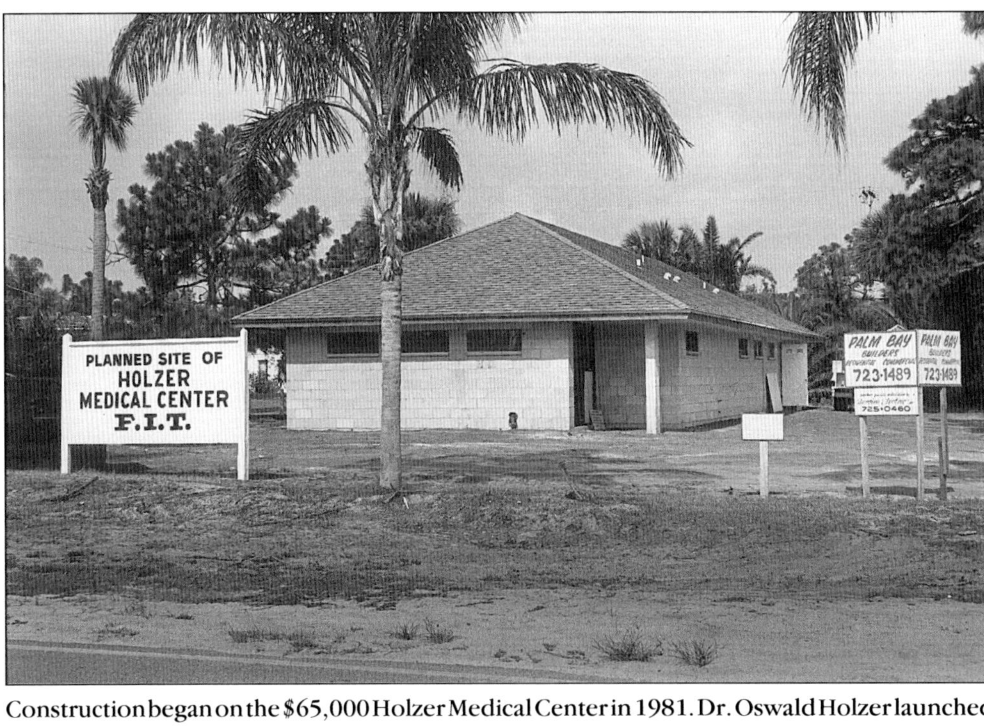

Construction began on the $65,000 Holzer Medical Center in 1981. Dr. Oswald Holzer launched the college's student health service in April 1975. (Courtesy of University Publications.)

Pictured here is the unveiling of the Chao Tsu-Yu Chinese Clock. During the 1970s and 1980s, Florida Tech was one of the leaders in granting graduate fellowships to Chinese students. Taiwanese officials presented the clock to the university in August 1981. (Courtesy of University Publications.)

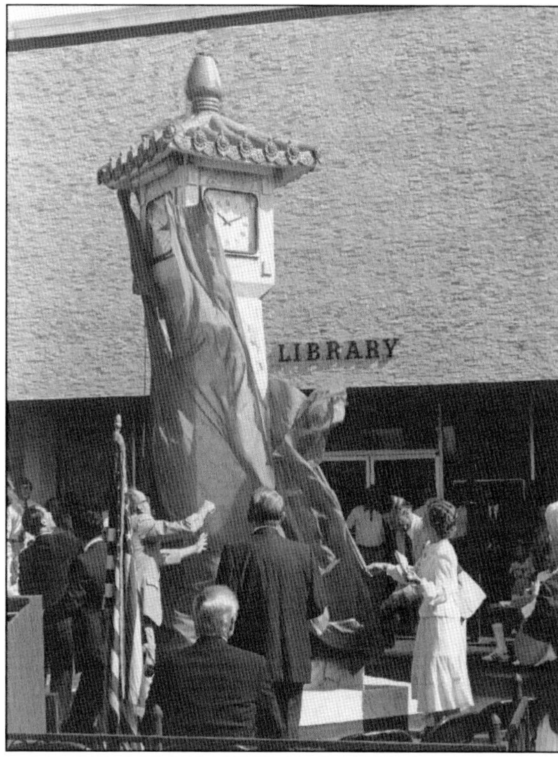

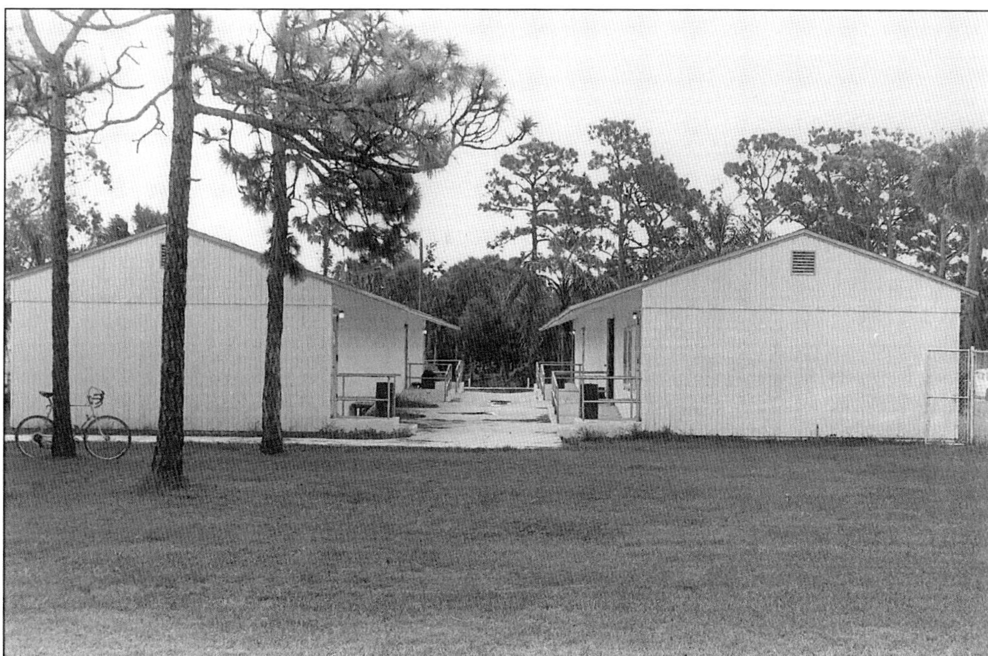

Skyrocketing student enrollment in the 1970s forced the university to create a classroom annex behind the gymnasium. These temporary classrooms were removed when the site was prepared for the Charles and Ruth Clemente Center for Sports and Recreation in 1999. (Courtesy of University Publications.)

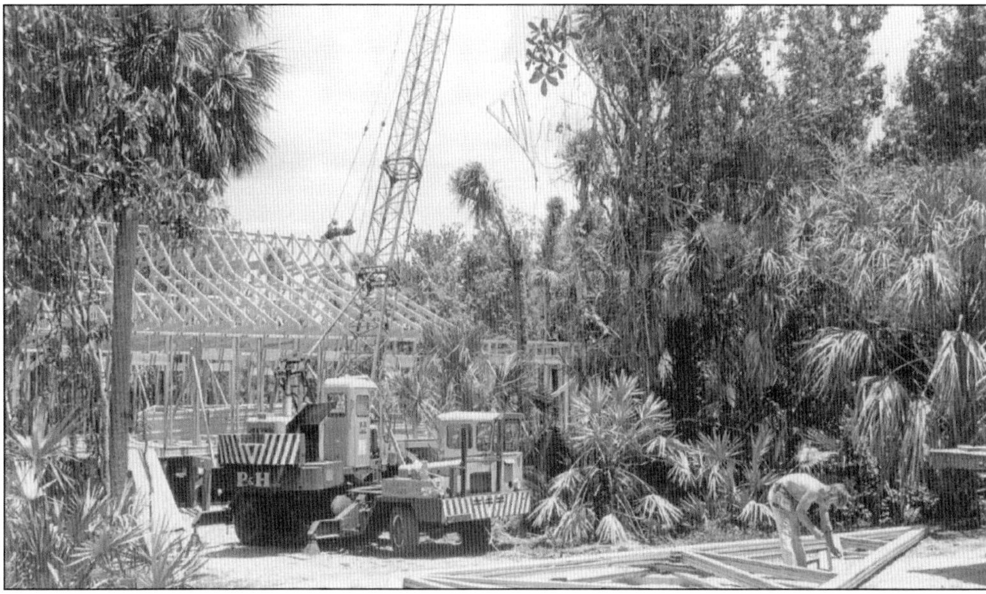

Construction of the Shephard Seminar Building, named in honor of Donald and Helen Shephard, trustees and founders of the Empire Tool Company, began in 1981. The Shephard Building houses the science education department. (Courtesy of University Publications.)

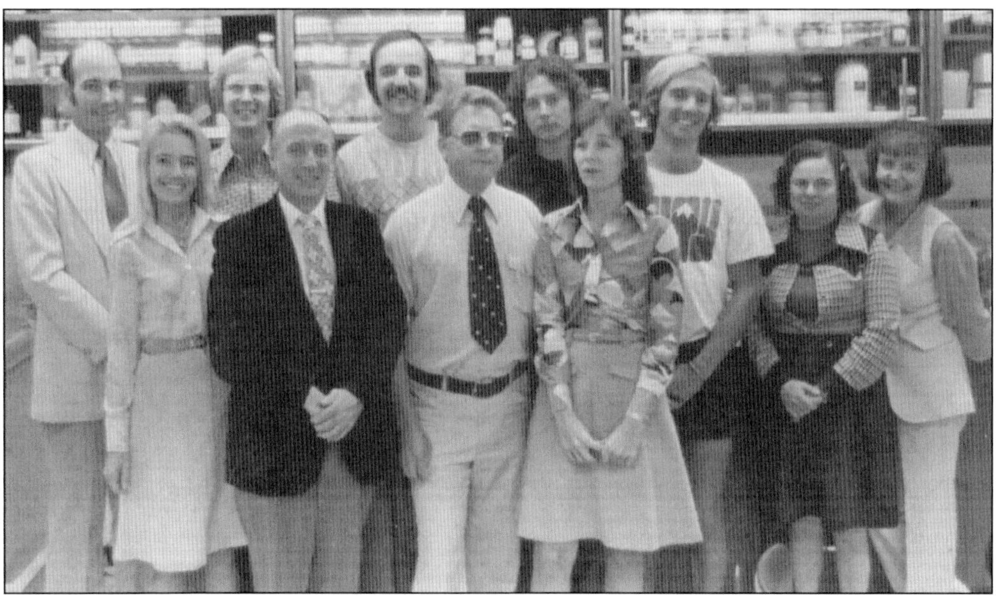

Science education and environmental science faculty, staff, and students from 1976–1977 are shown here. They are, from left to right, as follows: J. Taylor, P. Cooper, R. Fronk, D. Woodbridge (head), D. Marvel, R. Richmond, R. Murphy, A. Deblaiso, B. Peplin, B. Katz, and J. Vaught. In 1977, Dr. Robert Fronk became head of the science education department. (Courtesy of *Ad Astra*.)

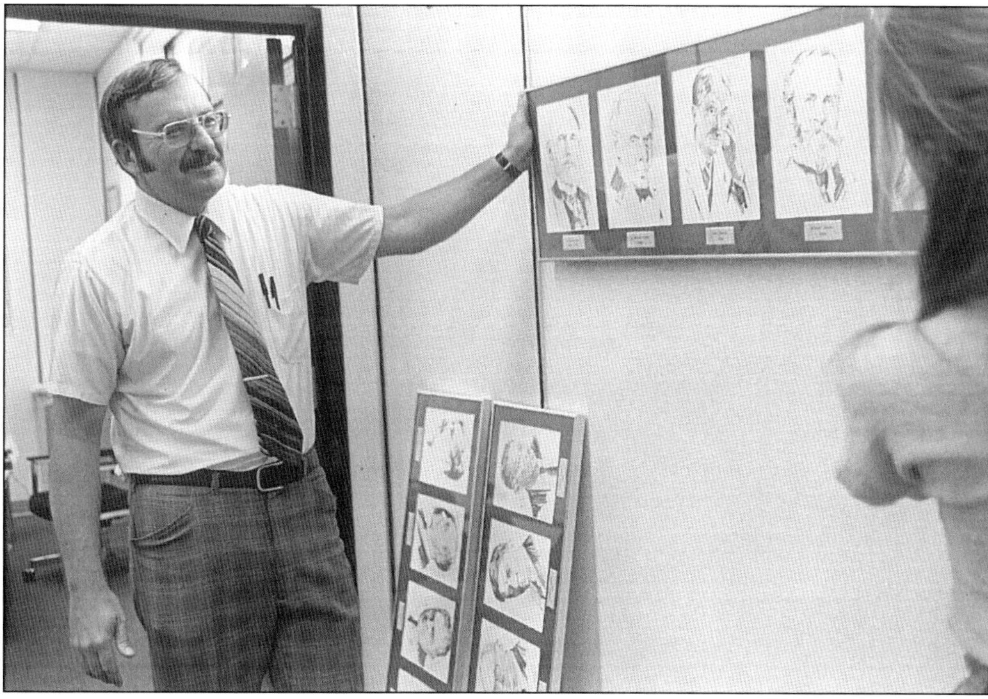

Psychologist Charles Corman (above) joined the university in 1977. John Miller charged Corman with creating an undergraduate and graduate program in psychology. Initially, the psychology program was part of the School of Engineering and Science. (Courtesy of University Publications.)

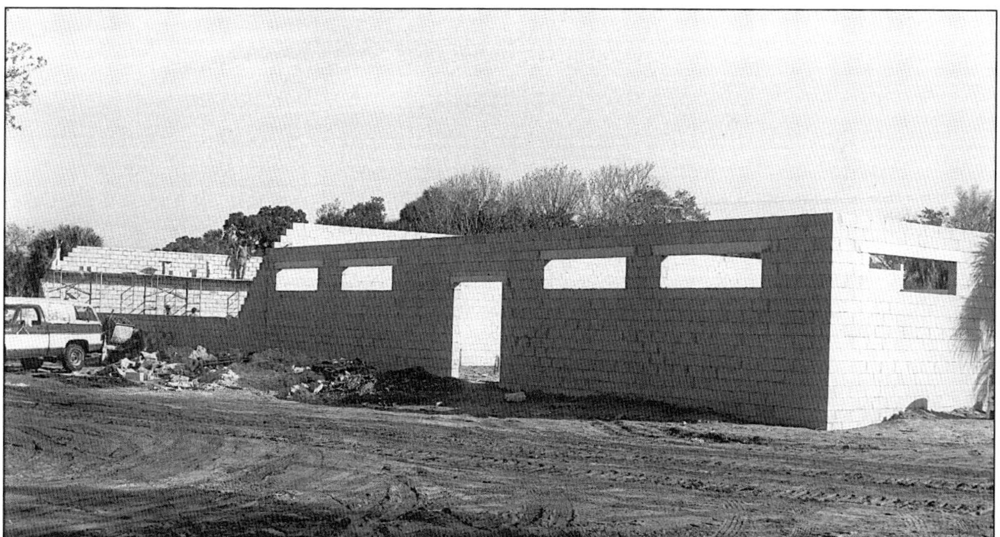

John Miller ordered a major academic reorganization in January 1980. Two new schools were created: the School of Psychology (Charles Corman, dean) and the School of Management and Humanities (Jim Stoms, dean). Miller named Andy Revay dean of the School of Science and Engineering when Harry Weber was promoted to associate vice-president for academic affairs. Pictured here in 1982 is construction on the new School of Psychology Building. (Courtesy of University Publications.)

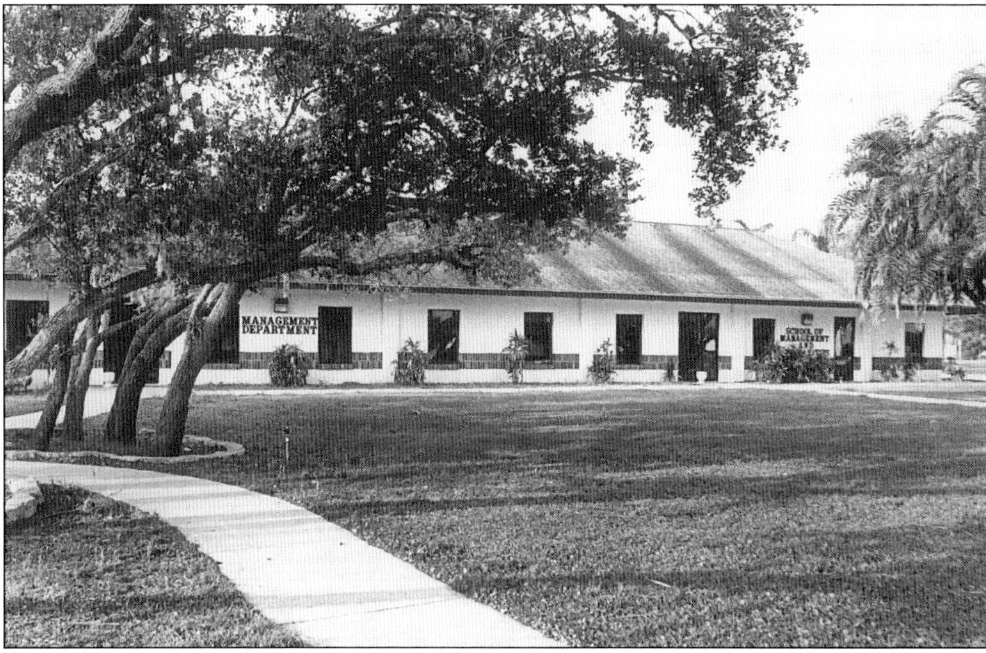

In 1982, management faculty members moved into new offices in the School of Management and Humanities Building (shown here). The humanities department remained in the Crawford Science Building. Jim Stoms appointed Gen. Ed Gudgel to lead the college's Off-Campus Programs. In 1972, the U.S. Navy asked Florida Tech to offer courses at the Patuxent River Naval Air Station in Maryland. (Courtesy of University Publications.)

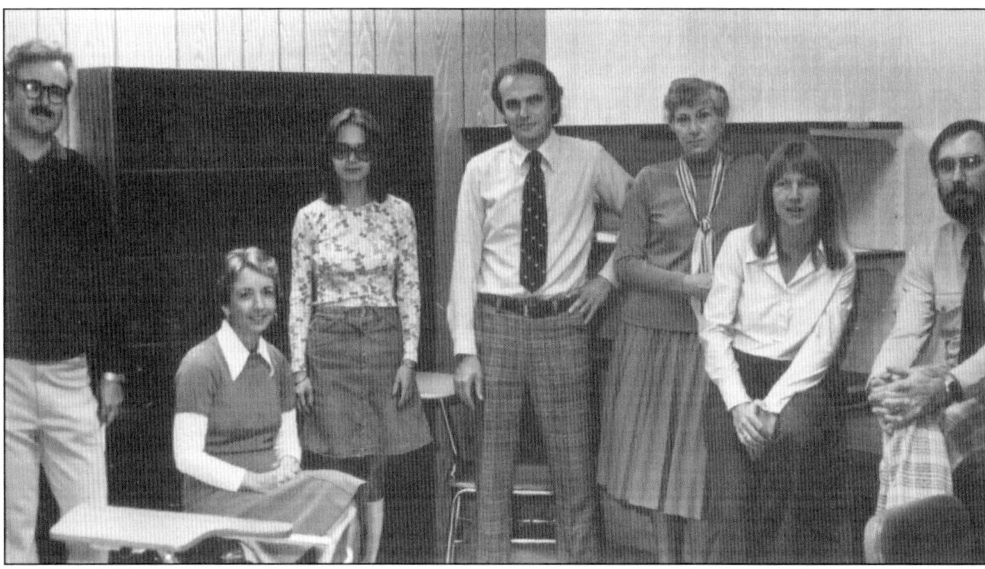

Florida Tech's forensic teams (Mona Davisson and Ed Harrell, coaches) won national recognition in 1975. Reporter and novelist Carl Hiassen praised Florida Tech's "brain stimulating alternative to athletics" in a *Florida Today* article. Pictured here is the 1978–1979 humanities department. They are, from left to right, D. Arnold, J.Patrick (head 1982–1997), D. Stevenson (secretary), J. Carter (head), M. Haberhern, C. Shehadeh, and E. Durfee. S. Irvin is not shown. (Courtesy of University Publications.)

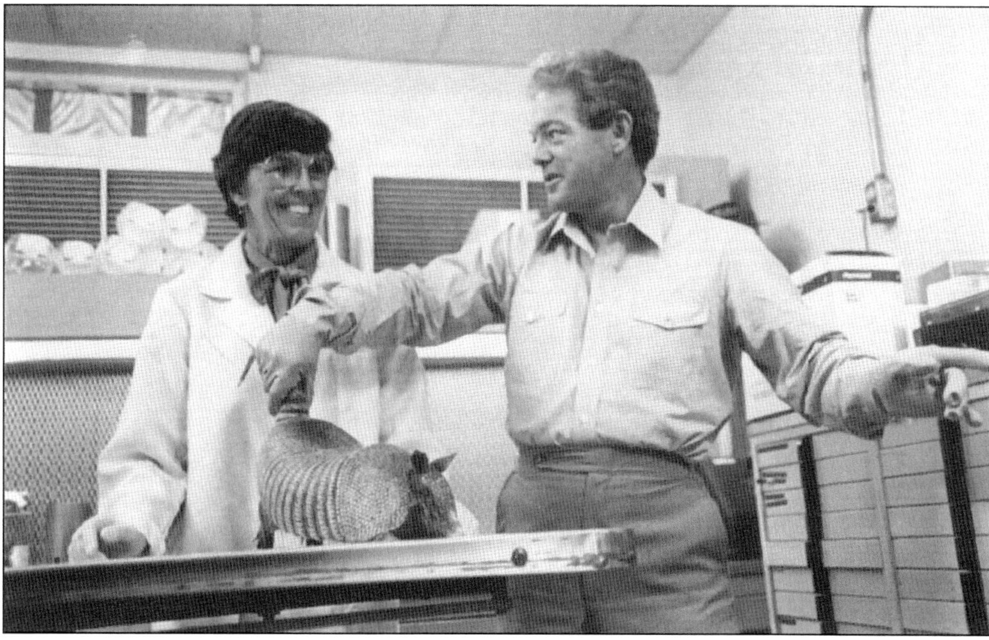

Eleanor E. Storrs, research professor in biology at Florida Tech's Medical Research Institute (MRI), is explaining how to nab an armadillo to television actor James MacArthur (*Hawaii-Five 0*) for the Disney Channel's *Scheme of Things*. From 1971 until the late 1980s, MRI researchers R. Jones, A. Dhople,E. Storrs, and J. Thomas conducted research on infectious diseases and other medical topics. (Courtesy of University Publications.)

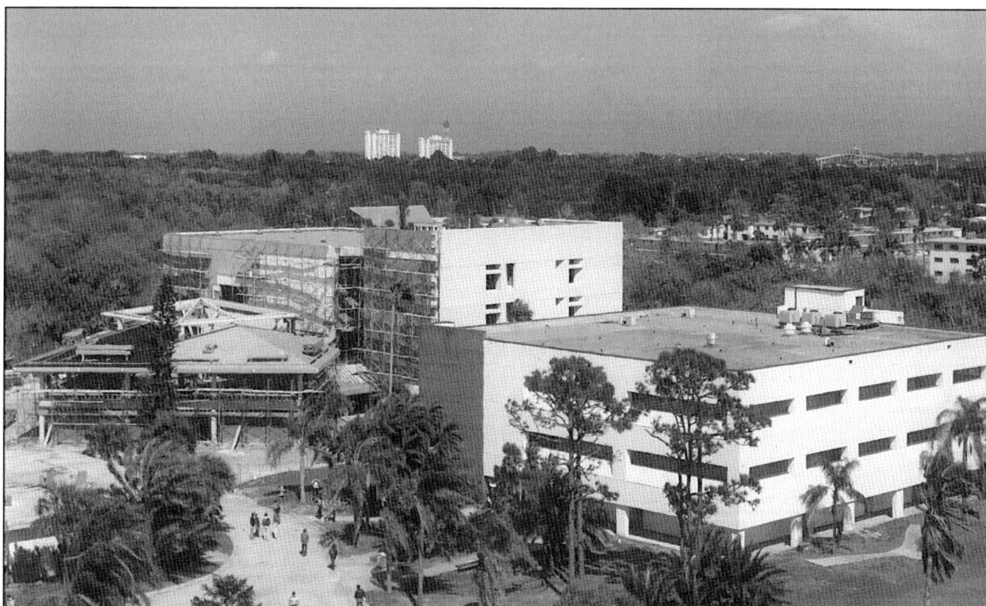

Construction started on a new university library in May 1983. Located to the north (left in photograph) of the Link Engineering Building, the $4-million, 68,915-square-foot facility was designed by the Skidmore, Owings & Merrill architectural firm. (Courtesy of University Publications.)

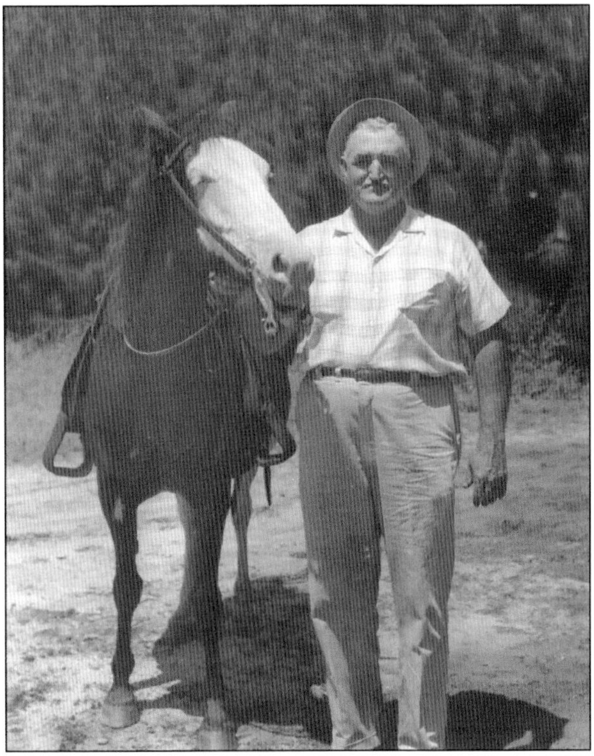

Pictured here is John Evans, a Florida citrus grower and cattleman who bequeathed to the university his extensive property holdings on New Haven Avenue. This property (purchased by the DeBartolo Corporation) was used as the site of the Melbourne Square Mall. The library is dedicated to the memory of both Evans' mother and Evans' wife. (Courtesy of Evans Library.)

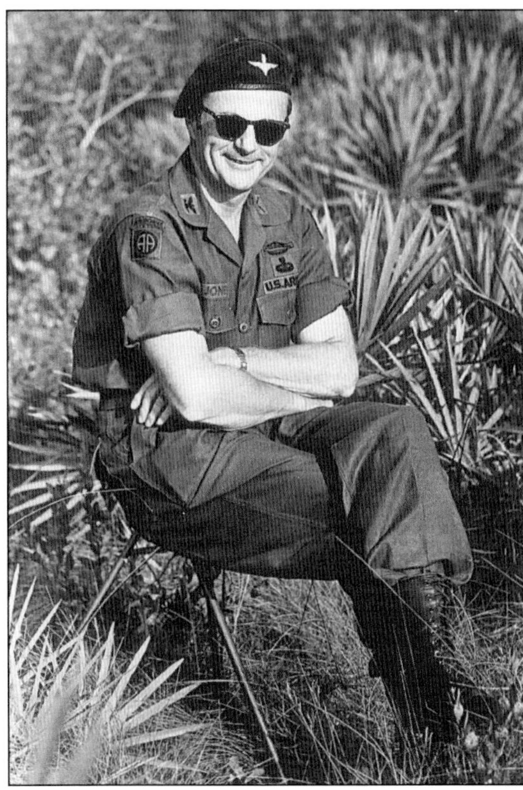

Col. George Jones served as the second commander from 1972 to 1975 of Florida Tech's ROTC program. The campus ROTC program began in 1969. After his retirement, Jones served Florida Tech as acting head of the oceanography and ocean engineering department and university registrar. (Courtesy of University Publications.)

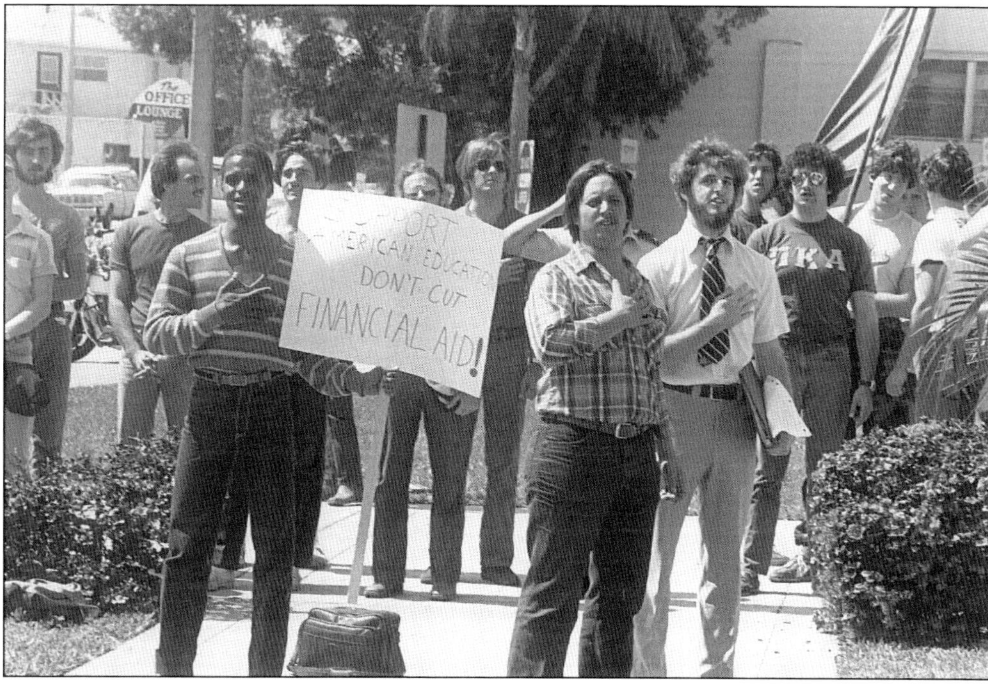

Pictured here in March 1982 is a group of Florida Tech students protesting President Reagan's proposed $3-billion cut in aid to education. Florida Tech student aviators flew over the protest in a plane trailing a banner declaring "Reagan is wrong. We need books not bombs." (Courtesy of University Publications.)

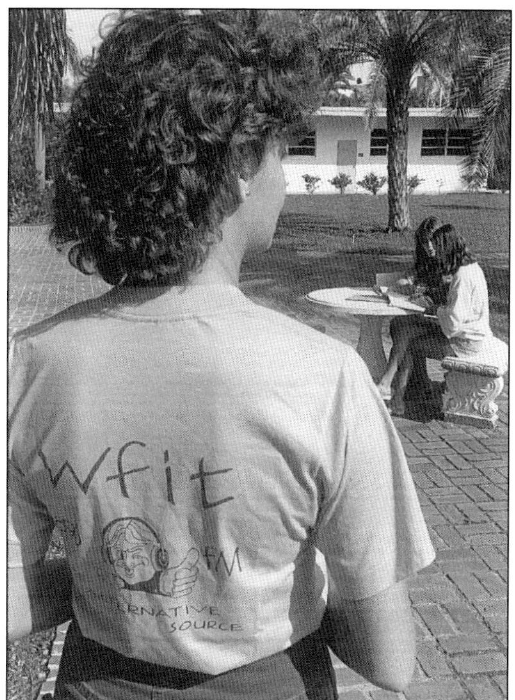

Students proposed the idea of a campus radio station in 1969. In February 1972, WFIT received its FCC license, but the 10-watt transmitter did not go on the air until March 1975. In 1979, the station increased its power to 3,000 watts. During the 1980s, the station won national recognition for its alternative programming. Pictured here is a WFIT supporter standing in the Quad. (Courtesy of University Publications.)

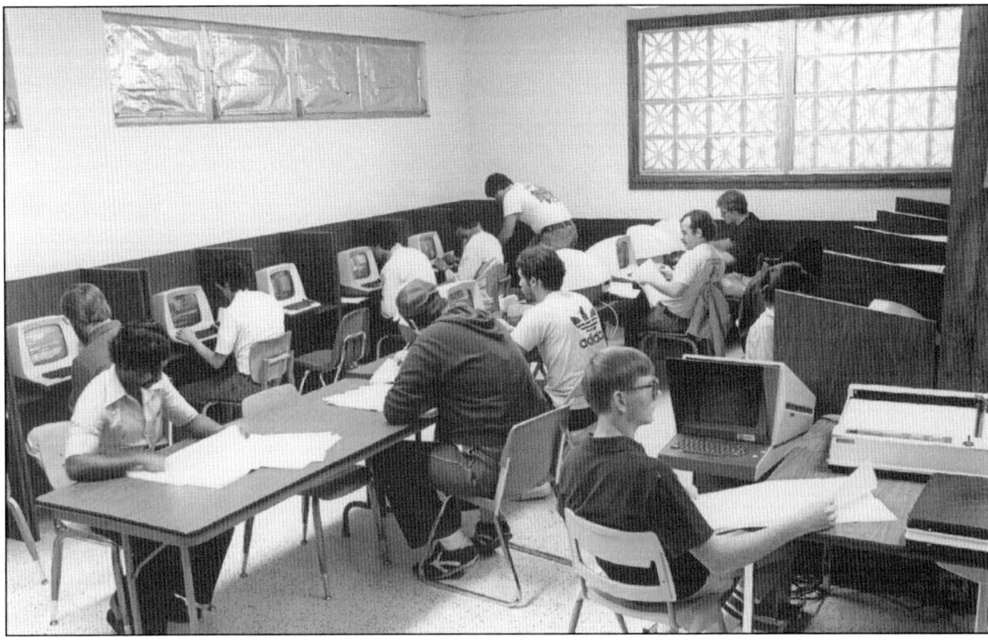

In 1966, Florida Tech offered its first degree in computer science. In 1980, Dee Dee Pannell served as director of the Academic Computer Center located in the Quad. The then state-of-the-art lab had 15 terminals. "Students," Pannell explained, "take a seat in the center and actually interact with a DEC computer." The center was open from 8 a.m. to 10 p.m. (Courtesy of University Publications.)

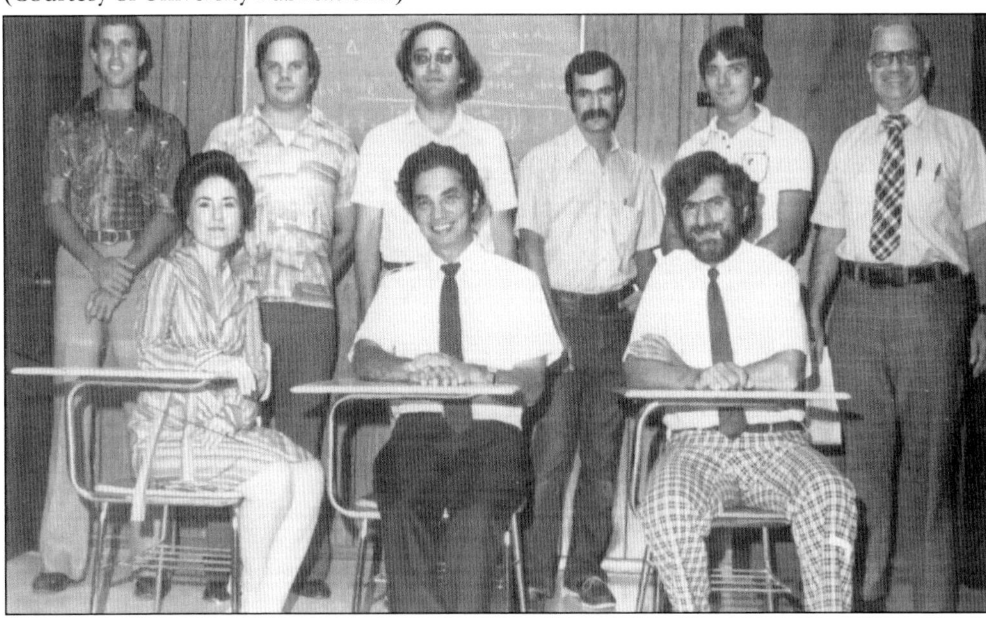

Mathematics, engineering sciences, and physics department students relied on the Academic Computer Center for support. Pictured here are members of the mathematics department in 1976–1977. They are, from left to right, (front row) V. Evans, F. Desua, and G. Abdo; (back row) R. Wollkind, T. McDonald, D. Jackson, W. Campopipano, J. Newman, and D. Clutterham (head). (Courtesy of *Ad Astra*.)

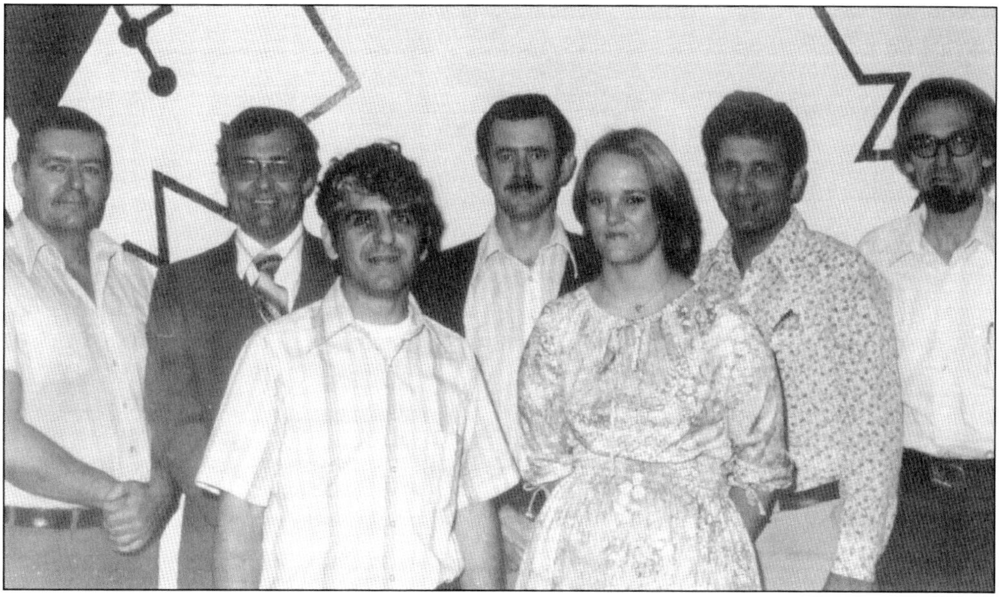

Pictured here are engineering faculty and staff in a 1979 yearbook photo. They are, from left to right, as follows: G. Campbell, A. Revay; E. Kalajian, W. Shelton, C. Harris, J. Hadjilogiou Jr., and M. Drake. (Courtesy of *Ad Astra*.)

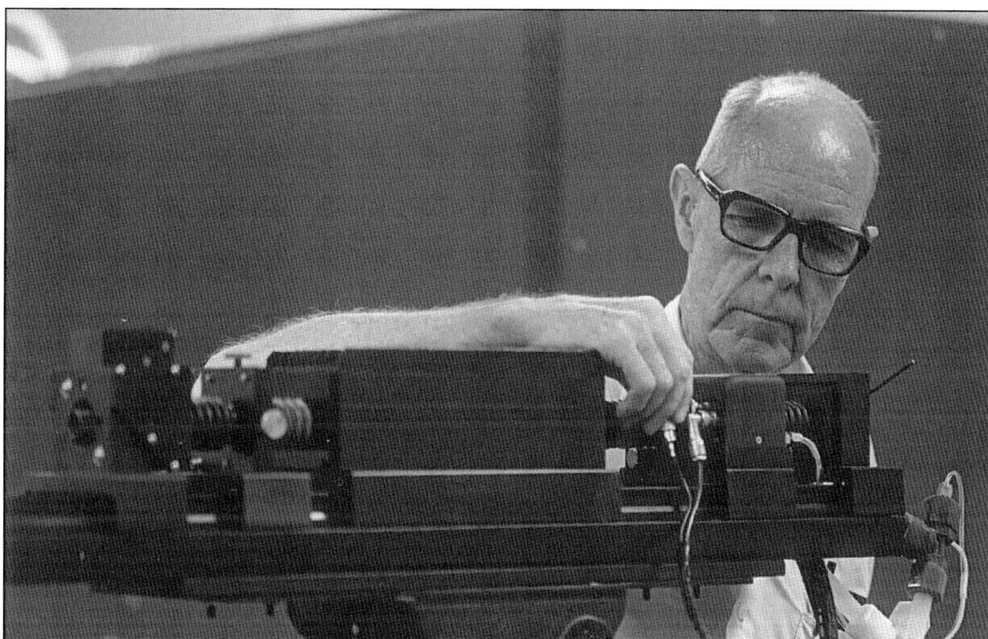

Electrical engineering Professor Walter Nunn is shown here adjusting a laser. Nunn, renowned for his dedication to teaching, played an instrumental role in developing Florida Tech's program in electrical engineering. (Courtesy of University Publications.)

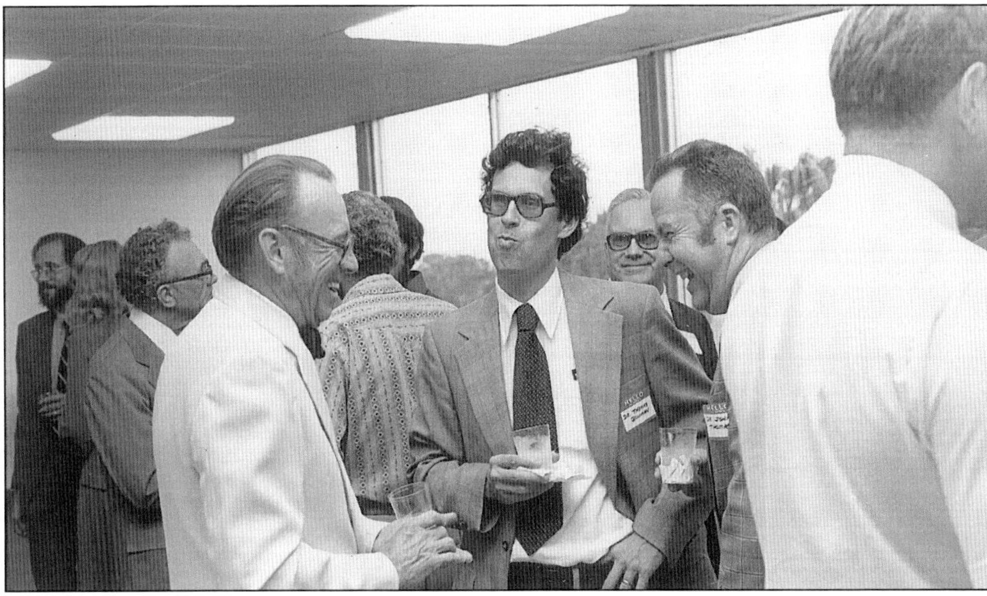

Jerry Keuper is shown here hosting the 1979 president's faculty reception. Keuper is exchanging quips with veteran professors Tom Bowman (mechanical engineering, center) and John Thomas (Medical Research Institute). David Clutterham, head of the mathematics department, is looking over Bowman's shoulder. Clayton Baum, chemistry, is at the far left. (Courtesy of University Publications.)

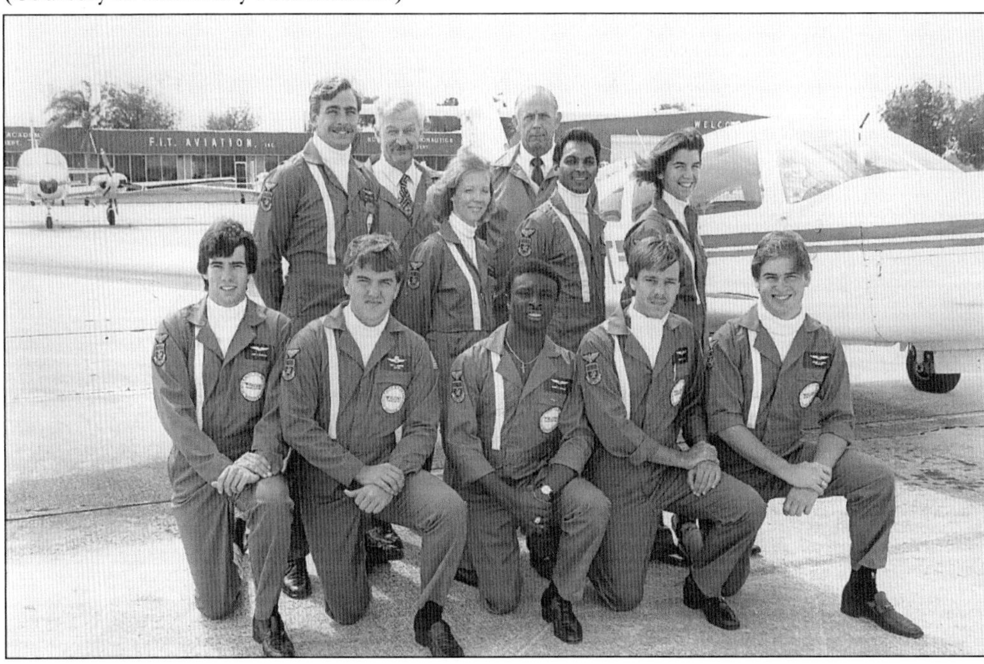

The School of Aeronautics "Flying Falcons" (above) won national recognition for Florida Tech's aviation program in the 1980s. Pictured here, from left to right, are members of the 1984 team: (kneeling) J. Blackford, K. Anderson, D. Anderson, R. Allen, and M. Weaver; (standing) B. Shortly, J. Derrick (faculty advisor), and E. Everette (faculty advisor); (center), P.Sobala, R. Persaud, and P. Smith. (Courtesy of University Publications.)

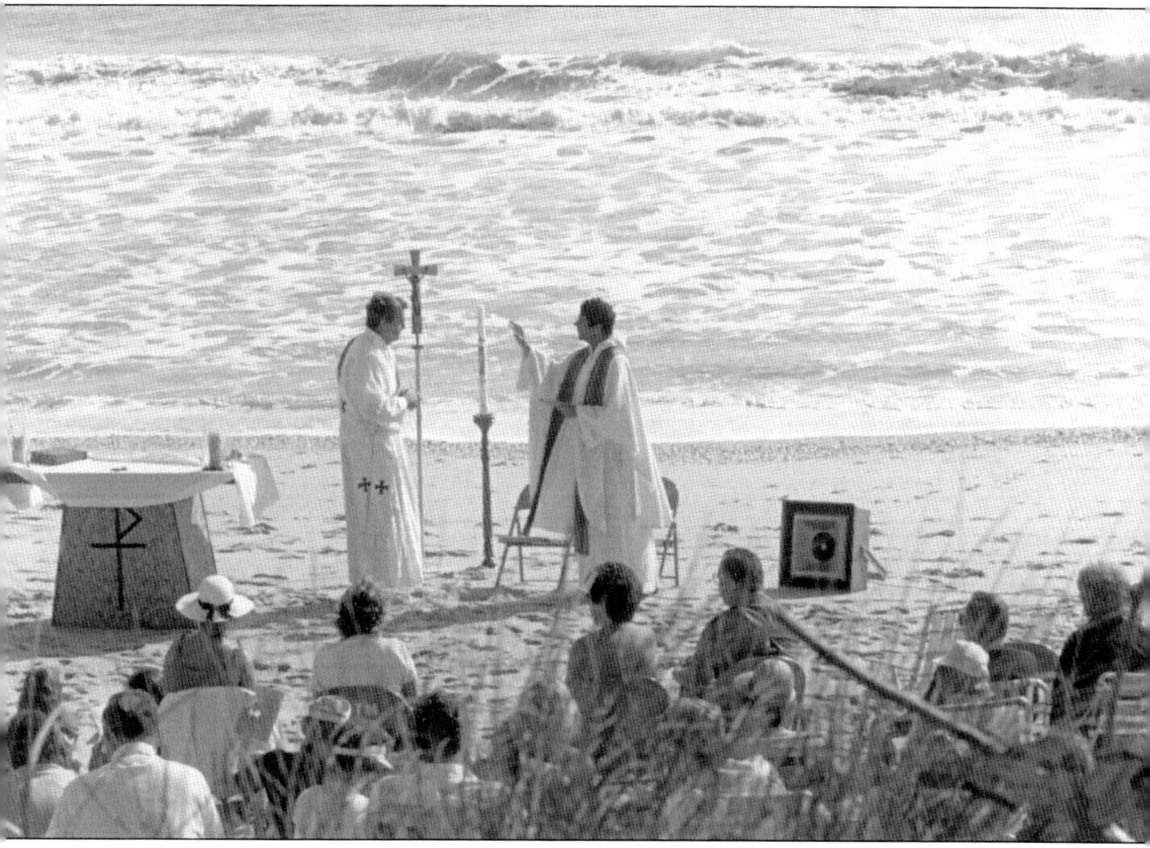

Fr. Doug Bailey (right, campus ministry) and Professor Maurice Pujol (management, with cross) are shown here at the Easter sunrise beach service in 1983. Florida Tech's Campus Ministry opened in 1971. In 1974, Fr. George Moreau expanded the ministry to include a counseling center. The School of Psychology assumed responsibility for the counseling center in the 1980s. In 1994, the university dedicated the new home for the All Faiths Center and United Campus Ministry at the south end of campus. (Courtesy of University Publications.)

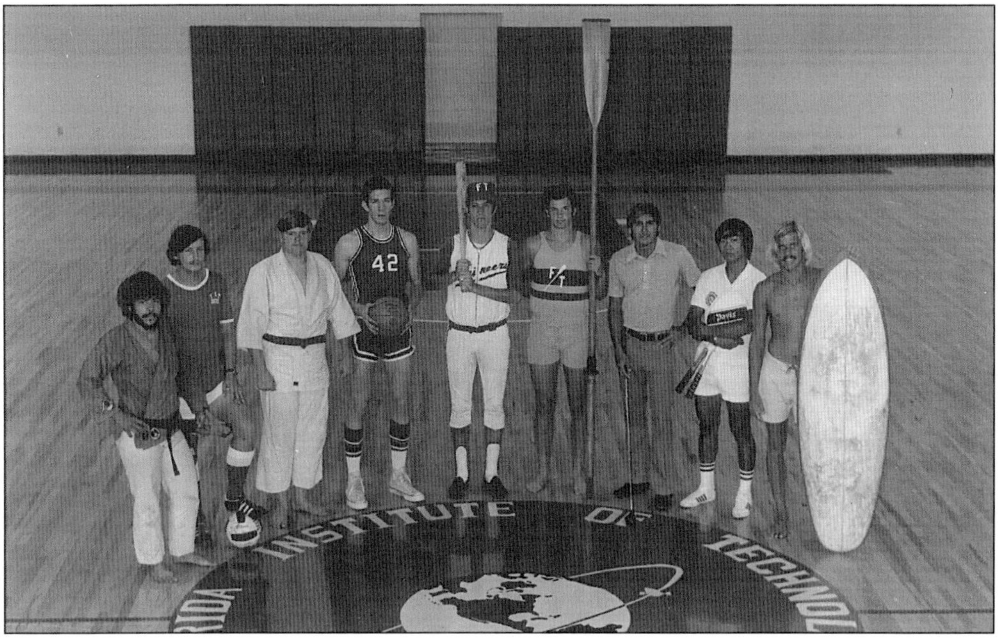

Since 1979, Florida Tech's athletic teams have competed within Division II of the National Collegiate Athletic Association (NCAA). The college joined the Sunshine State Conference in 1981. Pictured here are student athletes representing the men's athletic programs in the mid-1980s. (Courtesy of University Publications.)

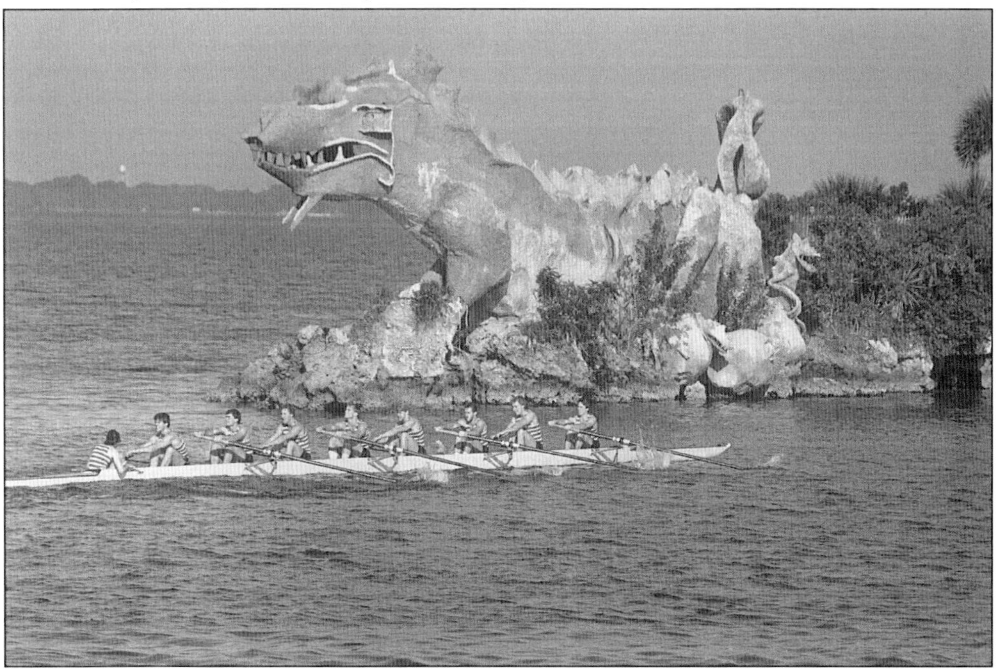

The men's varsity 8 crew team is shown here in a morning practice session in 1984 on the Indian River near the end of Merritt Island. In 1983, the college adopted the panther as the school mascot. (Note the Indian River landmark "Dragon" and "baby dragons" in the background.) (Courtesy of University Publications.)

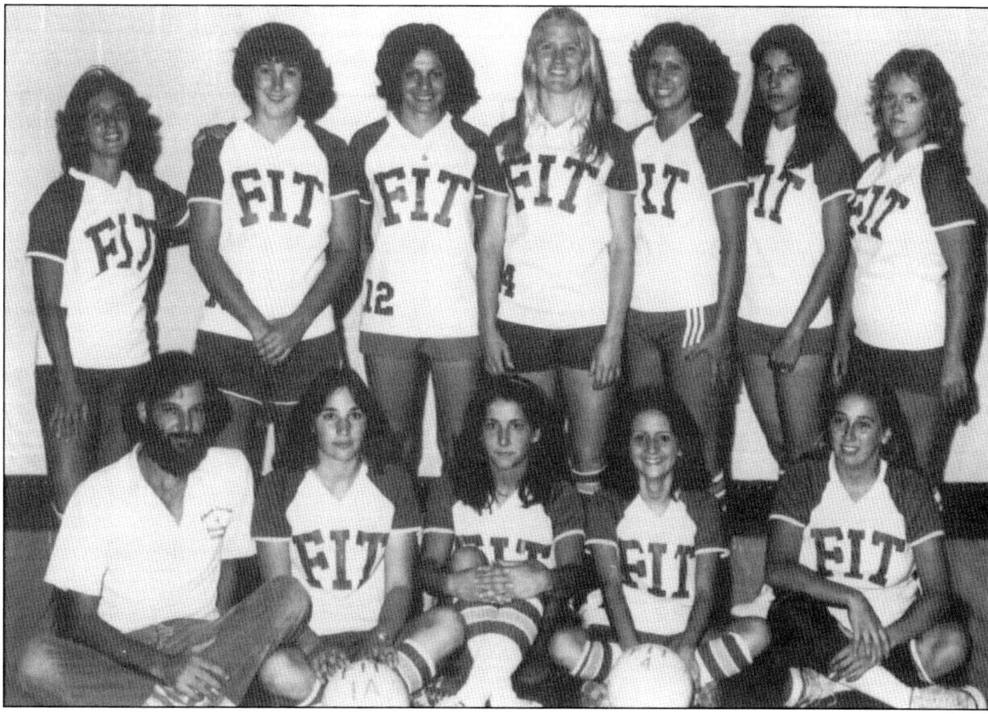

Women's sports began in 1972 with crew. Volleyball was added in 1978. Pictured here are members of the 1978–1979 women's volleyball team. From left to right are (front row) Dave Clay (coach and faculty member), K. Chaffe, K. Alexion, I. Astor, and D. D'Angelo; (back row) I. Meisel, D. Radcliff, E. Mendez, S. DeMoss, D. Clegg, M. Rondon, and L. Cucchiara. (Courtesy of *Ad Astra*.)

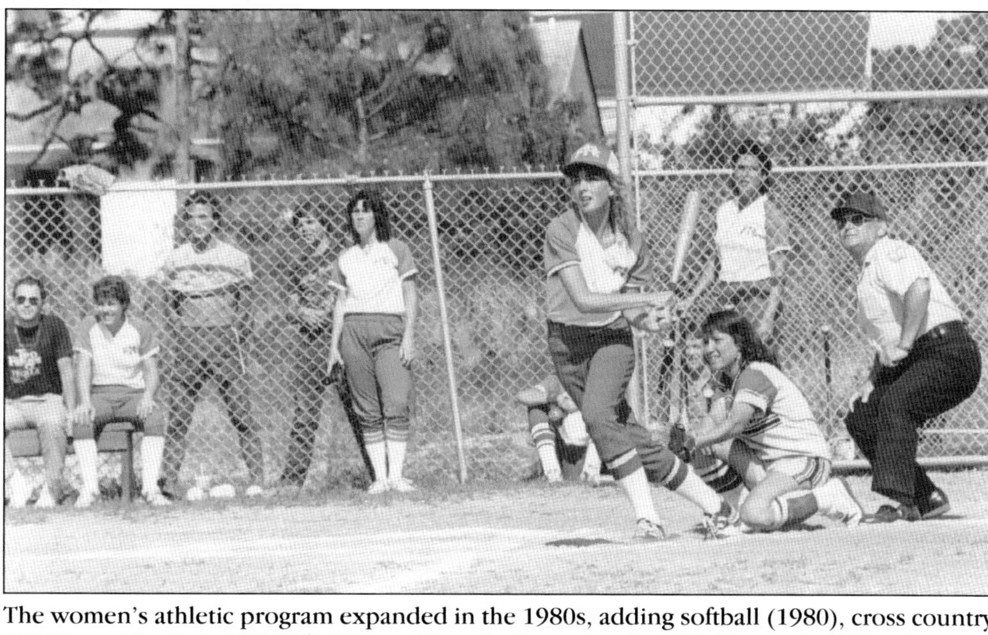

The women's athletic program expanded in the 1980s, adding softball (1980), cross country (1982), and basketball (1986). Pictured here is the women's softball team in 1983. (Courtesy of University Publications.)

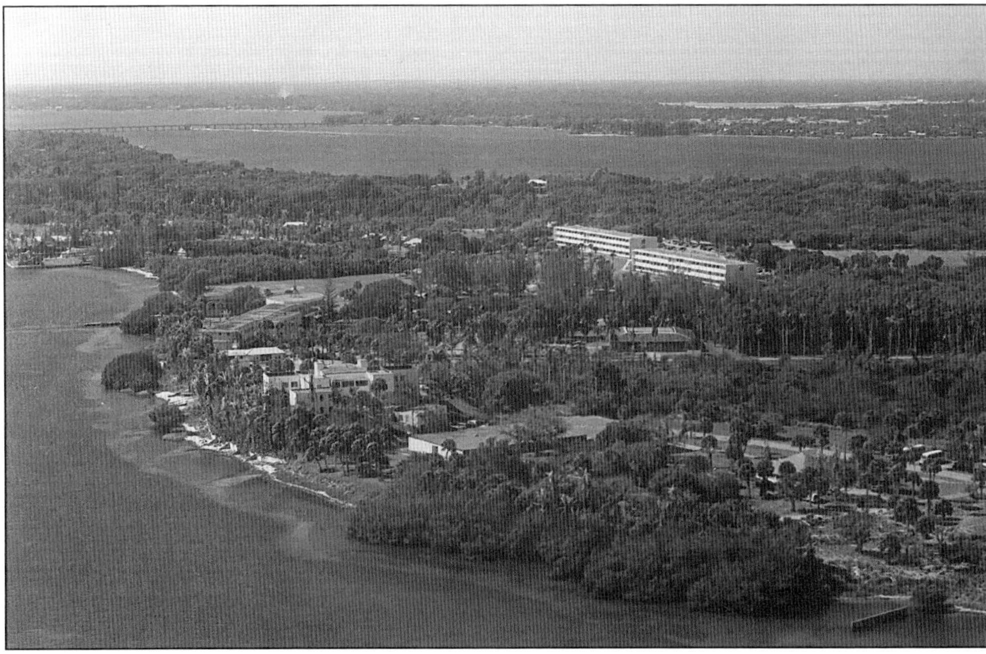

Jerry Keuper learned in April 1972 that St. Joseph's College in Jensen Beach (70 miles south of Melbourne) was closing. Florida Tech purchased the 84-acre campus to serve as the new home for the university's Hydrospace Technical Institute (formerly located in Cocoa Beach). Pictured here is the Jensen Beach Campus. (Courtesy of University Publications.)

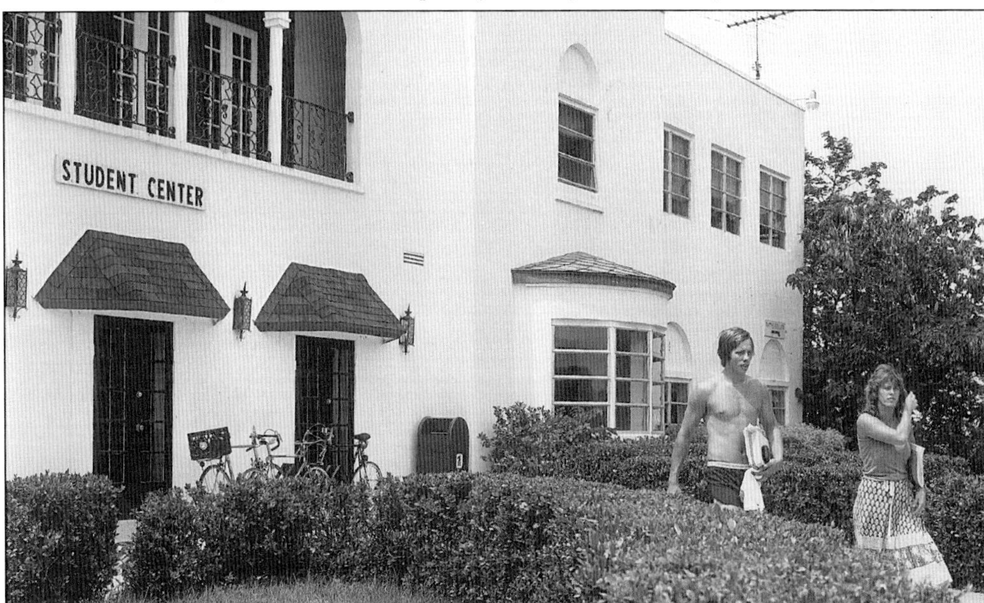

In 1973, the Hydrospace Technical Institute was renamed the School of Marine and Environmental Technology (SOMET). Two years later, Jensen Beach dean E. (Tim) Tealey announced the full integration of SOMET into Florida Institute of Technology. Pictured here is the student center at Jensen Beach. (Courtesy of University Publications.)

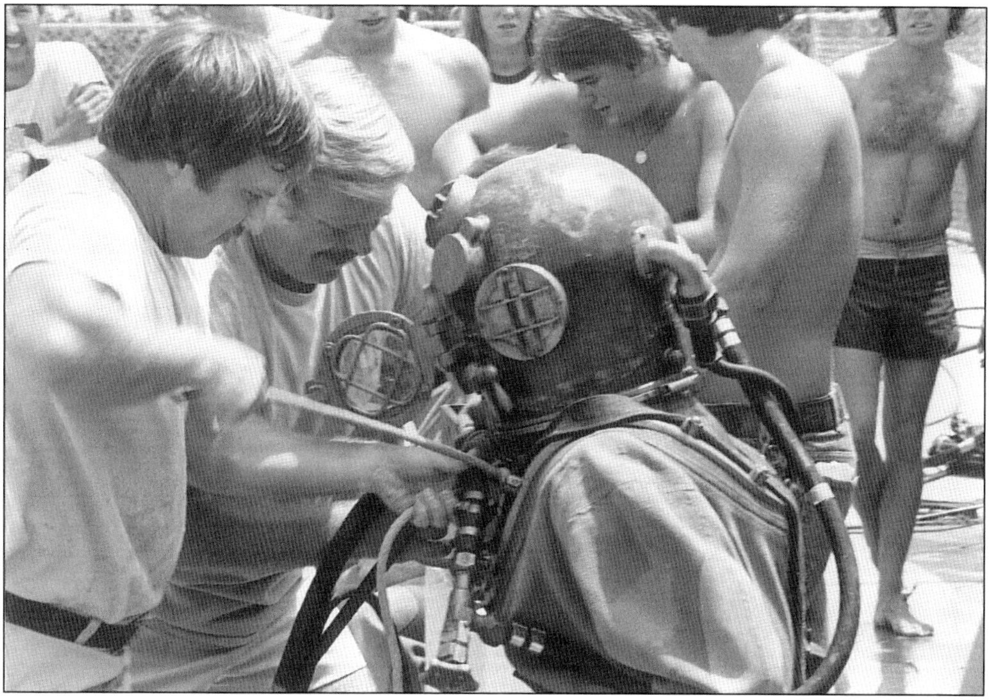

In 1982, nearly 7,000 students were enrolled in Florida Institute of Technology (Melbourne, Jensen Beach, and Off-Campus Programs). The majority of the Jensen Beach students were enrolled in two-year specialized programs. Pictured here is a Jensen Beach student preparing for a dive. (Courtesy of University Publications.)

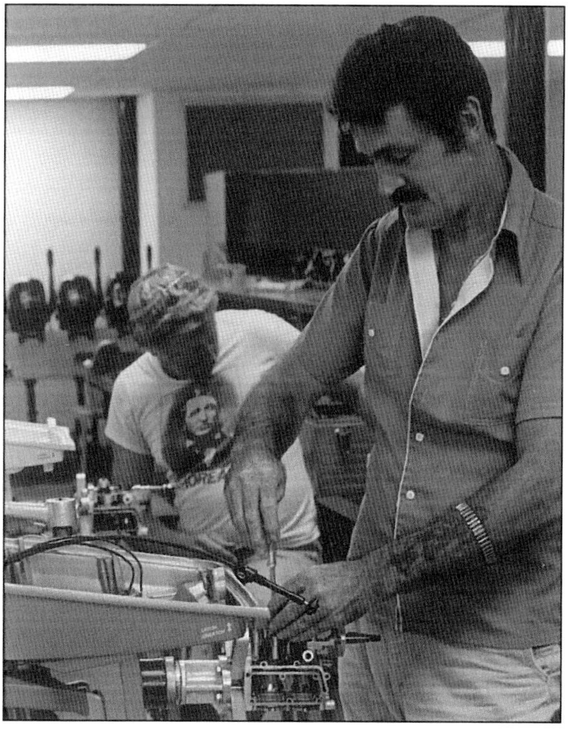

Ralph Evinrude (founder of the Outboard Motor Company and trustee) played a crucial role in acquiring the Jensen Beach campus. Pictured here is an outboard motor technology class in 1979. (Courtesy of University Publications.)

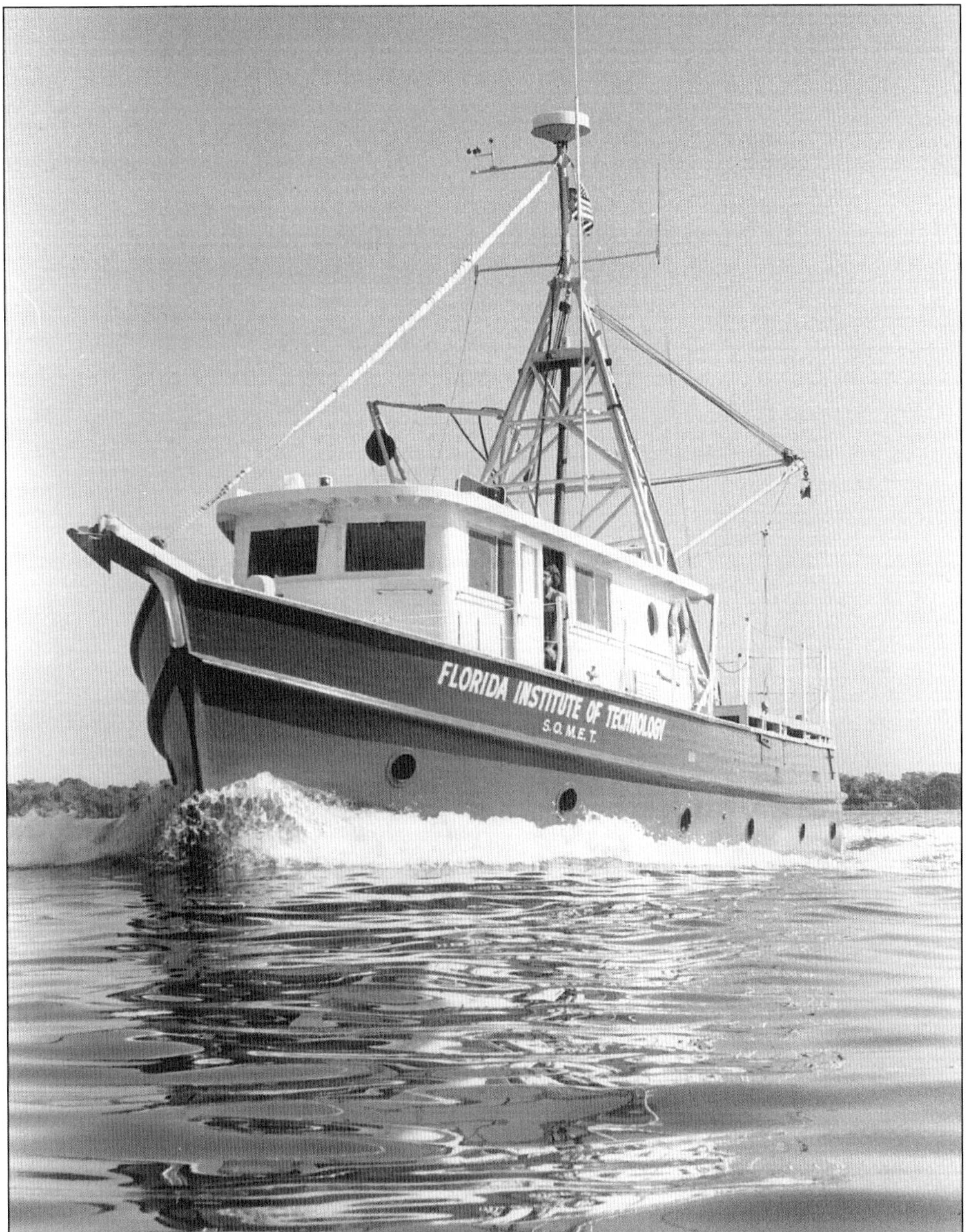

Jensen Beach served as the home port for the School of Marine and Environmental Technology. Pictured here is one of the research ships in the mid-1970s. (Courtesy of University Publications.)

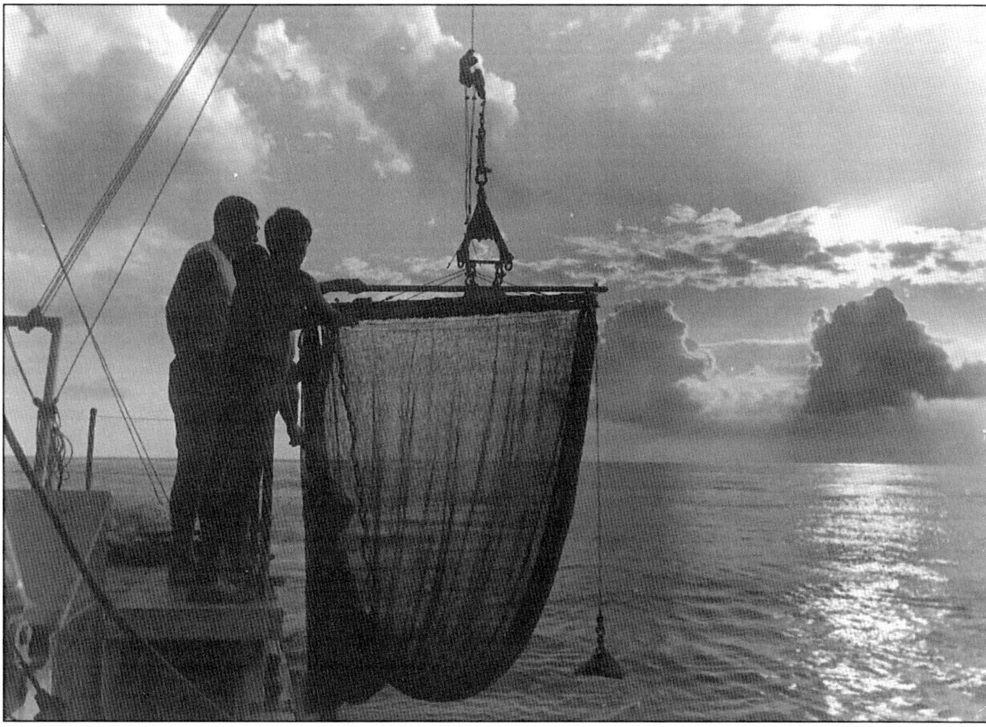

Declining student enrollments at Jensen Beach and a growing budget deficit led to the decision to close the Jensen Beach campus in 1986. Students and faculty protested. Robert Heidinger directed the transfer of Jensen Beach to the Melbourne campus. Pictured here is a Jensen Beach student research team. (Courtesy University Publications.)

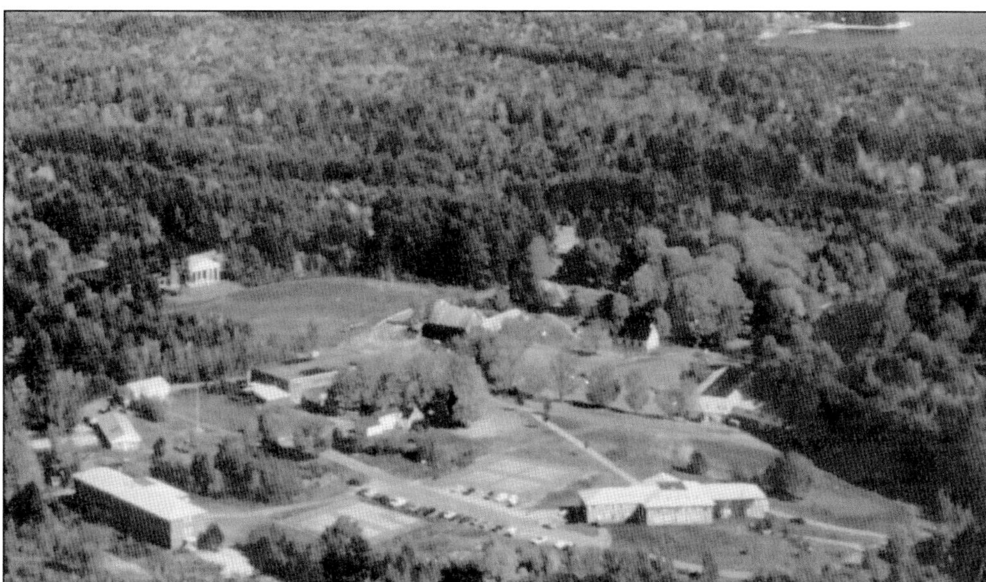

In 1981, Florida Tech had acquired an interest in Hawthorne College located in New Hampshire. Millions of dollars were lost in the effort to save the New Hampshire school. Pictured here is the Hawthorne campus. (Courtesy of University Publications.)

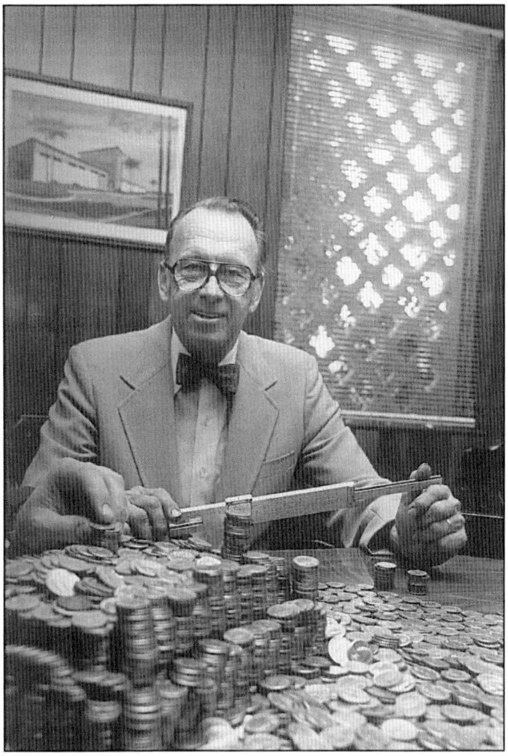

Pictured here is Jerry Keuper in 1983 preparing for the college's twenty-fifth anniversary celebration. Keuper reminded the audience that the college had begun with a single 37¢ contribution. (Courtesy of University Publications.)

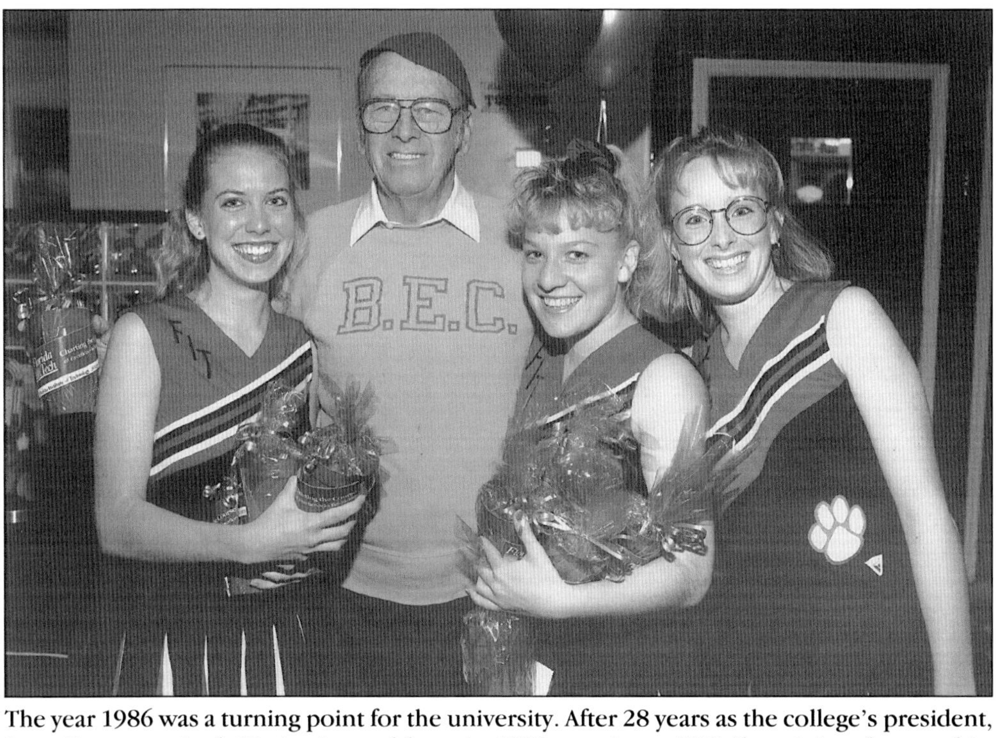

The year 1986 was a turning point for the university. After 28 years as the college's president, Jerry Keuper retired. He is pictured here in 1993 wearing a BEC "beanie" and sweatshirt with a group of Florida Tech cheerleaders. (Courtesy of University Publications.)

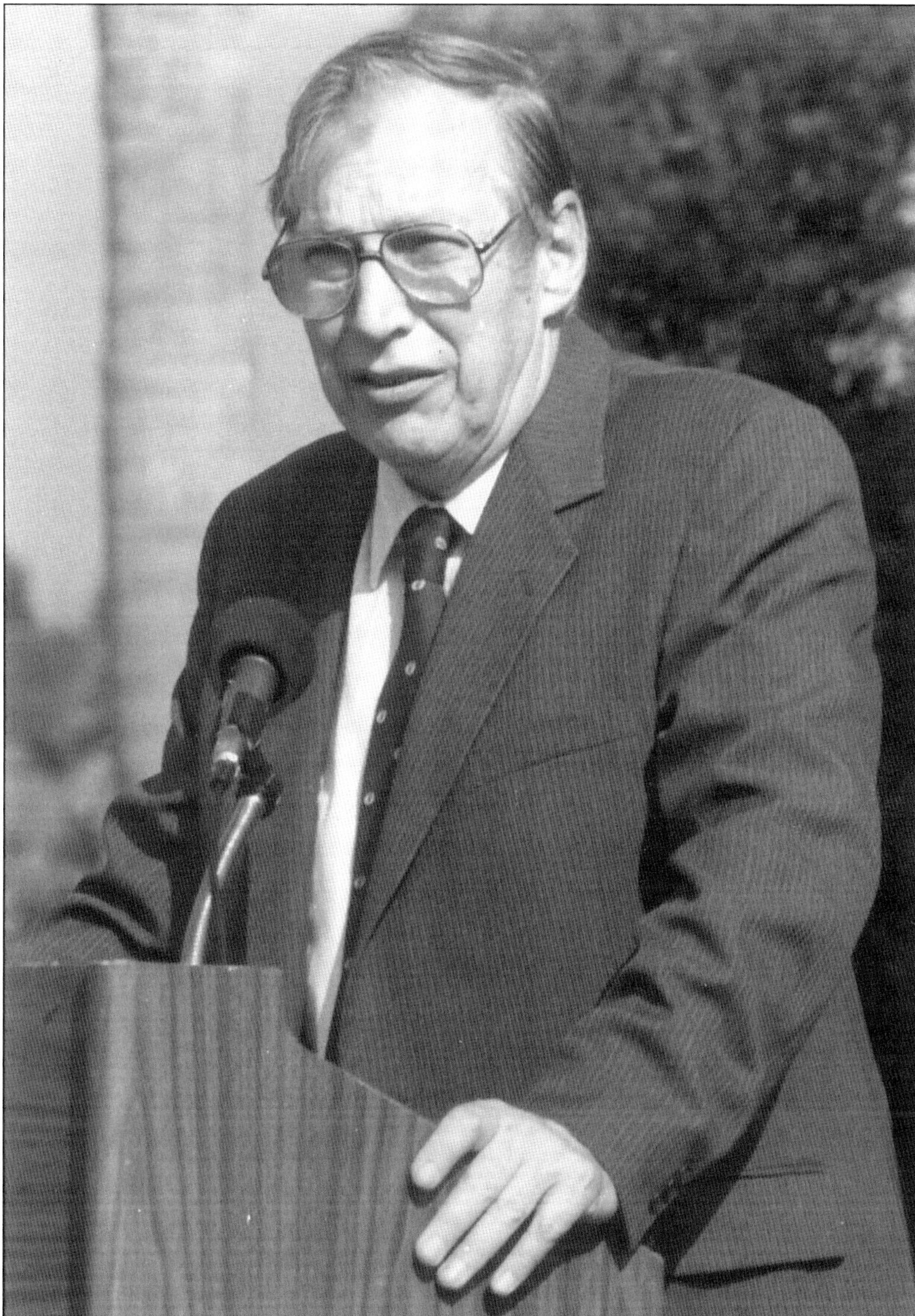

John Miller served as Florida Tech's second president in 1986–1987. In 1993, the president's office building was renamed the John Miller Administrative Building. (Courtesy of University Publications.)

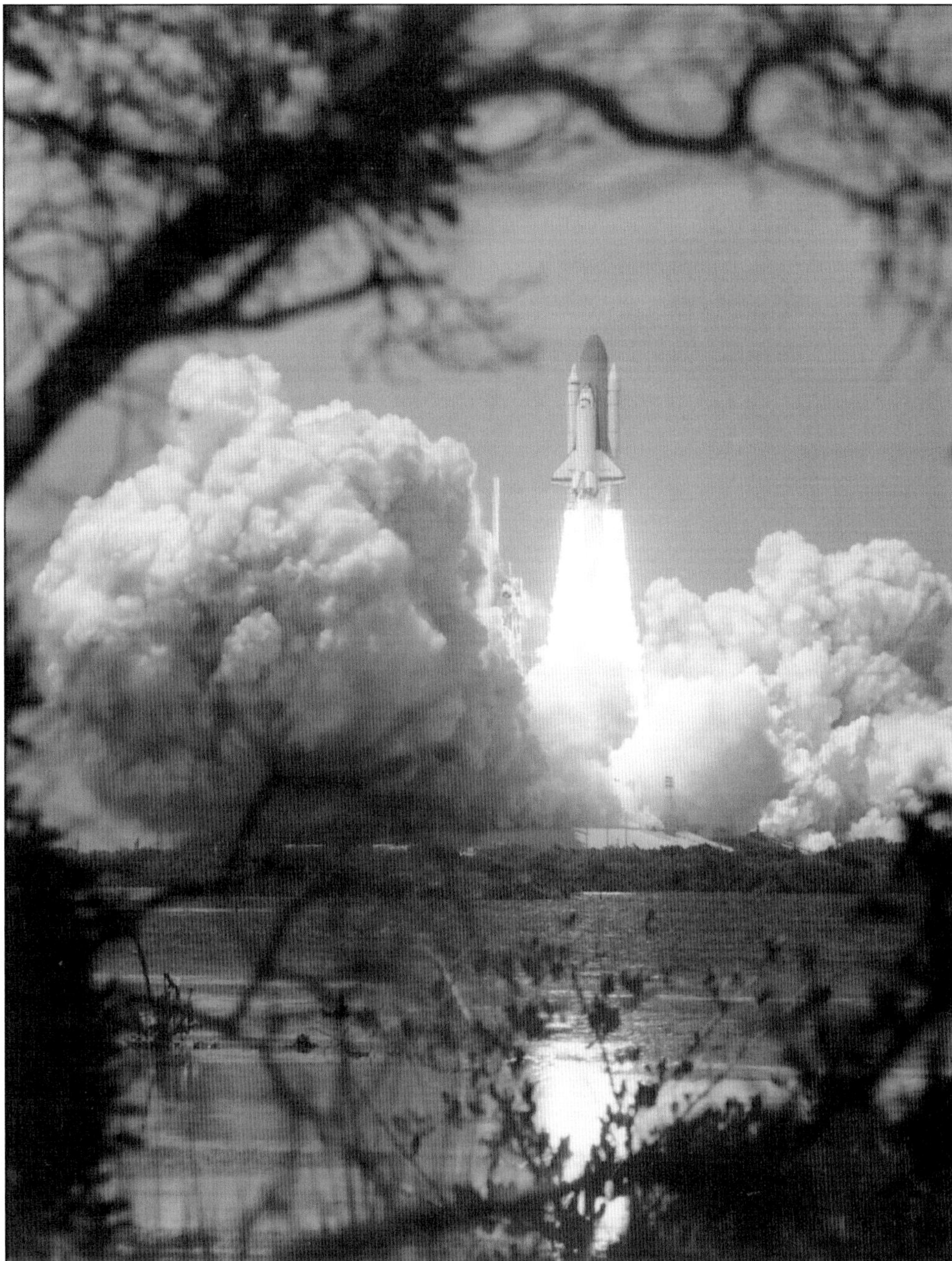

Mission specialist Kathryn (Kay) Hire, Florida Tech's first astronaut, was one of the crew aboard the Space Shuttle Columbia, which lifted off from Launch Pad 39B on April 17, 1998. Many Florida Tech faculty members and alumni have contributed to the Shuttle program. In 1978, Florida Tech professor Tom Bowman was named "lead scientist" for a liquid reorientation experiment to be performed in an early Spacelab mission. (Courtesy of NASA.)

Five

At the Edge of History: 1988–Present

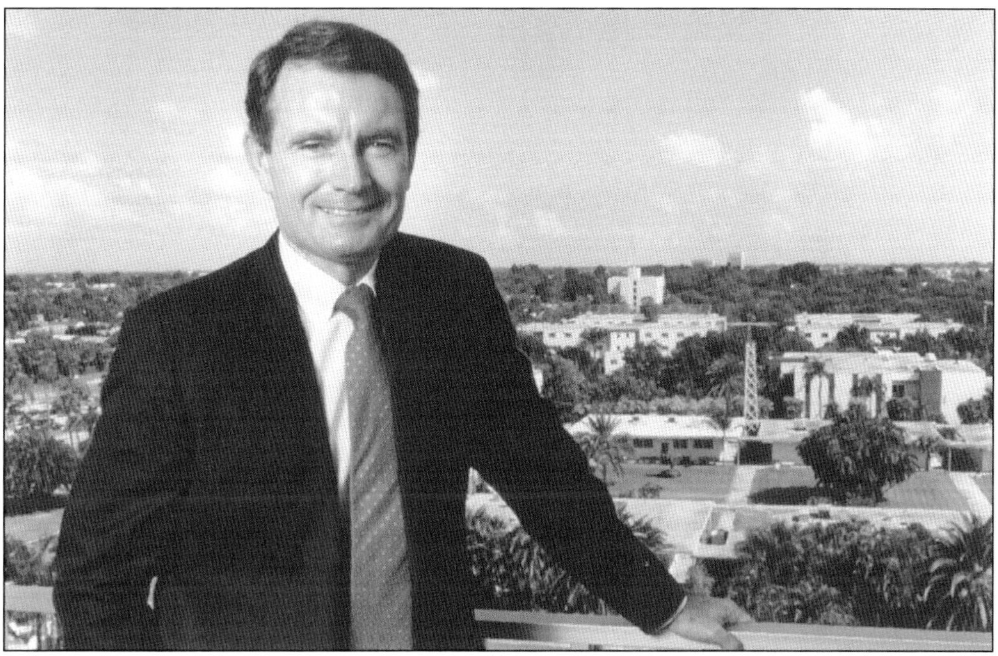

Lynn Edward Weaver became Florida Tech's third president in 1987. Weaver, a distinguished nuclear engineer and former dean at Auburn, brought new energy and direction to the university. Emphasizing the importance of research, President Weaver announced an ambitious ($25 million) capital campaign in November 1987 to improve the university's facilities. In 1988, Weaver called for the reorganization of the university's academic units. (Courtesy of University Publications.)

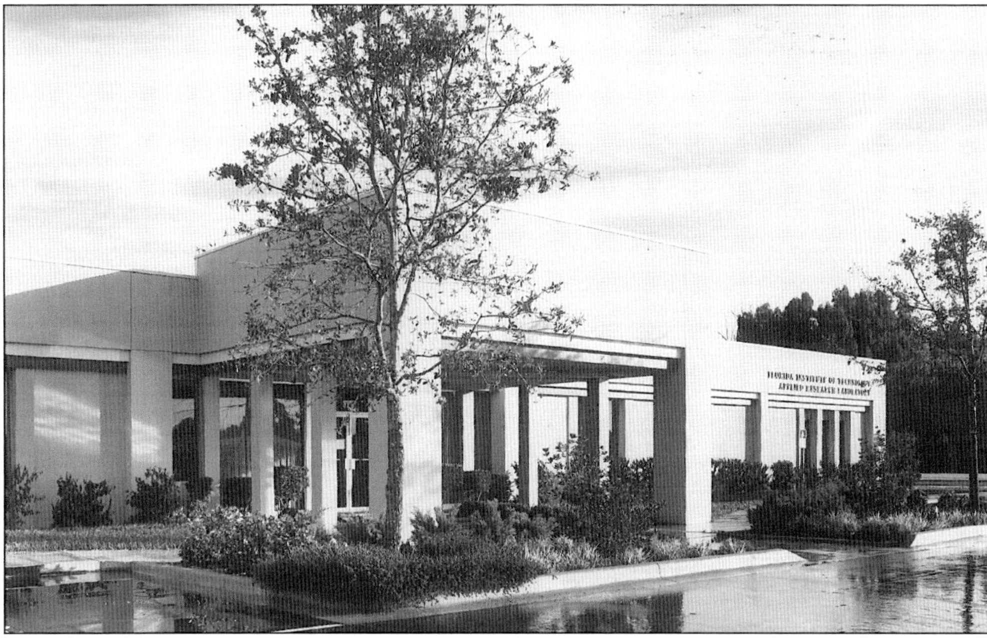

Faced with a shortage of laboratory space for faculty and student research, the university purchased an off-campus facility in 1988. The Advanced Research Laboratory (ARL) also serves as home for Florida Tech's Office of External Affairs. (Courtesy of University Publications.)

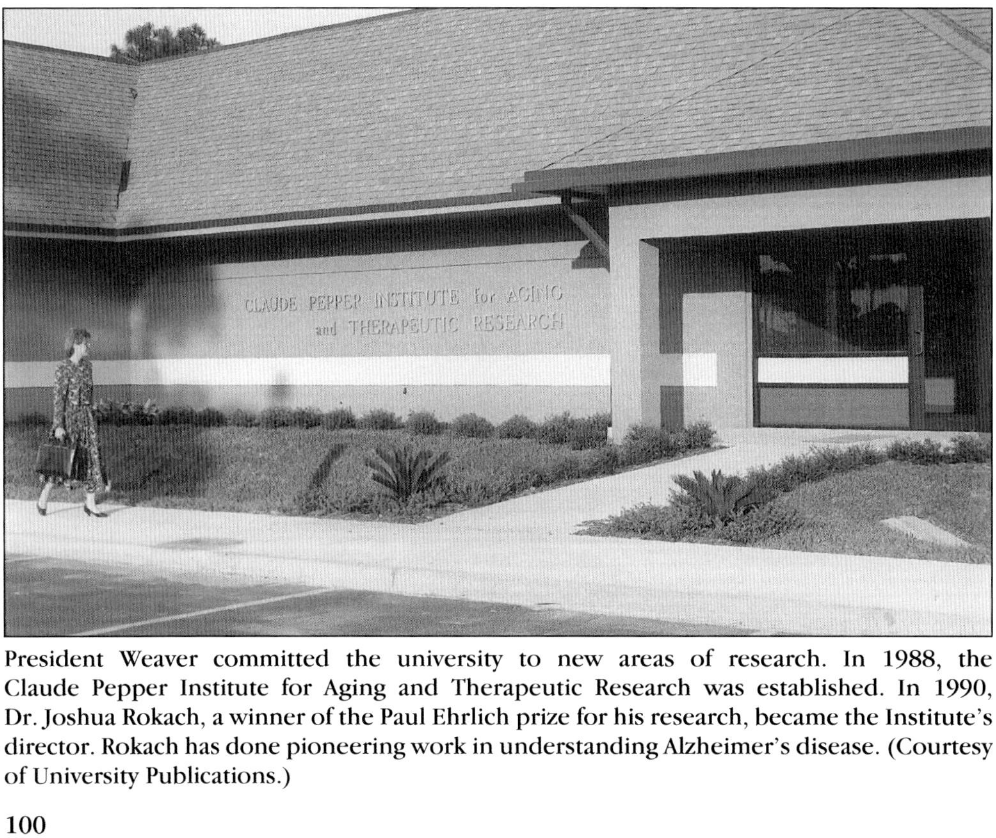

President Weaver committed the university to new areas of research. In 1988, the Claude Pepper Institute for Aging and Therapeutic Research was established. In 1990, Dr. Joshua Rokach, a winner of the Paul Ehrlich prize for his research, became the Institute's director. Rokach has done pioneering work in understanding Alzheimer's disease. (Courtesy of University Publications.)

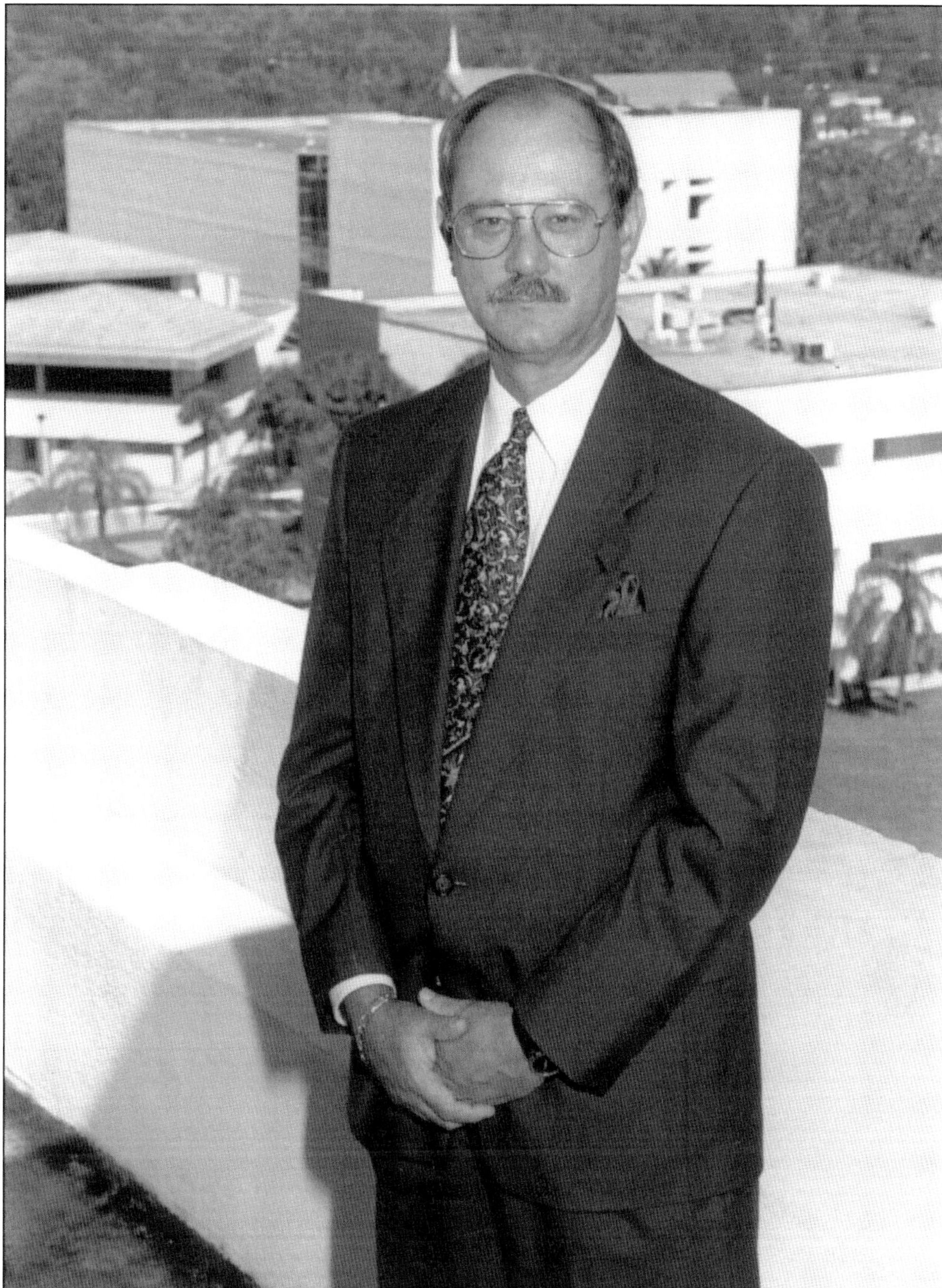

In 1988, President Weaver directed that the College of Engineering and Sciences be divided into the College of Science and Liberal Arts and the College of Engineering. Robert Sullivan (above), formerly head of the University of Florida's Electrical Engineering Department, was named dean of the College of Engineering in 1990. In 2000, Weaver promoted Sullivan to vice president of research. J. Ronald Bailey became the new dean of the College of Engineering. (Courtesy of University Publications.)

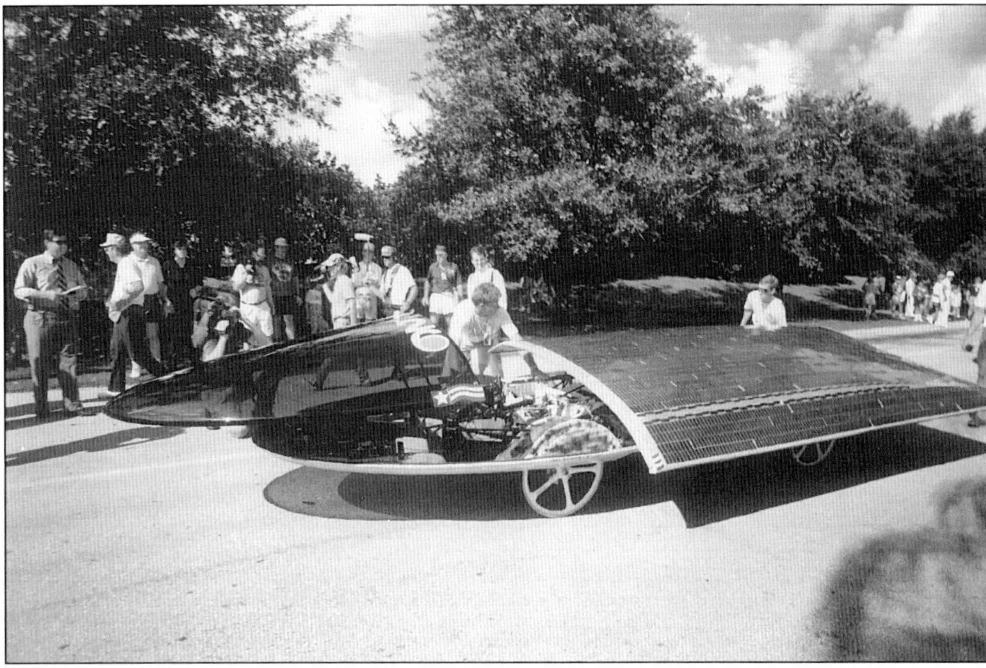

Florida Tech's engineering students and their professors won national recognition throughout the 1990s. In 1991, a student team competed in the GM Sunrayce. Florida Tech's Solar 1 (pictured here) took part in a challenging 11-day, 1,600-mile cross-country race. (Courtesy of University Publications.)

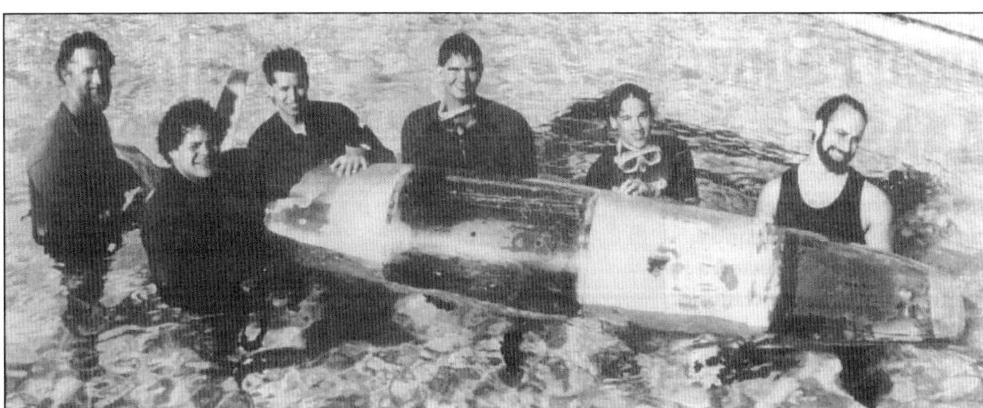

Florida Tech's 1994 Sea Spot team placed fourth in the national human powered submarine competition held in California. Pictured here, from left to right, are members Professor Lee Harris, Norman Badenhop, Eric Roehl, Steven Barow, Andrew Major, and Eric Handel. (Courtesy of University Publications.)

Mechanical engineering students are shown here making a test run for the 1998 Midwest SAE Mini Baja competition. Florida Tech's off-road vehicle placed third in top speed in the grueling competition. (Courtesy of University Publications.)

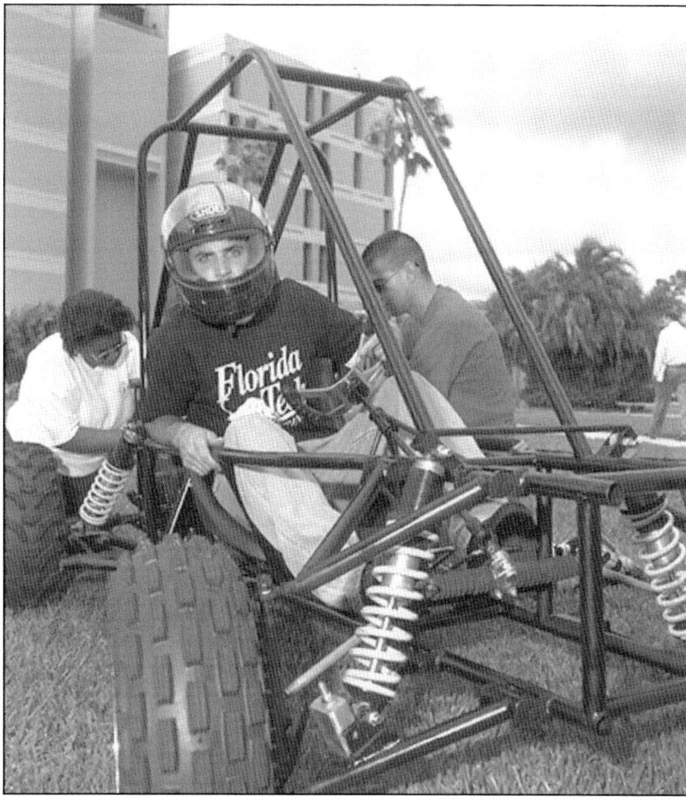

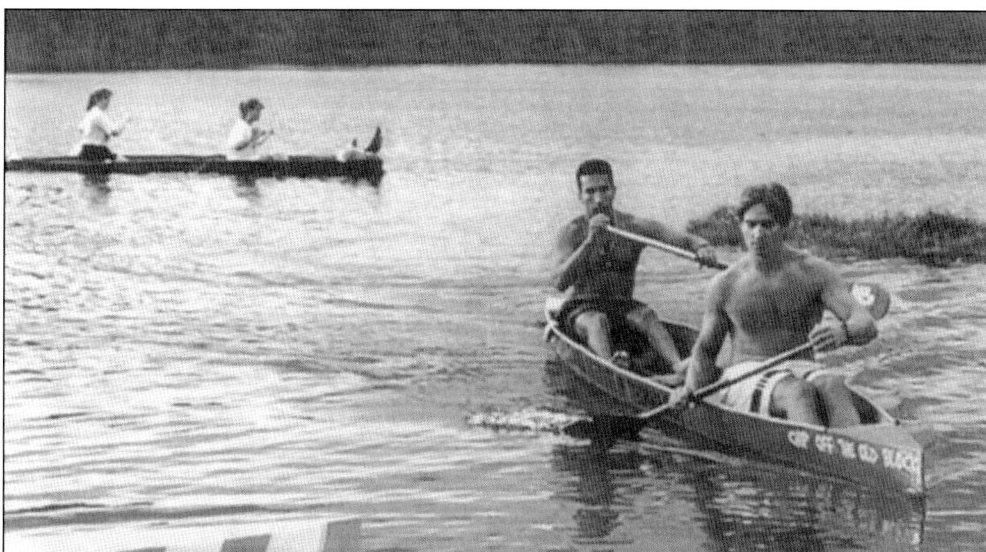

Florida Tech's civil engineering students, Tomas Montemayor (stern) and Chris Peterson (bow), are shown here practicing paddling "Chip off the Old Block," the first-place winner of the 1997 ASCE-Master Builders National Concrete Canoe Competition. Other team members included Heather Audet, Kari Chaney, Kama Dobbs, Jason Mapanoo, Nathaniel Tarbox, Jerry Butler, George Criss, Marc Leonard, and Paul Cosentino (faculty advisor). (Courtesy of University Publications.)

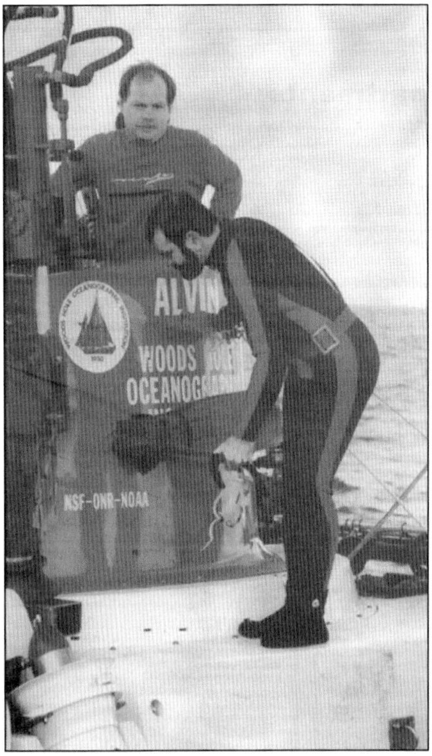

Oceanography and environmental sciences Professor John Trefry is preparing for a dive aboard the Alvin to research hydrothermal vents at the Juan de Fuca Ridge (2,300 meters) in the Pacific (200 miles off the Oregon and Washington coast). (Courtesy of University Publications.)

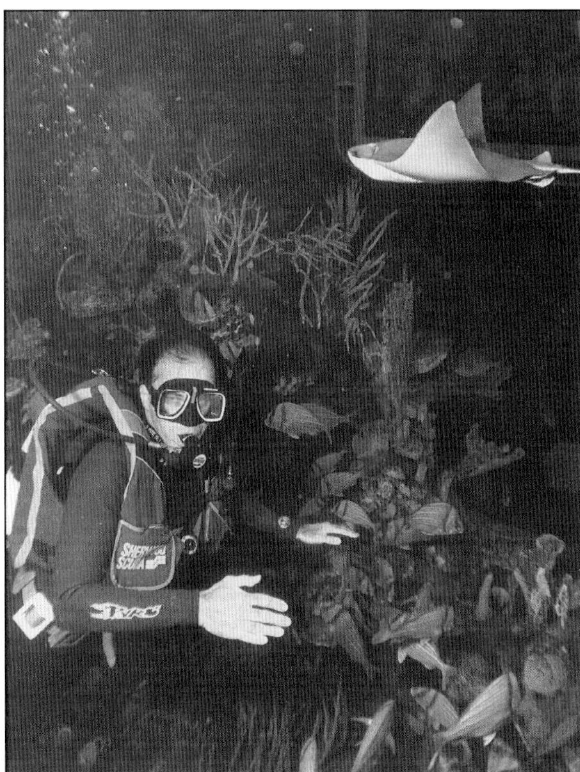

Disney World asked Florida Tech in 1991 to help in extending the life of the Epcot Center's Living Seas Aquarium. Geoffrey Swain (professor of ocean engineering and oceanography) led the team of Florida Tech faculty and graduate students who took on the problem of corrosion in the 5.7 million–gallon tank. (Courtesy of University Publications.)

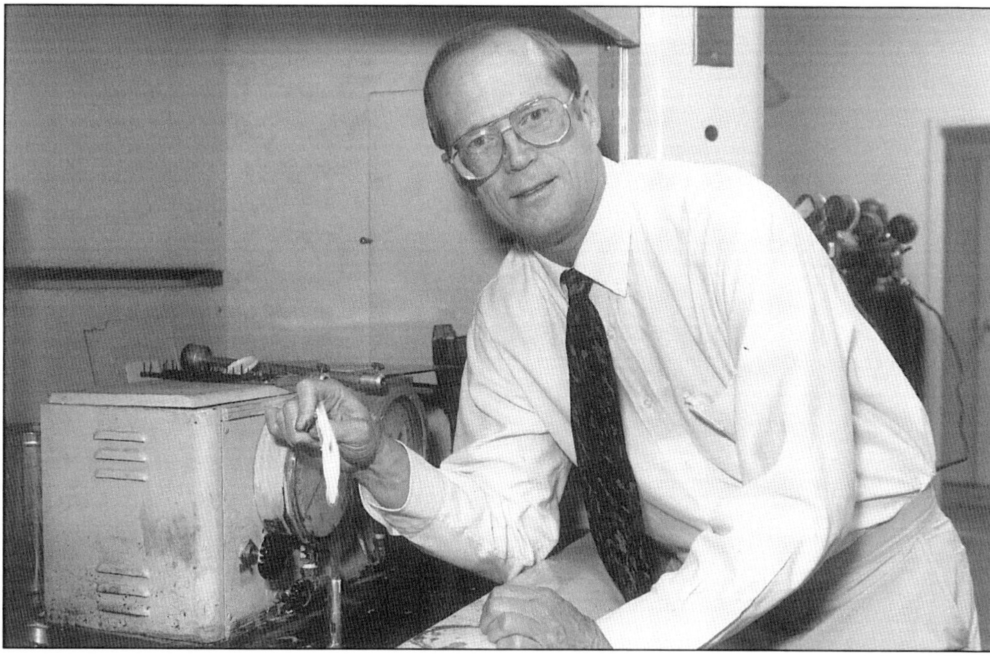

Gordon Nelson, shown here, was named the first dean of the College of Science and Liberal Arts in 1989. Nelson, a former president of the American Chemical Society, has won numerous awards for his research in polymers. (Courtesy of University Publications.)

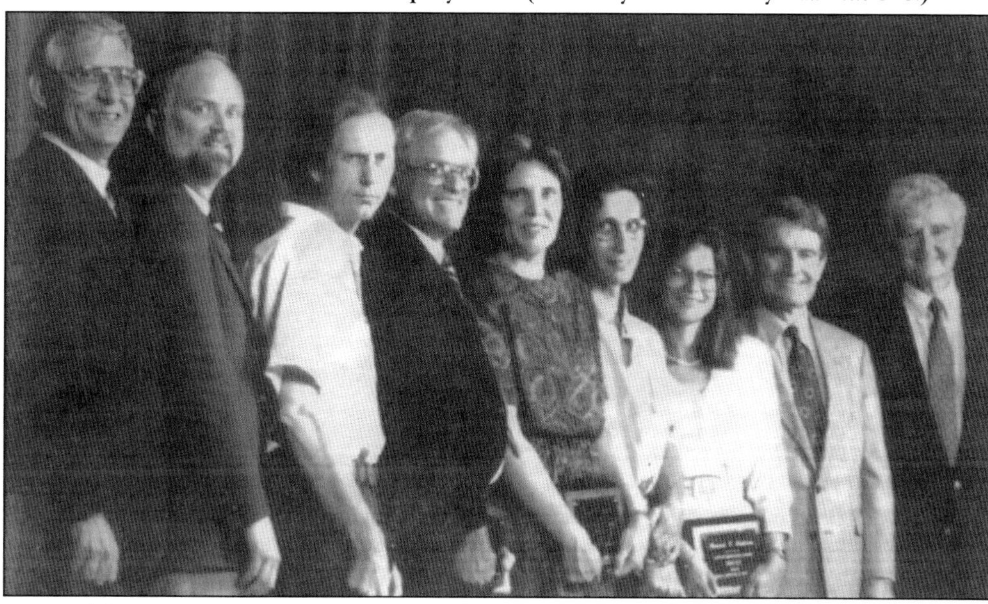

Pictured here are the 1992 winners of the faculty senate awards for teaching, research, and service. They are, from left to right, Andy Revay, vice president academic affairs; Terry Oswalt, research (physics and space sciences); Benjamin Sawyer, teaching (physics and space sciences); Kerry Clark, teaching (biology); Cecilia Knoll, service (mathematics); Nikolaos Papageorgiou, research (mathematics); Deborah Anderson, service (library); Lynn Weaver; and Gerard Cahill, faculty senate president. In 1999 the teaching award was renamed in Kerry Clark's memory. (Courtesy of University Publications.)

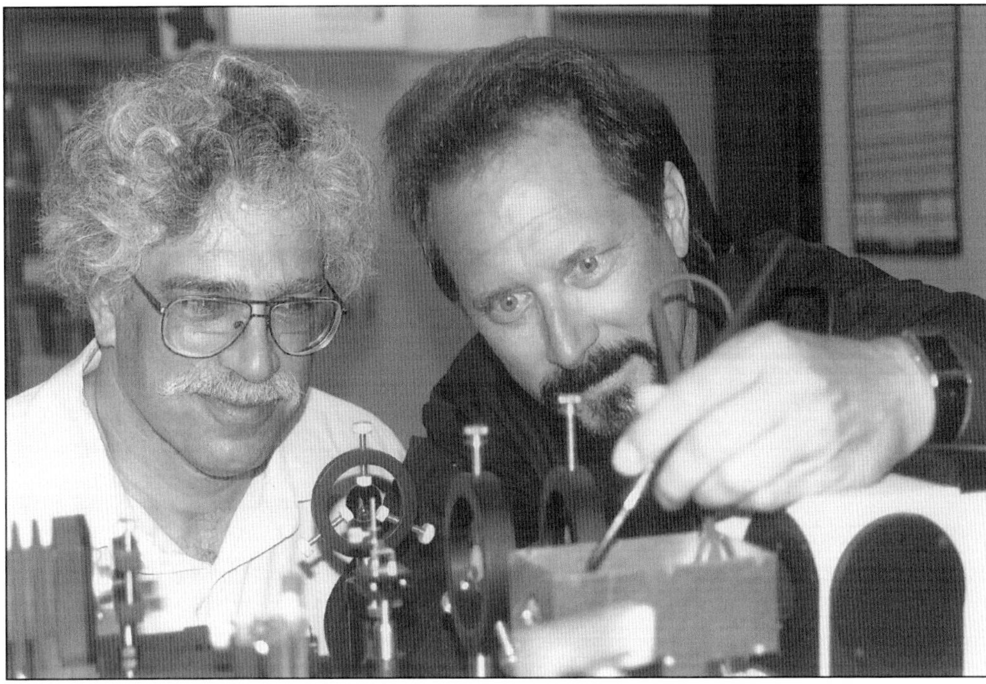

Biologist Glenn Cohen and Fredric Ham (Harris Professor) are pictured working on a device that would use infrared light to scan a diabetic's finger to monitor glucose. (Courtesy of University Publications.)

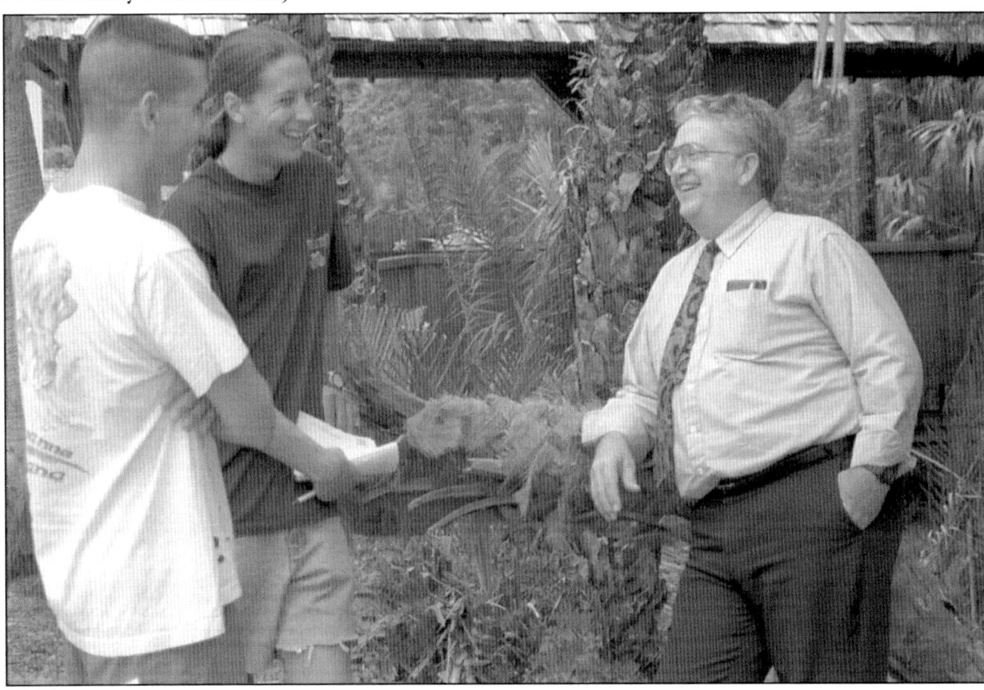

Biology is the largest undergraduate major in the College of Science and Liberal Arts. Professor Gary Wells, right, head of the biology department, is pictured here with two undergraduate students. (Courtesy of University Publications.)

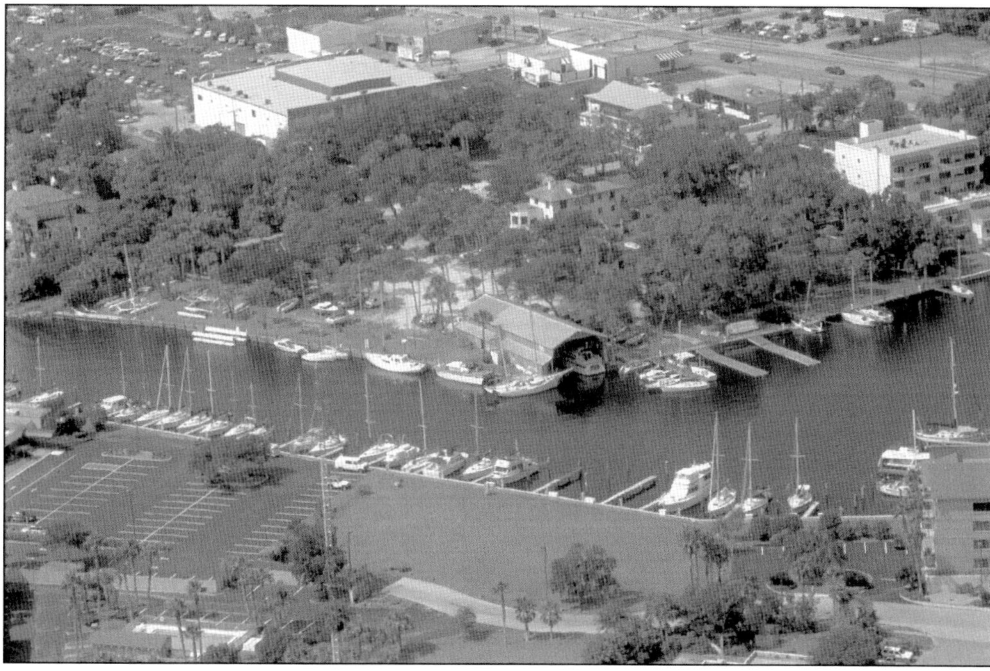

In 1994, Florida Tech's anchorage was renamed the Ralph S. Evinrude Marine Operations Center. The Evinrude Center serves as a base for crew team training, the university's research vessels, and boat donations. (Courtesy of University Publications.)

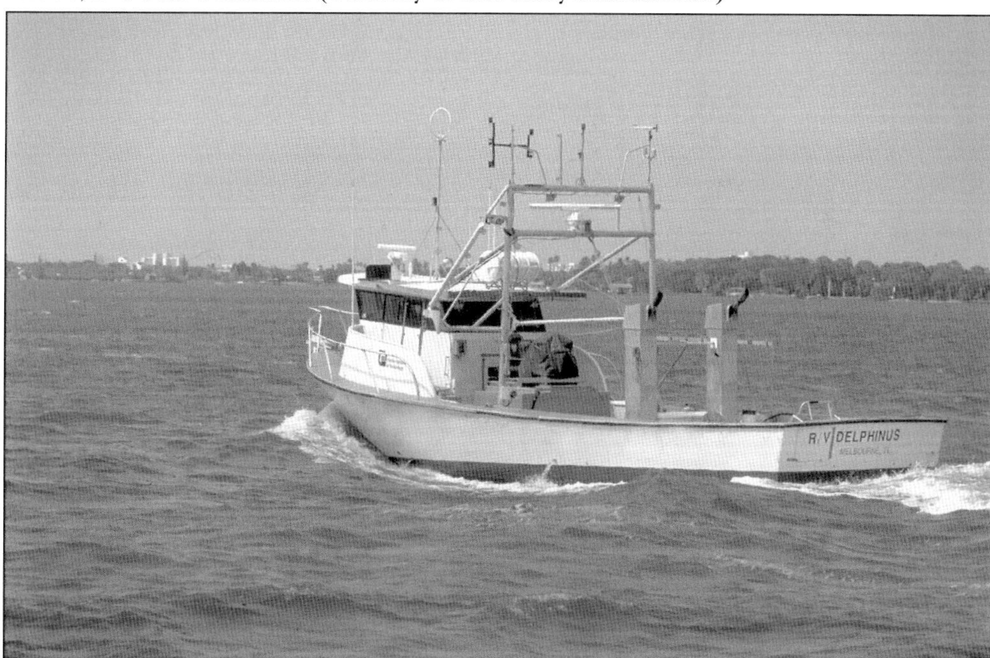

The 60-foot, gray and white, diesel powered *R/V Delphinus* (shown here) is the latest addition to Florida Tech's ocean and estuarine research program. Since 1992, the *R/V Delphinus* has served the oceanography, ocean engineering, environmental sciences, biological sciences, and science education programs. (Courtesy of University Publications.)

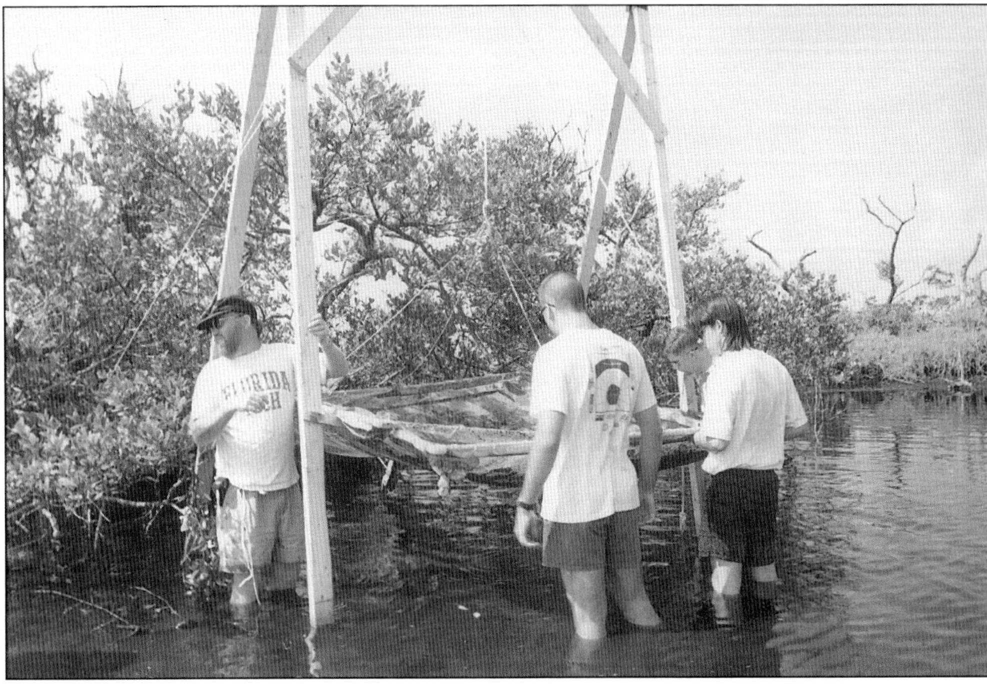

Professor Jon Shenker and students are pictured here gathering research data on tarpon near Sebastian Inlet. (Courtesy of University Publications.)

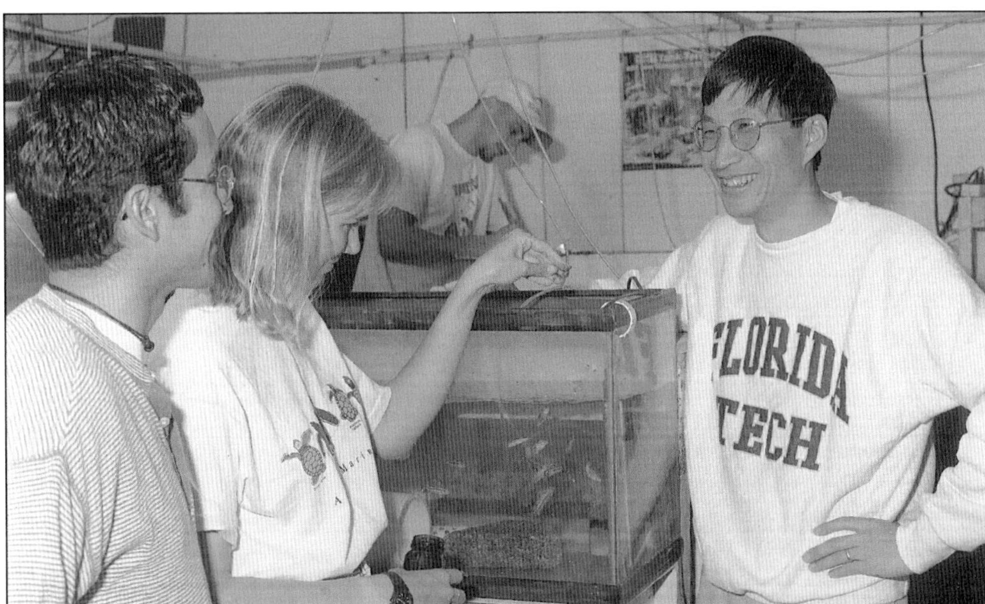

Professor Junda Lin, an expert on molluscan and crustacean aquaculture, is shown here with two students in one of the biology department's aquaculture labs. The biology department has offered a major in aquaculture since 1986. Courses in aquaculture technology were first offered at Jensen Beach in the 1970s. (Courtesy of University Publications.)

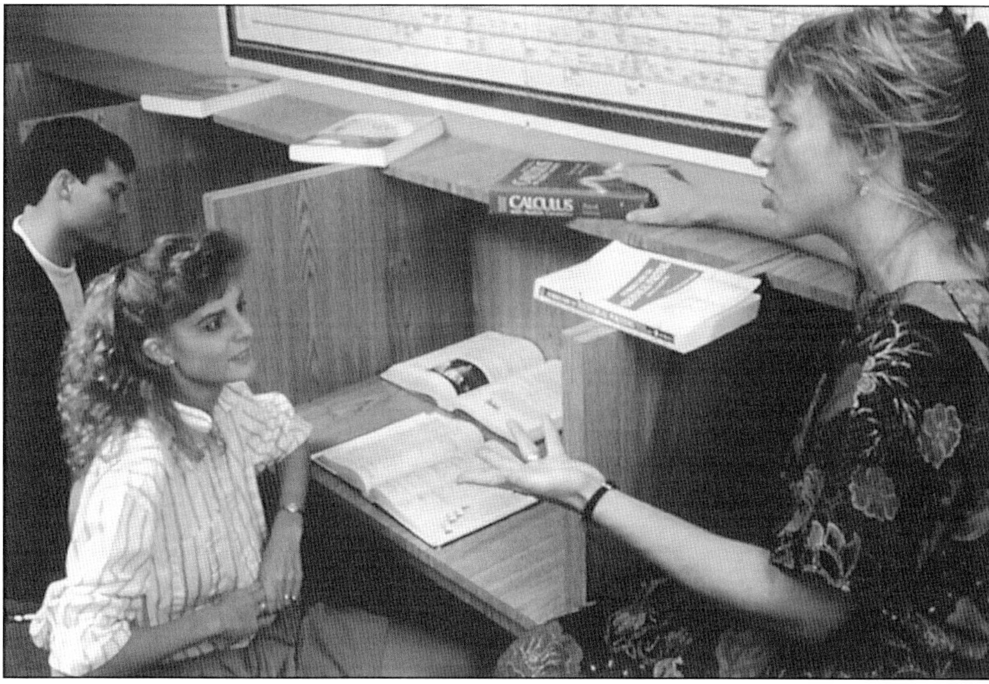

The Department of Humanities and Communication (Nabil Matar, head) offers both undergraduate and graduate degrees. Professor Carol Shehadeh (pictured here) serves as program chair for the undergraduate communication program. Professor Judith Strother leads a master's degree program in technical and professional communication. (Courtesy of University Publications.)

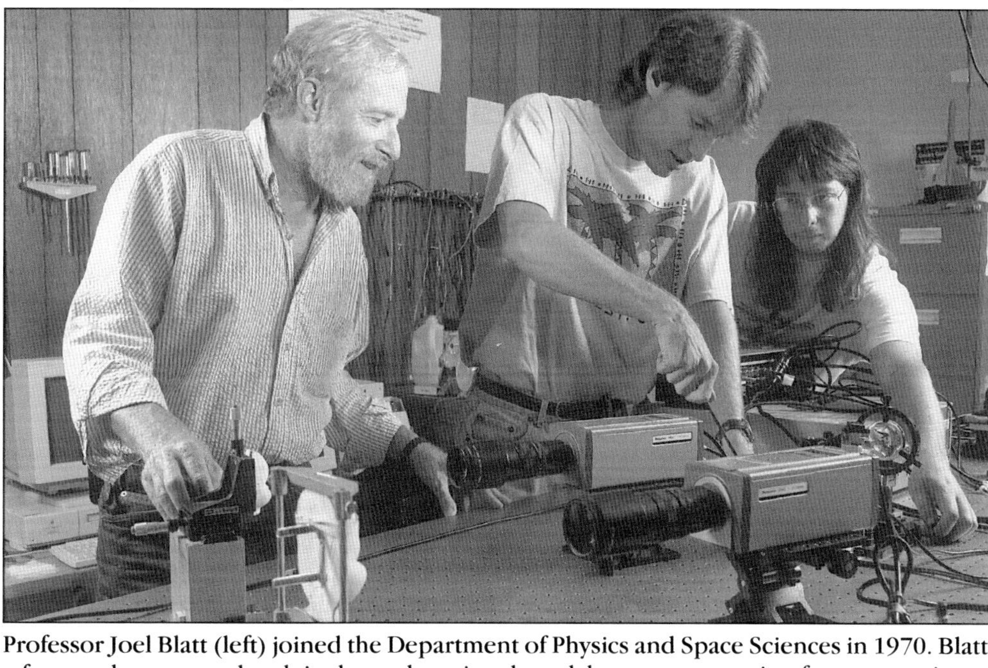

Professor Joel Blatt (left) joined the Department of Physics and Space Sciences in 1970. Blatt, a former department head, is shown here in a laser laboratory preparing for an experiment in 3-D imaging. (Courtesy of University Publications.)

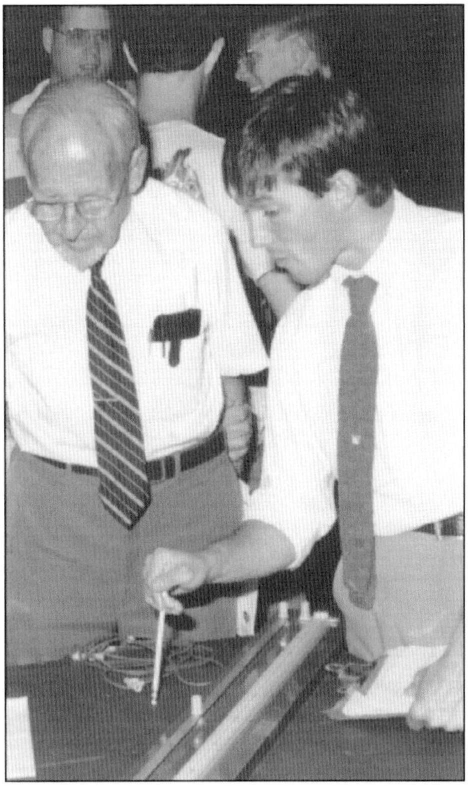

Science education graduate and high school teacher Tracey Bailey ('88 science education) is showing Professor Emeritus James Potter, left, an experiment he is preparing for his Satellite Beach students. In 1993, Bailey was named U.S. Teacher of the Year. (Courtesy of University Publications.)

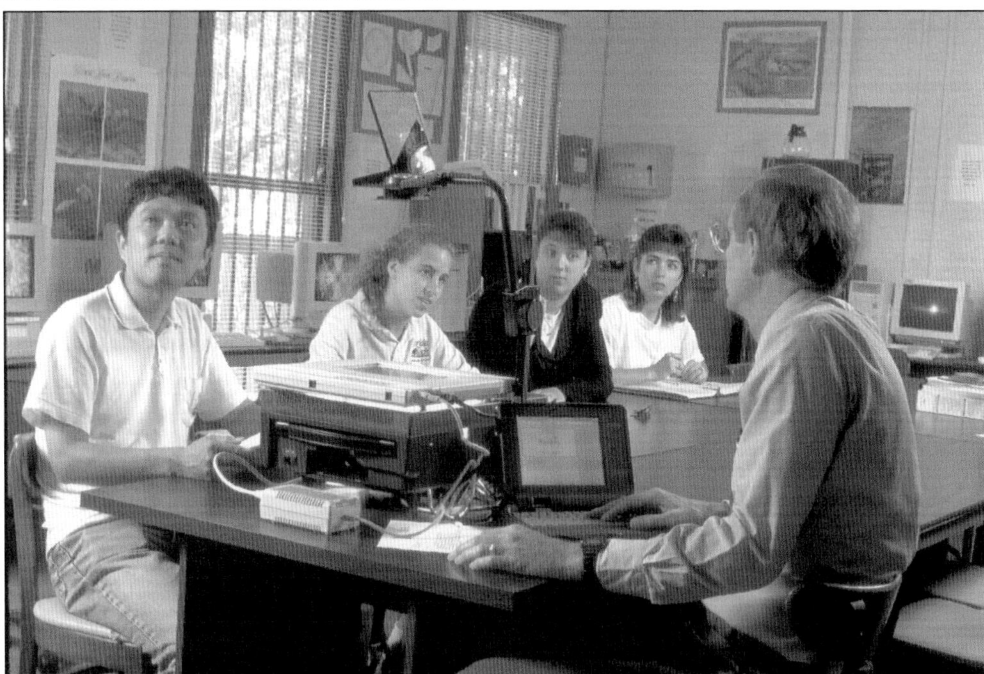

Robert Fronk (head, science education) is shown here meeting with a group of students in the Shephard Seminar Building. (Courtesy of University Publications.)

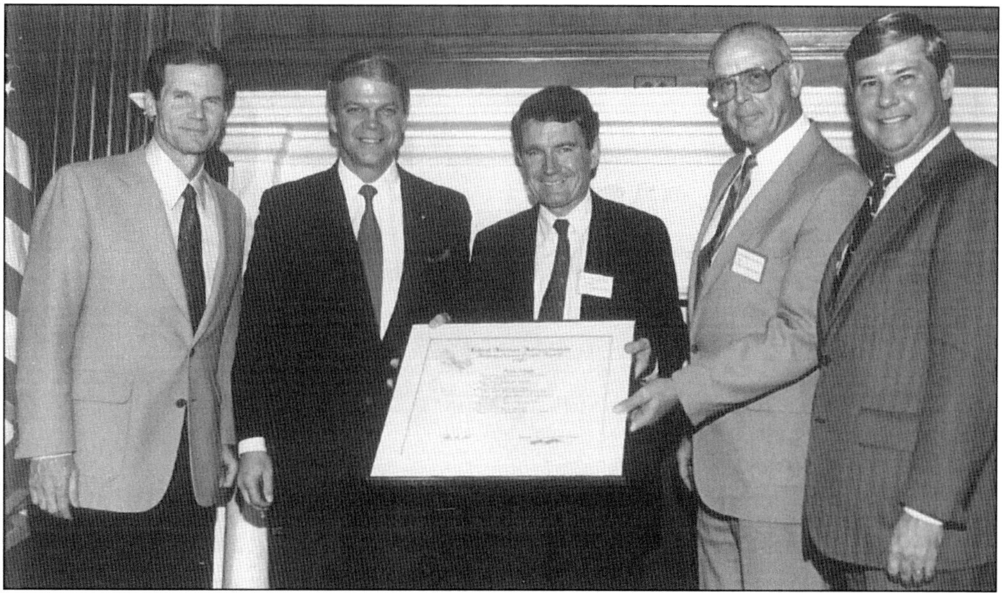

In 1990, Florida Tech received a $1.2-million grant from the Federal Aviation Administration for the construction of an Airways Sciences Building. Pictured here, from left to right, are Congressman Bill Nelson; Allan McArtor, FAA administrator; Lynn Weaver; Edmund Everette, dean of School of Aeronautics; and Senator Bob Graham. (Courtesy of University Publications.)

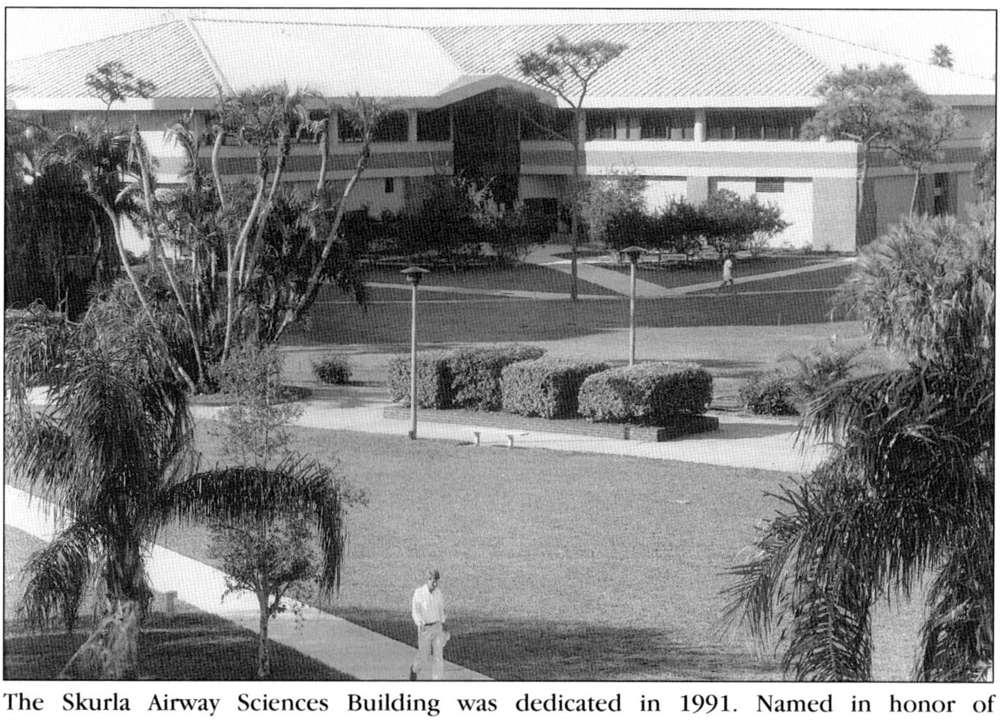

The Skurla Airway Sciences Building was dedicated in 1991. Named in honor of George Skurla, university trustee and retired CEO of the Grumman Corporation, this building provided needed classroom and laboratory space for the School of Aeronautics. (Courtesy of University Publications.)

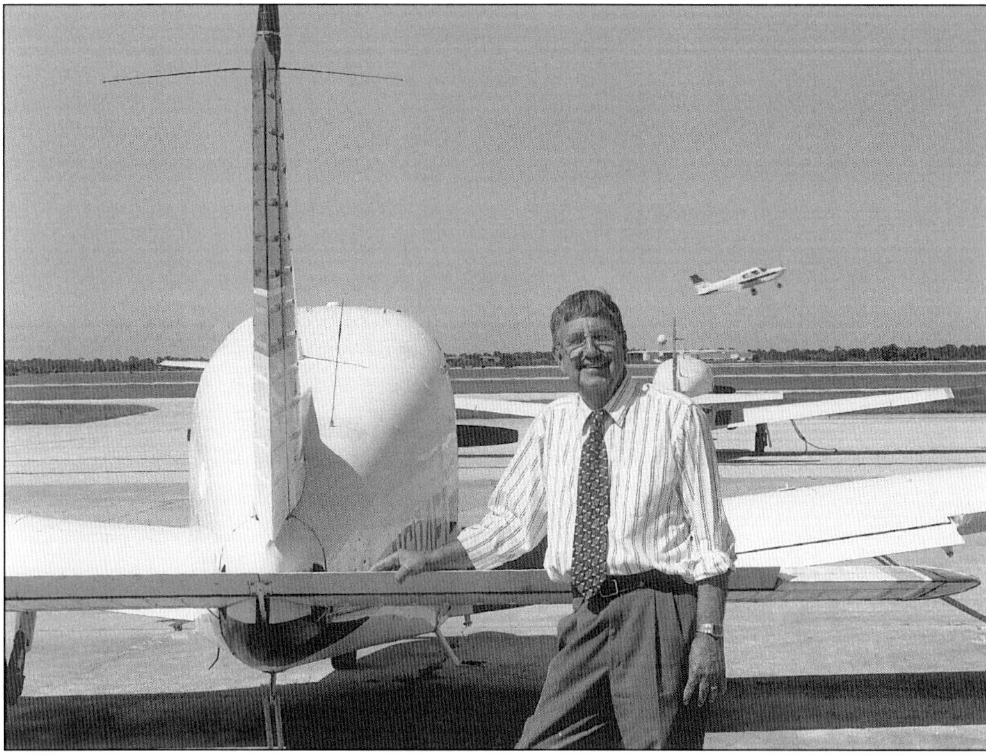

Tom Stephens is shown here at the School of Aeronautics Melbourne Airport facility. Stephens became dean of the School of Aeronautics in 1993 after Edmund Everette's retirement. (Courtesy of University Publications.)

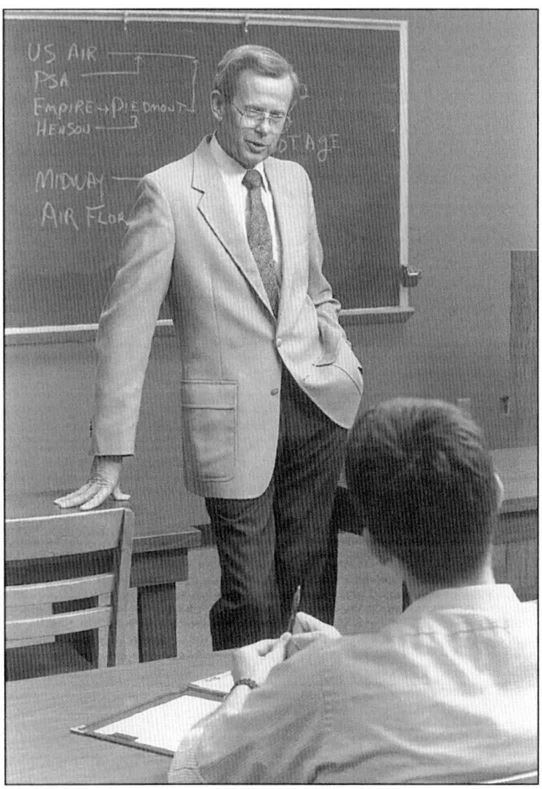

The School of Aeronautics has a reputation for excellence in teaching. Pictured in one of the new Skurla Building classrooms is Professor Paul Davis, a winner of the faculty senate award for outstanding teaching. (Courtesy of University Publications.)

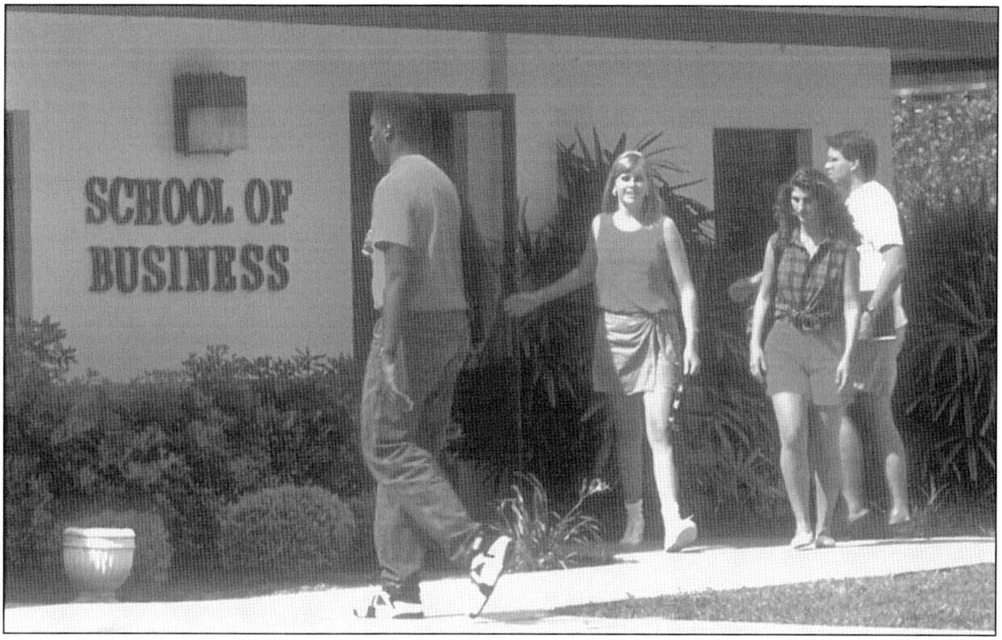

President Weaver's 1988 decision to reorganize the university's academic units led to changes beyond the College of Engineering. In 1990, the School of Management was renamed the School of Business. Pictured here are students entering the School of Business Building. (Courtesy of University Publications.)

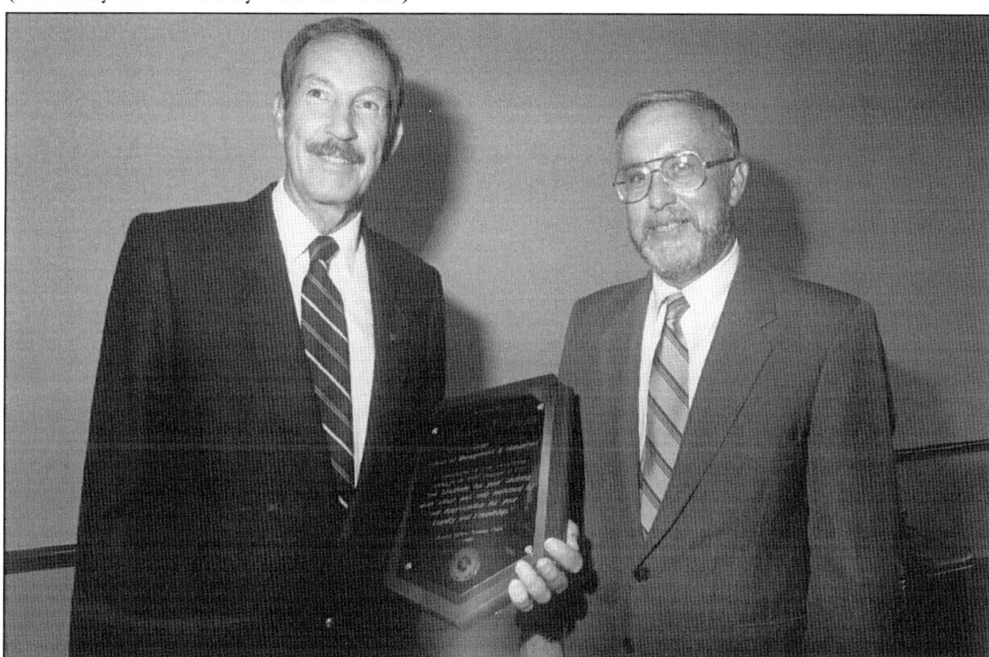

Jim Stoms, left, dean 1980–1988, and Roger Manley, right, dean 1988–1990, served as the first deans of the School of Management. Stoms and Joan Bixby organized the college's management program in the 1960s. Pictured here is Stoms receiving an award at his retirement. (Courtesy of University Publications.)

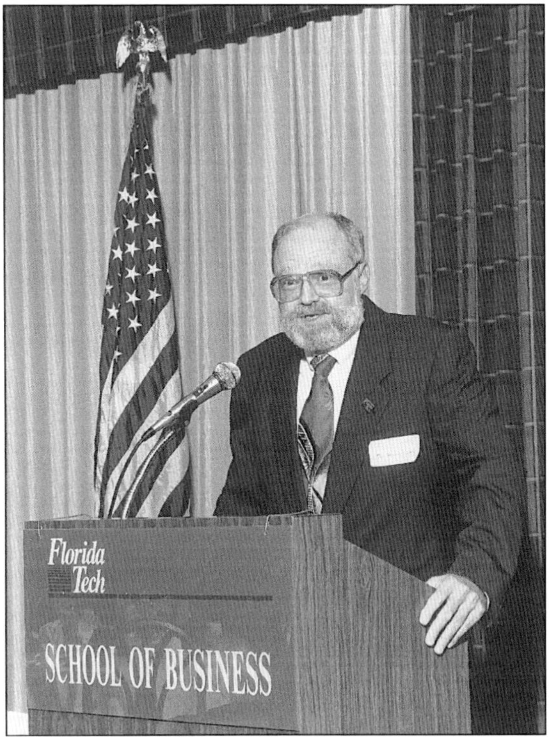

In 1990, President Weaver named A. Thomas Hollingsworth (pictured here) to succeed Roger Manley as dean of the School of Business. (Courtesy of University Publications.)

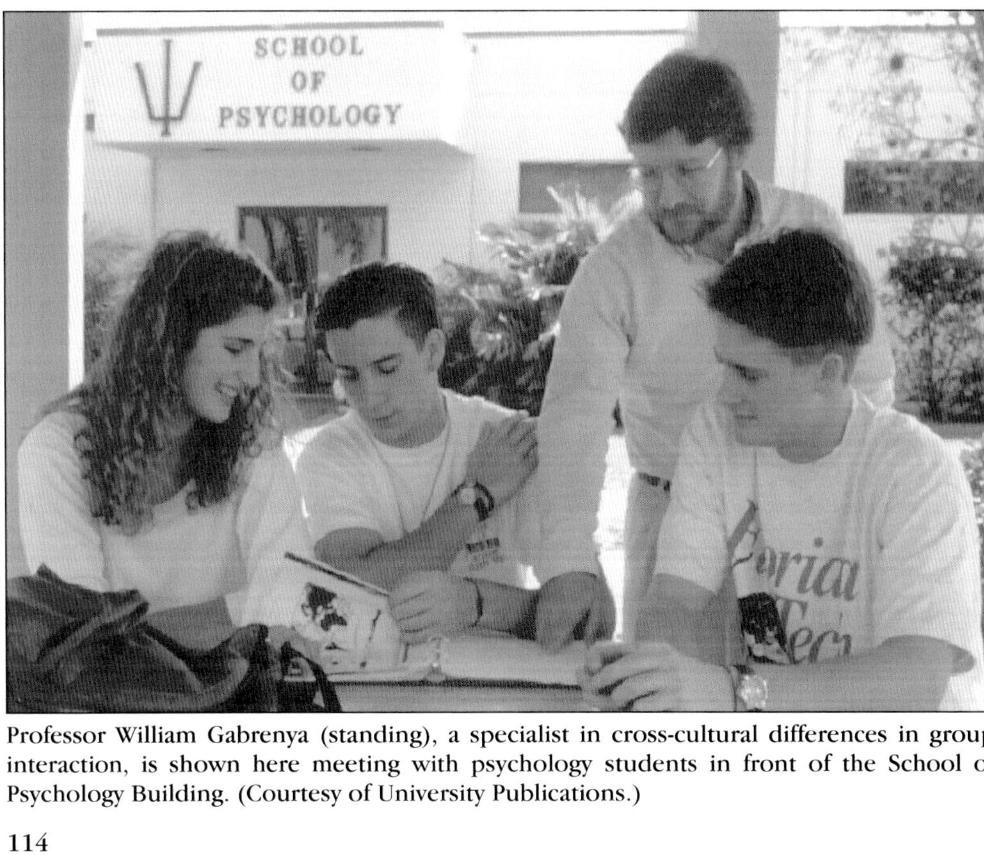

Professor William Gabrenya (standing), a specialist in cross-cultural differences in group interaction, is shown here meeting with psychology students in front of the School of Psychology Building. (Courtesy of University Publications.)

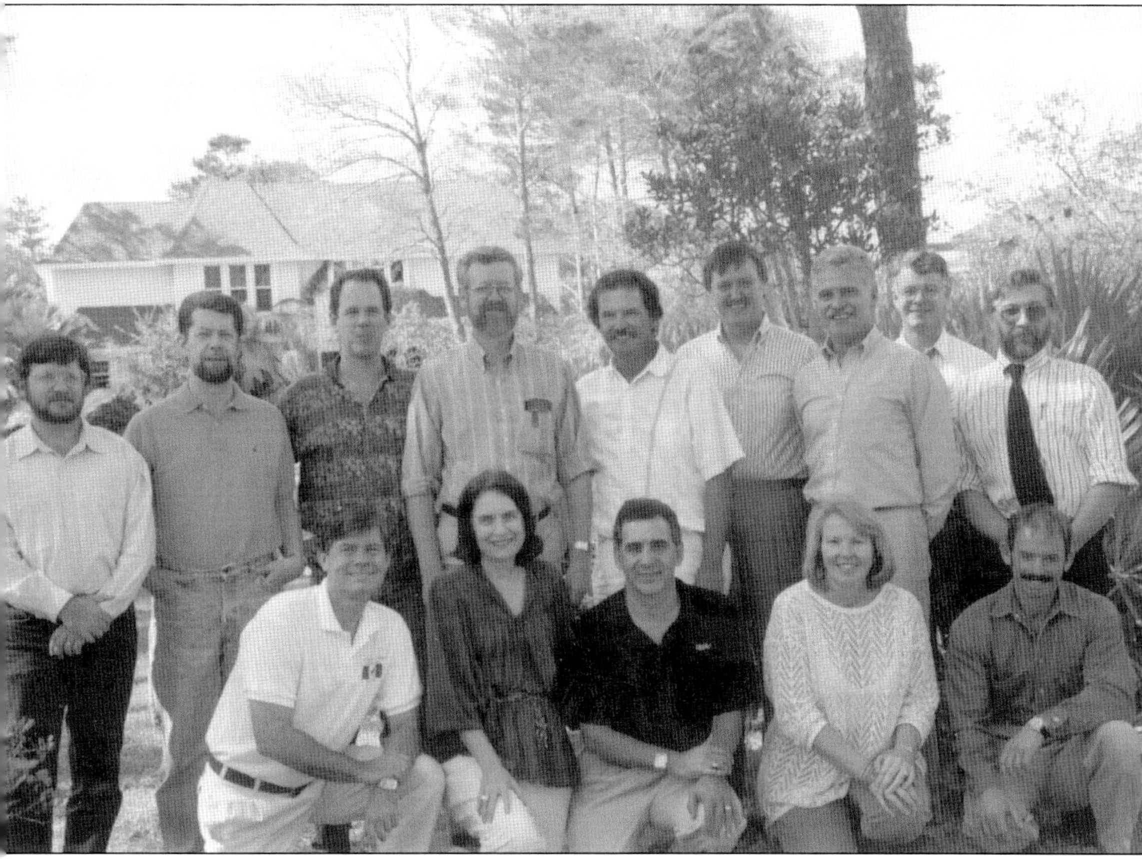

Members of the School of Psychology, pictured here at their 1993 faculty retreat, are, from left to right, (front) Frank Webbe (dean, 1985–1993), Juanita Baker, Philip Farber, Carol Philpot (dean, 1998–present), and Modesta Hevia; (back) William Gabrenya, Tom Harrell, Jeff Rain, Charles Prokop (dean, 1993–1998), Art Gutman, Richard Elmore Jr., Tom Peake, Don Smith, and Alan Stokes. (Courtesy of University Publications.)

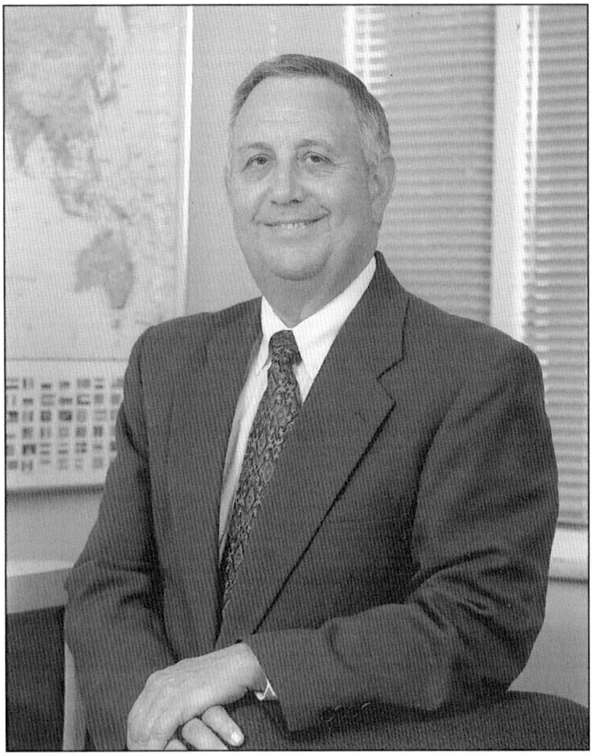

In 1990, Ron Marshall, shown here, succeeded Gen. Edward Gudgel, U.S.A. ret., as dean of the School of Extended Graduate Studies (SEGS). By 1995, Florida Tech SEGS had awarded more than 8,000 masters degrees in its off-campus programs. (Courtesy of University Publications.)

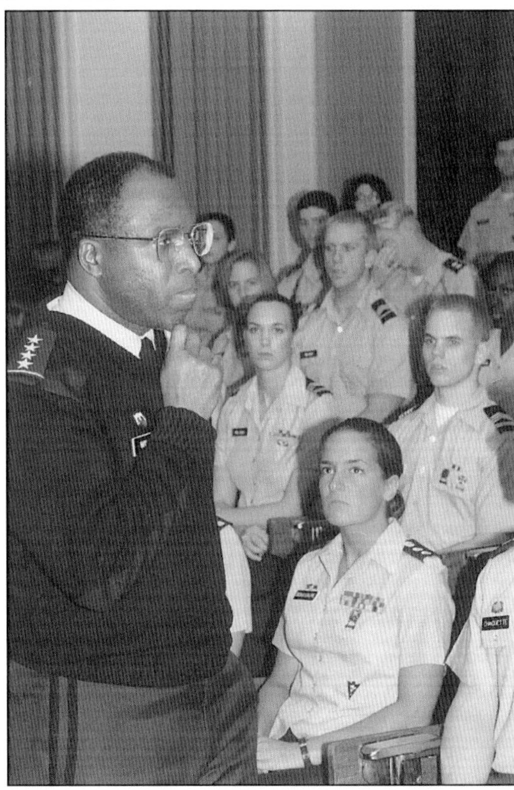

Four-star Army Gen. Johnnie Wilson is shown here meeting with Florida Tech ROTC students. General Wilson, the highest ranking African American serving in the U.S. military forces in 1998, earned his master's degree through Florida Tech's off-campus program (SEGS). (Courtesy of University Publications.)

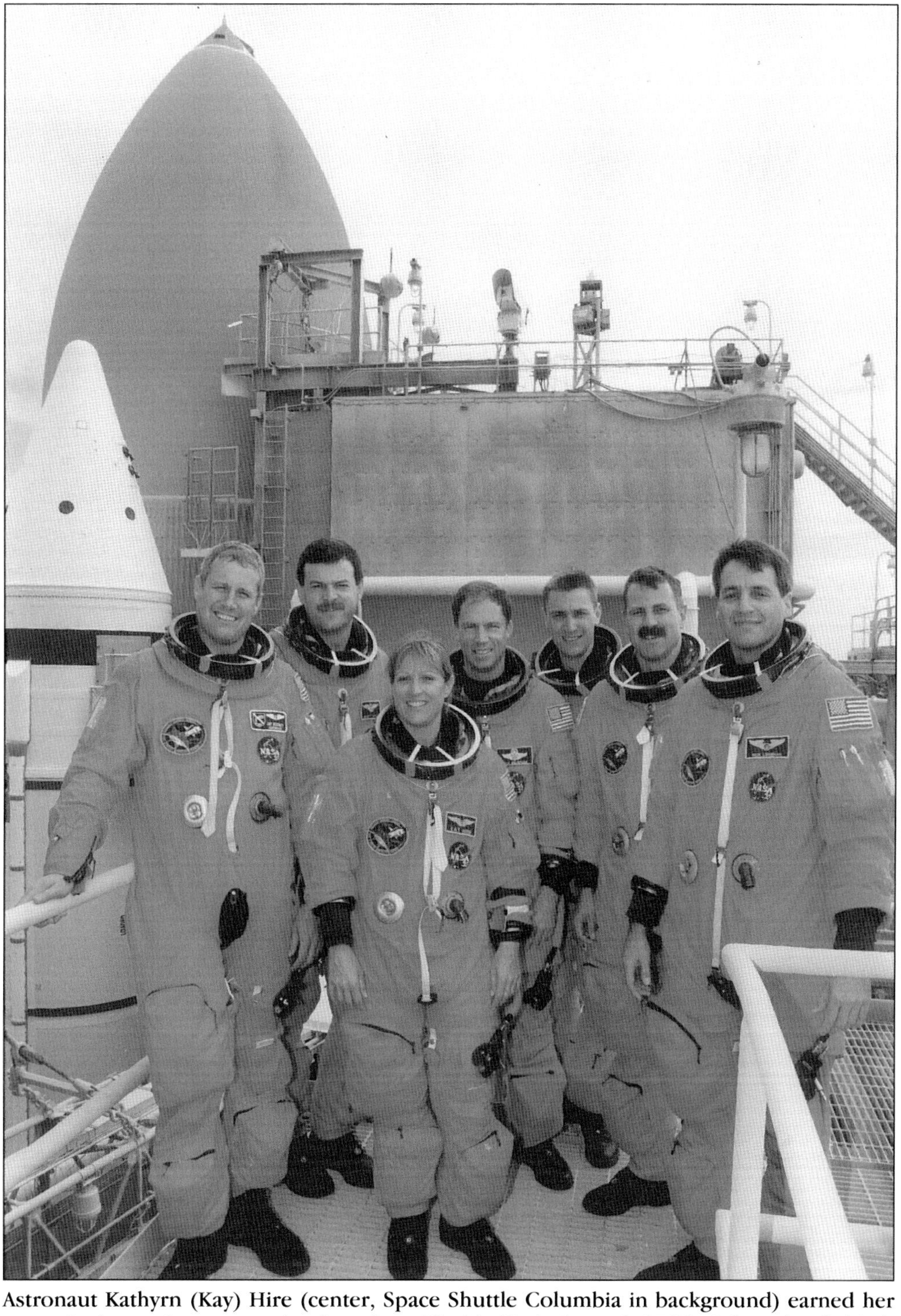

Astronaut Kathyrn (Kay) Hire (center, Space Shuttle Columbia in background) earned her master's degree in space technology from Florida Tech through SEGS. Other Florida Tech students serve in the astronaut corps. Joan Higginbotham ('92 MS, '96 MS) has completed her astronaut training and is awaiting assignment. (Courtesy of NASA.)

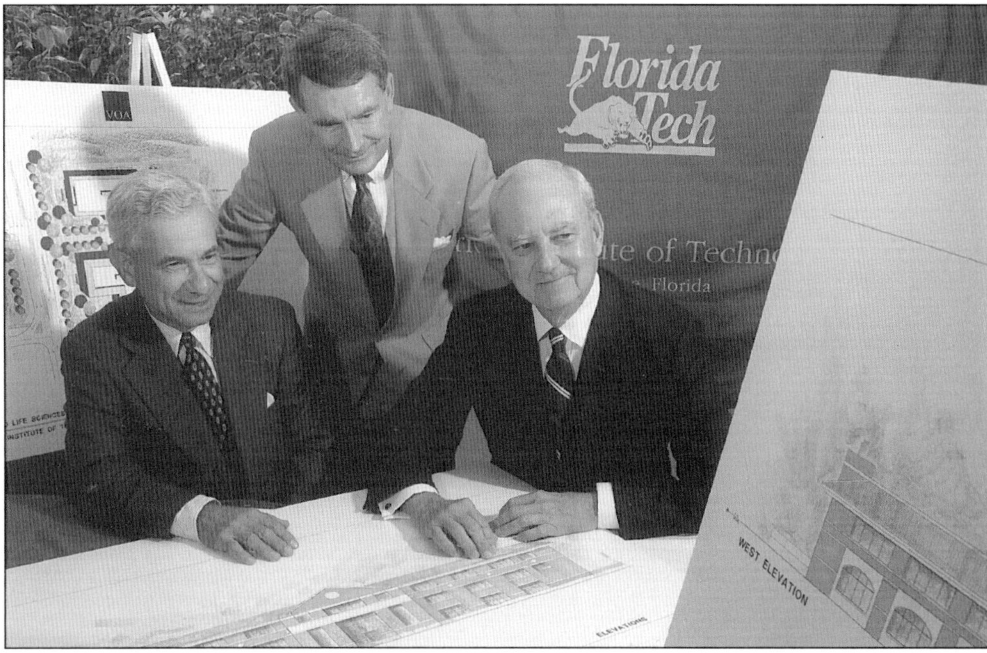

In 1997, the F.W. Olin Foundation awarded the university a $50-million grant. Lawrence Milas, left, F.W. Olin Foundation president, explained that the Olin Foundation had chosen Florida Tech for this award because the university possessed "unassailable academic quality and sound institutional management." President Lynn Weaver, center, and John T. Hartley, right, chairman of the board of trustees, are pictured here with Milas. (Courtesy of University Publications.)

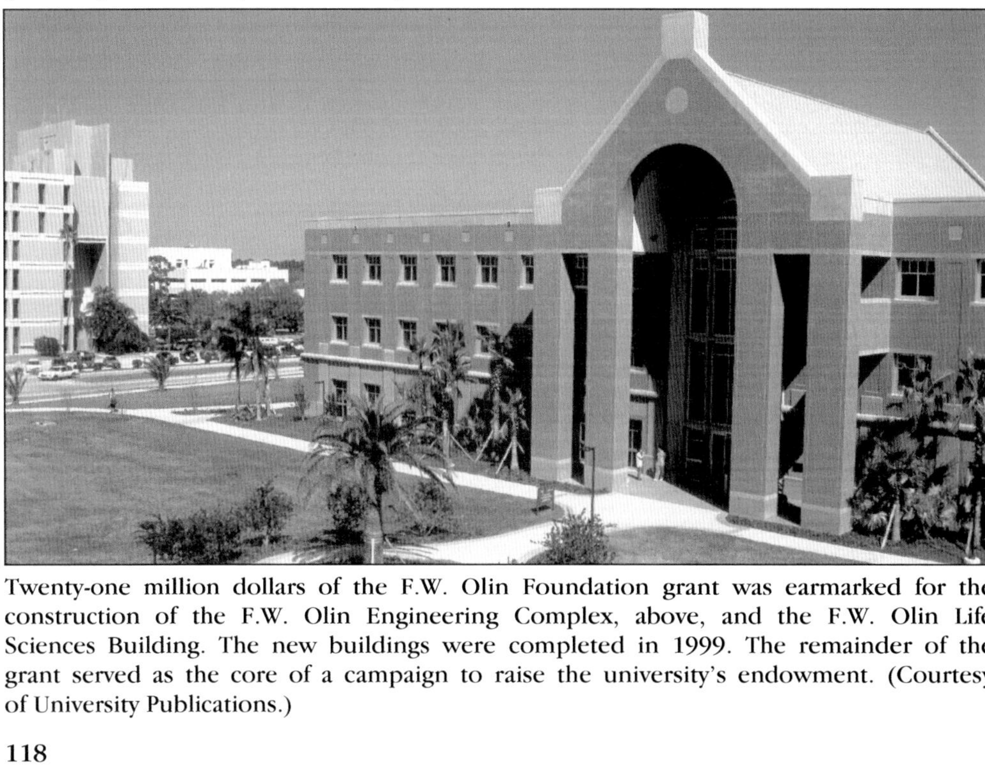

Twenty-one million dollars of the F.W. Olin Foundation grant was earmarked for the construction of the F.W. Olin Engineering Complex, above, and the F.W. Olin Life Sciences Building. The new buildings were completed in 1999. The remainder of the grant served as the core of a campaign to raise the university's endowment. (Courtesy of University Publications.)

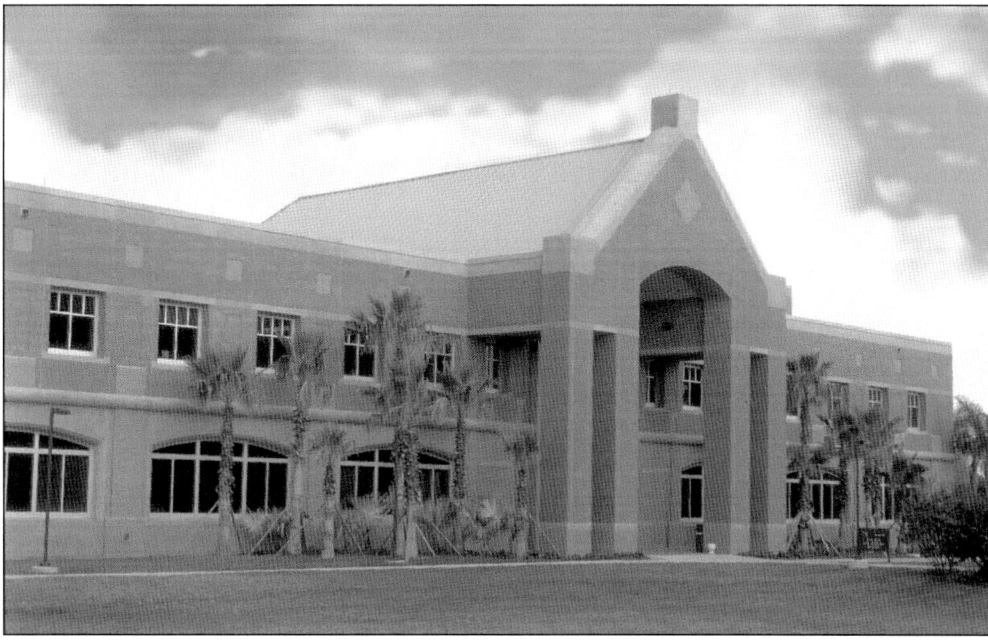

The F.W. Olin Life Science Building serves as home of Florida Tech's highly respected biology department. (Courtesy of University Publications.)

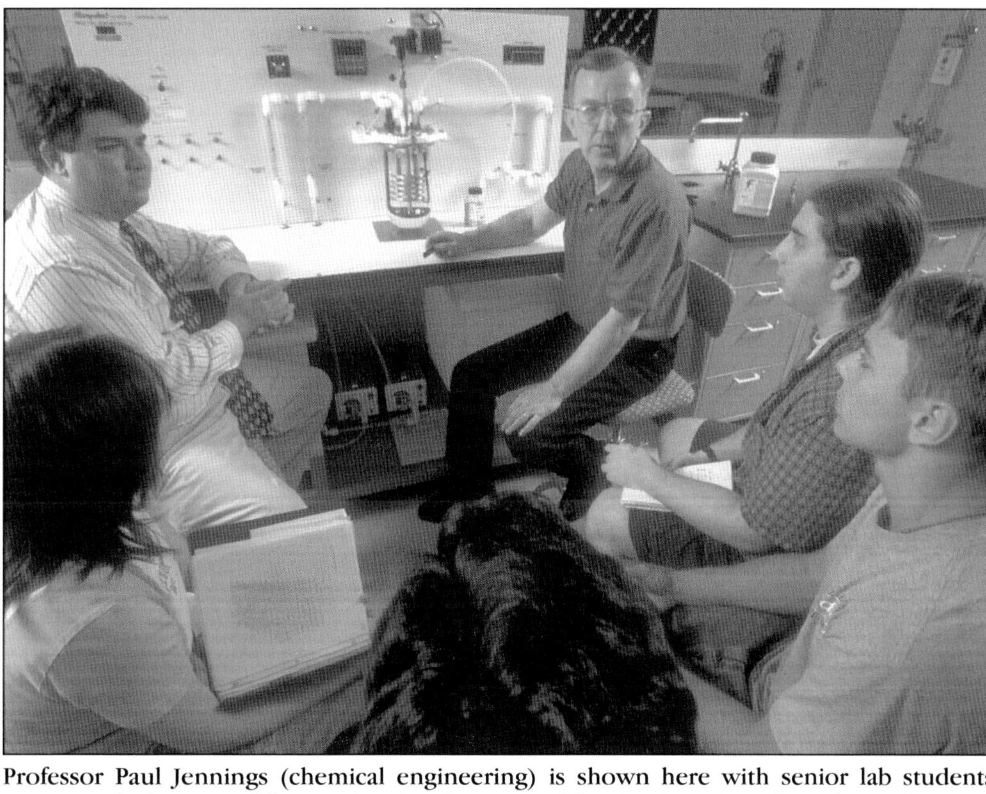

Professor Paul Jennings (chemical engineering) is shown here with senior lab students in one of the new laboratories in the F.W. Olin Engineering Complex. (Courtesy of University Publications.)

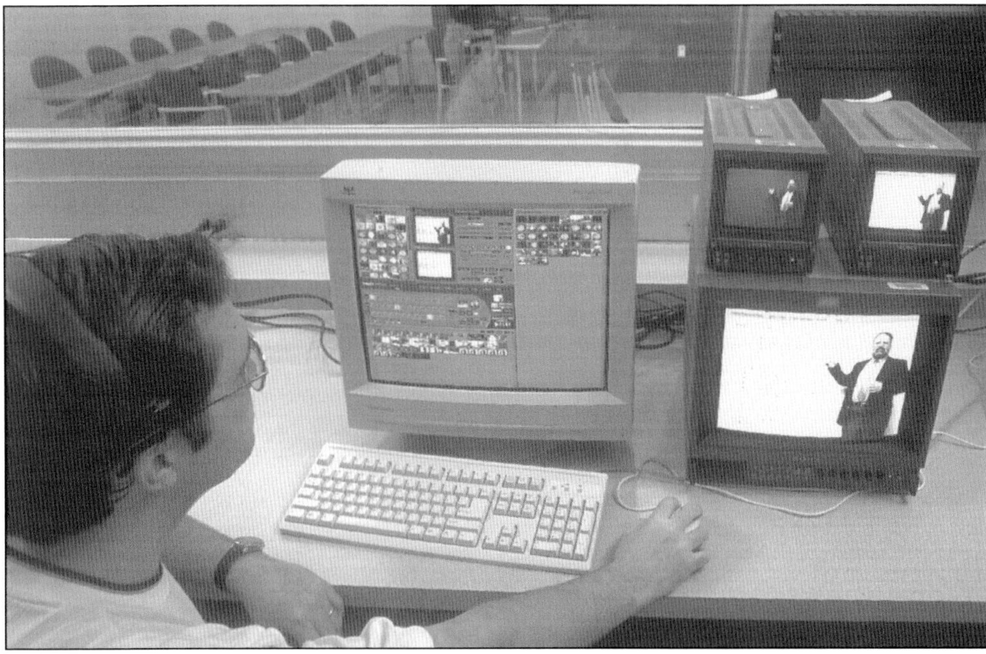

The Olin Engineering Complex and Olin Life Sciences Building allow Florida Tech faculty and students to explore new technologies. Here, Professor Hal Brown (on the monitor in the picture) is using one of the new laboratories to develop state-of-the-art distance learning strategies. (Courtesy of University Publications.)

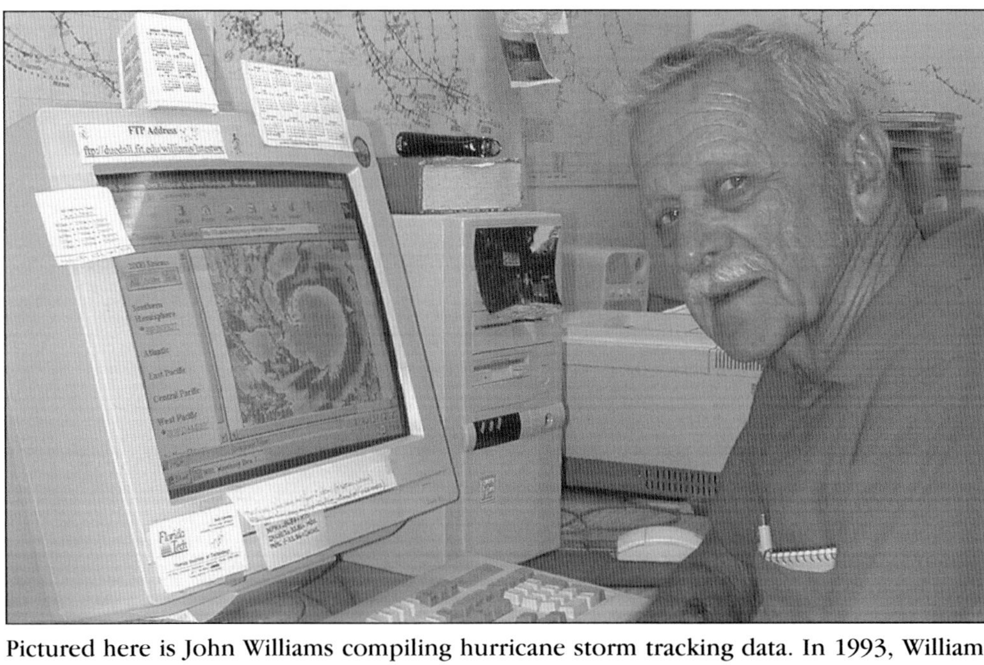

Pictured here is John Williams compiling hurricane storm tracking data. In 1993, Williams and Professor Iver Duedall (environmental sciences) authored a history of Florida hurricanes. Williams is a past winner of the Florida Tech Advocates' Most Valuable Panther Award (MVP) for his contributions to improving campus life.(Courtesy of University Publications.)

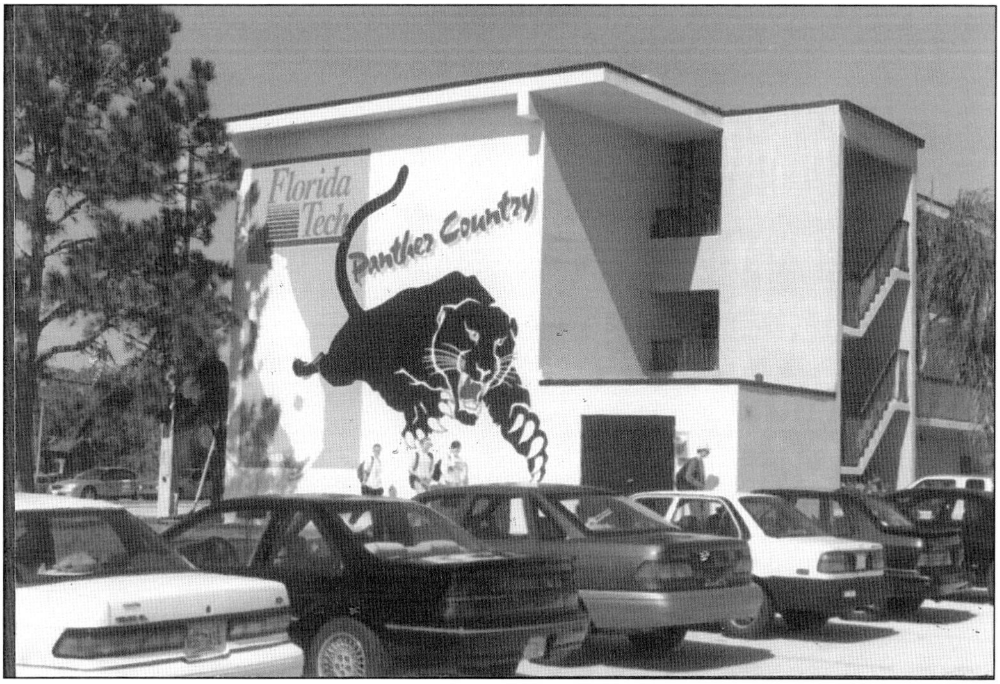

In 1992, President Weaver accepted the recommendation of the university's Identity Task Force. The new Florida Tech image (upper left) was used in official publications. The Florida Tech Panther became the new graphic identity for the athletic program. (Courtesy of University Publications.)

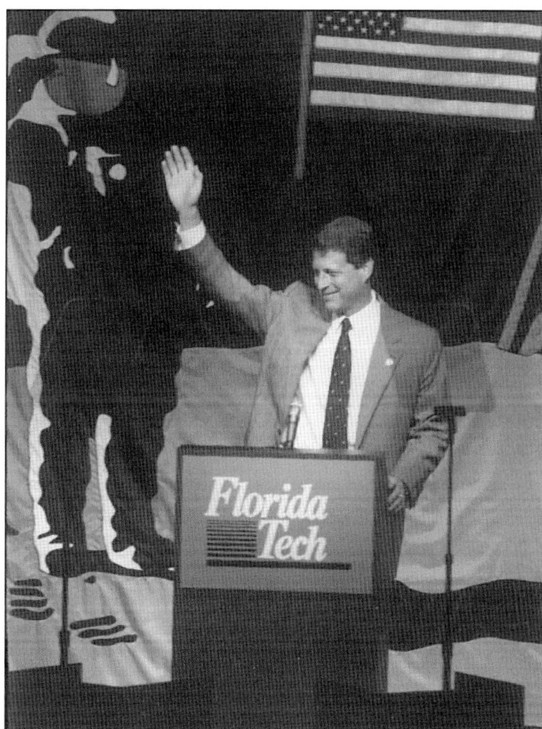

Many distinguished individuals visited Panther Country during the 1990s. Pictured here is vice presidential candidate Al Gore delivering a major policy address on the U.S. space program in Gleason Auditorium in 1992. Note the image of an American astronaut in the background. (Courtesy of University Publications.)

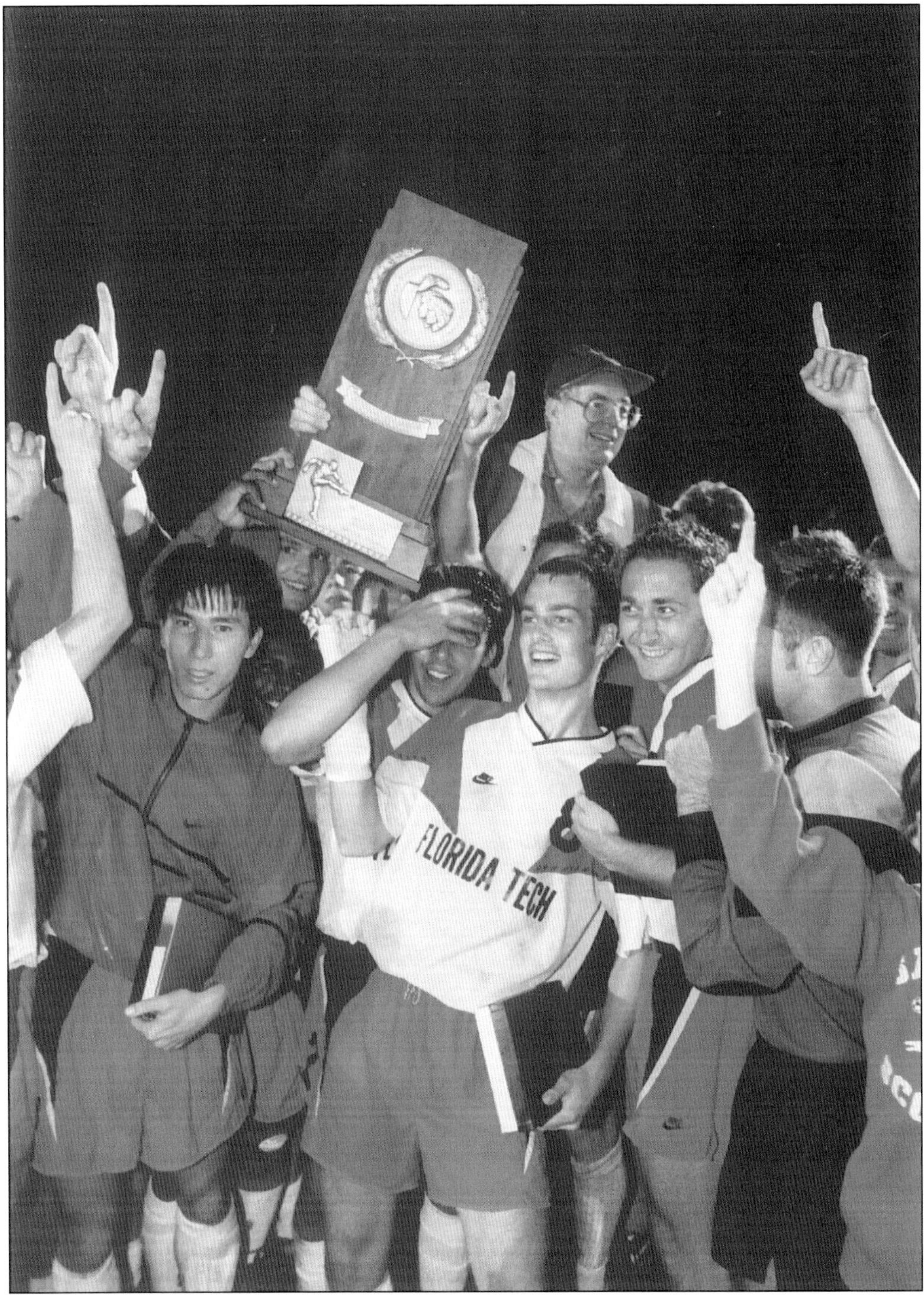

Florida Tech's Panthers won national recognition for their accomplishments in the late 1980s and 1990s. In 1988 and 1991, the men's soccer team won the NCAA Division II national championship. Pictured here is the 1988 national championship team and their Coach Rick Stottler (center) in their victory celebration. (Courtesy of University Publications.)

Coach John Reynolds led the Lady Panthers basketball team to back-to-back conference championships in 1991–1992 and 1992–1993. Here, Florida Tech's Candee Zepka drives past a Florida Southern defender. Zepka's four free throws in the final seconds of the game sealed the Panther's 71-66 victory. (Courtesy of University Publications.)

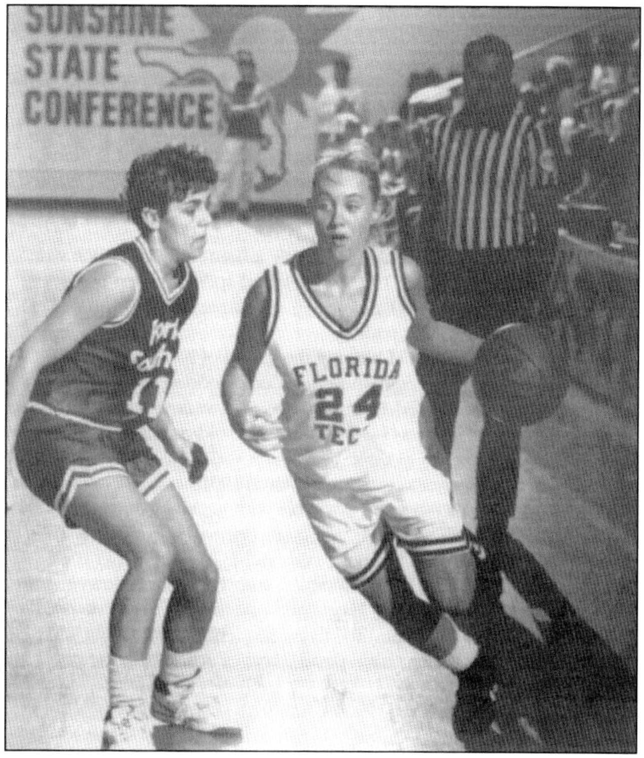

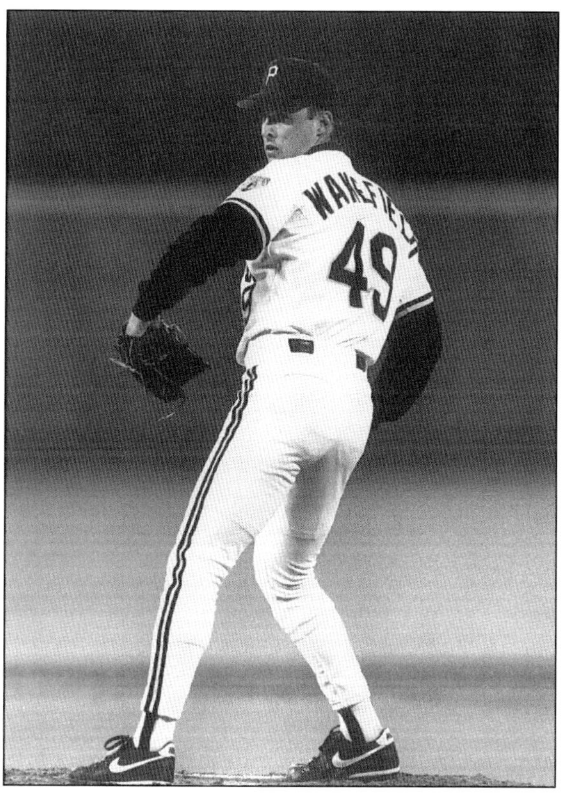

Tim Wakefield (Florida Tech baseball 1986-1988) was named National League Rookie Pitcher of the Year in 1992. Wakefield holds the school record for career home runs (40). Here, Wakefield is shown when he pitched for the Pittsburgh Pirates. He later joined the Boston Red Sox. (Courtesy of University Publications.)

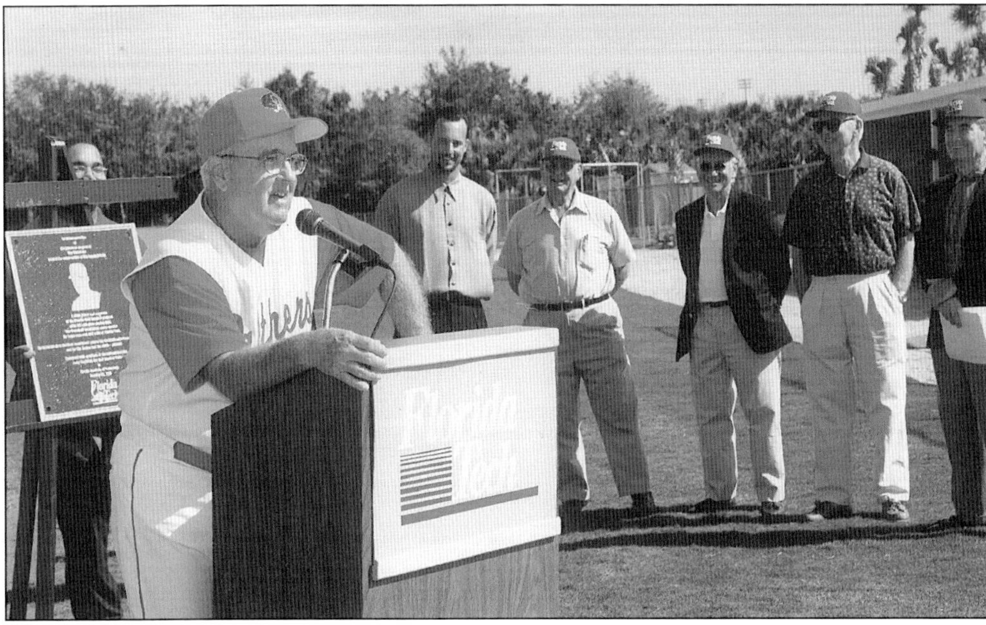

Les Hall, Florida Tech's baseball coach, speaks at the dedication of the Andy Seminick–Les Hall Baseball Fields in 1999. Tim Wakefield (right of Hall) donated $150,000 and Richard Muns $25,000 to help build the new facility. The F.W. Olin Foundation provided an additional $250,000. Pictured here, from left to right, are Hall, Wakefield, Andy Seminick, Lawrence Milas, John Hartley, and Lynn Weaver. (Courtesy of University Publications.)

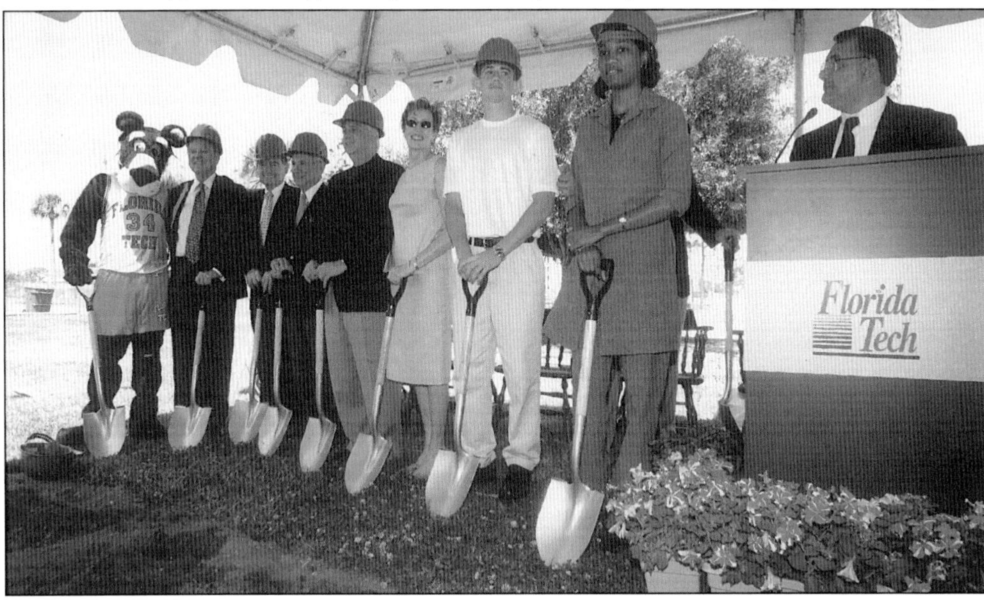

In June 1999, Charles and Ruth Clemente donated $3.3 million to build a new sports and recreational complex on the site of the Hedgecock Gymnasium and classroom annex. The F.W. Olin Foundation provided an additional $3.3 million. Pictured at the ground breaking ceremonies, from left to right, are Florida Tech Panther, John Hartley, Lynn Weaver, Lawrence Milas, Charles Clemente, Ruth Clemente, two representatives of the student body, and Jim DeSantis (vice president external affairs). (Courtesy of University Publications.)

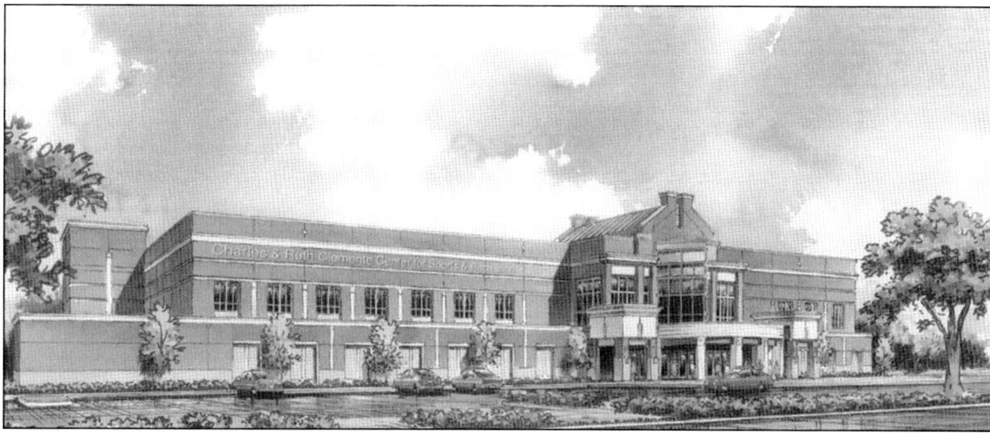

The Charles and Ruth Clemente Center for Sports and Recreation is scheduled for completion in 2001. Shown here is a rendering of the building. (Courtesy of University Publications.)

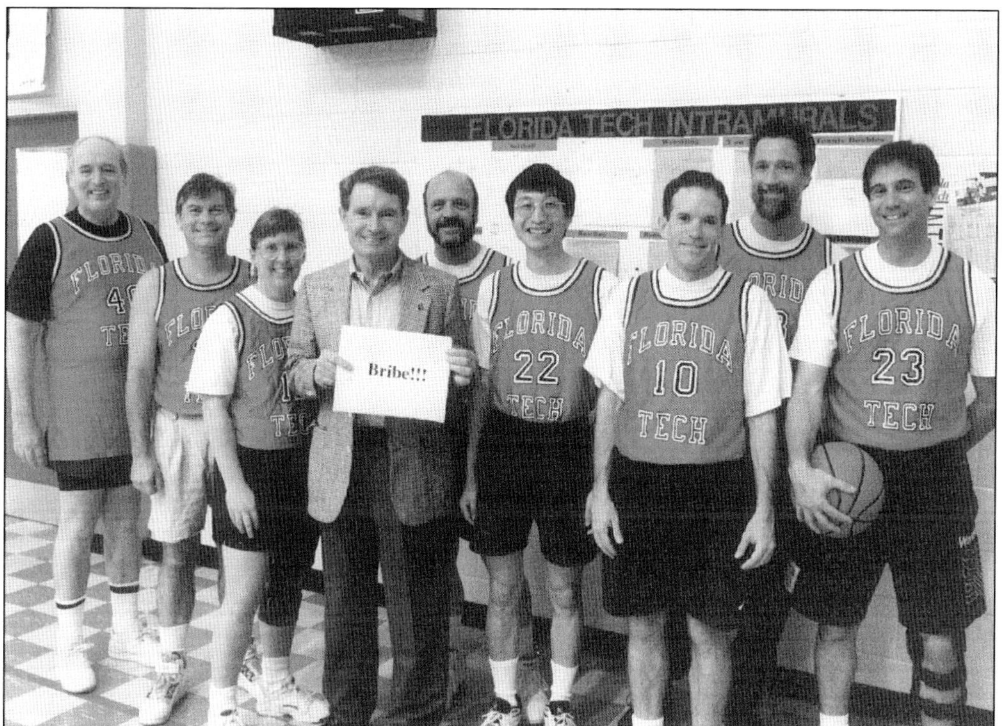

Alumni faculty basketball games are one of Florida Tech's Homecoming traditions. Pictured here is the faculty team in 1996. They are, from left to right, Fred Buoni, Frank Webbe, Sue Hann, Lynn Weaver (coach), David Hott, Junda Lin, Al Brown, Lee Harris, and Paul Cosentino. The alumni team won 8-0. (Courtesy of University Publications.)

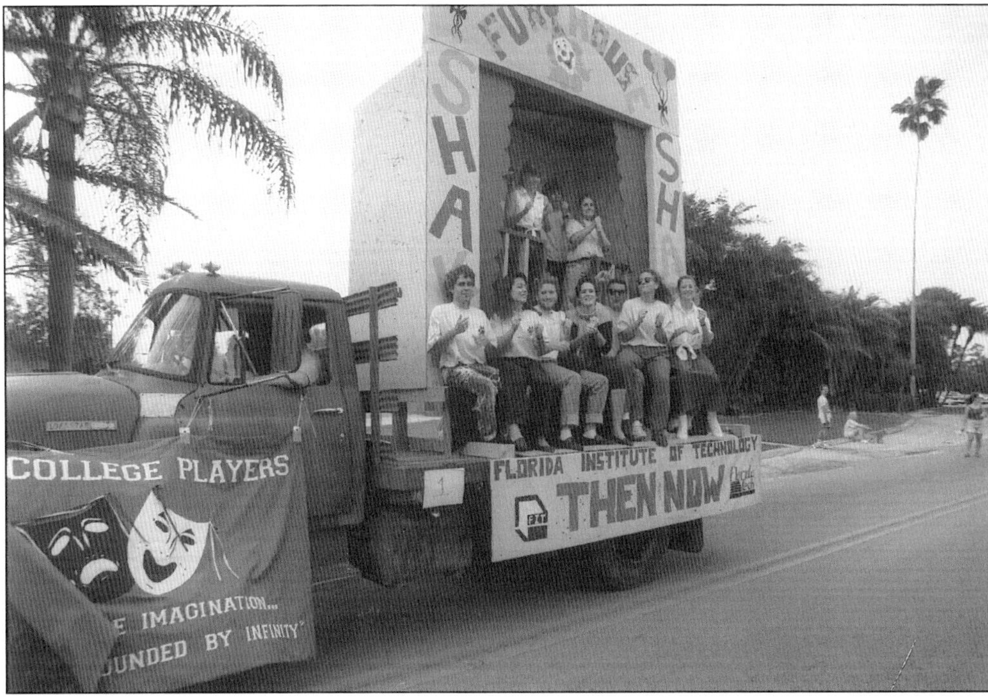

Homecoming is a time of reflection. Pictured here is the College Player's early 1990s float. Their theme was "Florida Institute of Technology: Then and Now." (Courtesy of University Publications.)

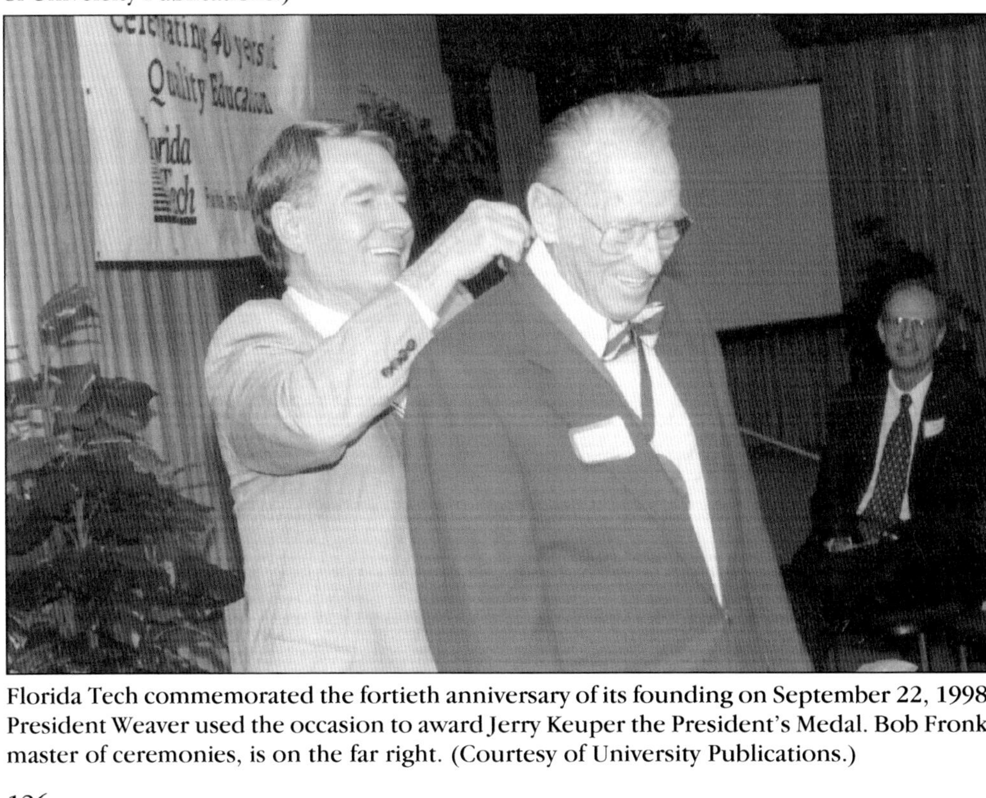

Florida Tech commemorated the fortieth anniversary of its founding on September 22, 1998. President Weaver used the occasion to award Jerry Keuper the President's Medal. Bob Fronk, master of ceremonies, is on the far right. (Courtesy of University Publications.)

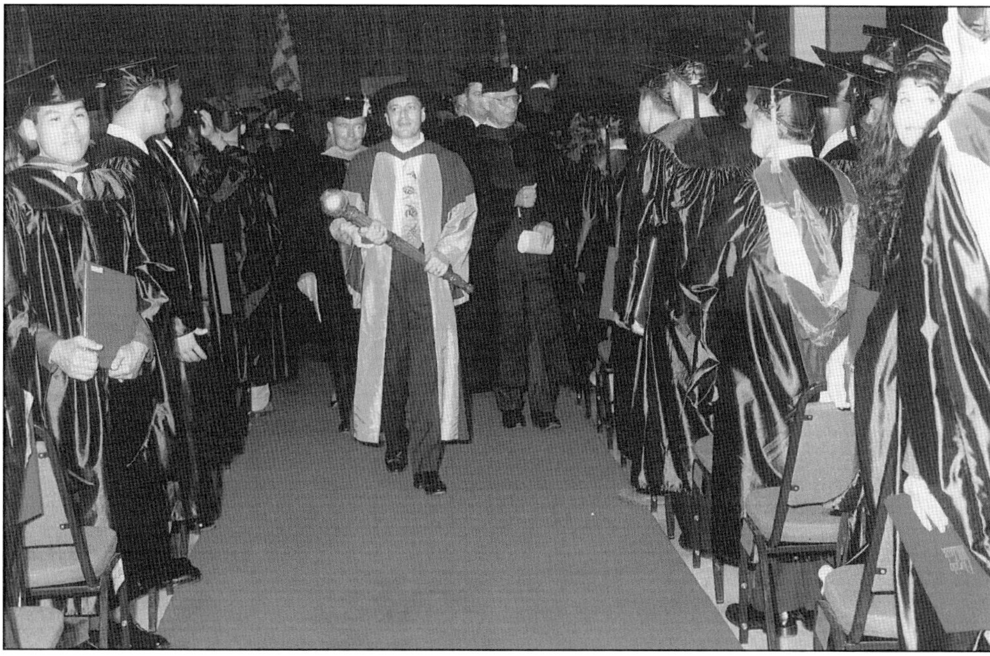

Grand Marshall Mark Bush is shown here leading the commencement party at the May 2000 graduation ceremony. President Weaver, left, and Academic Vice President Andy Revay, right, congratulate the members of the class of 2000. (Courtesy of University Publications.)

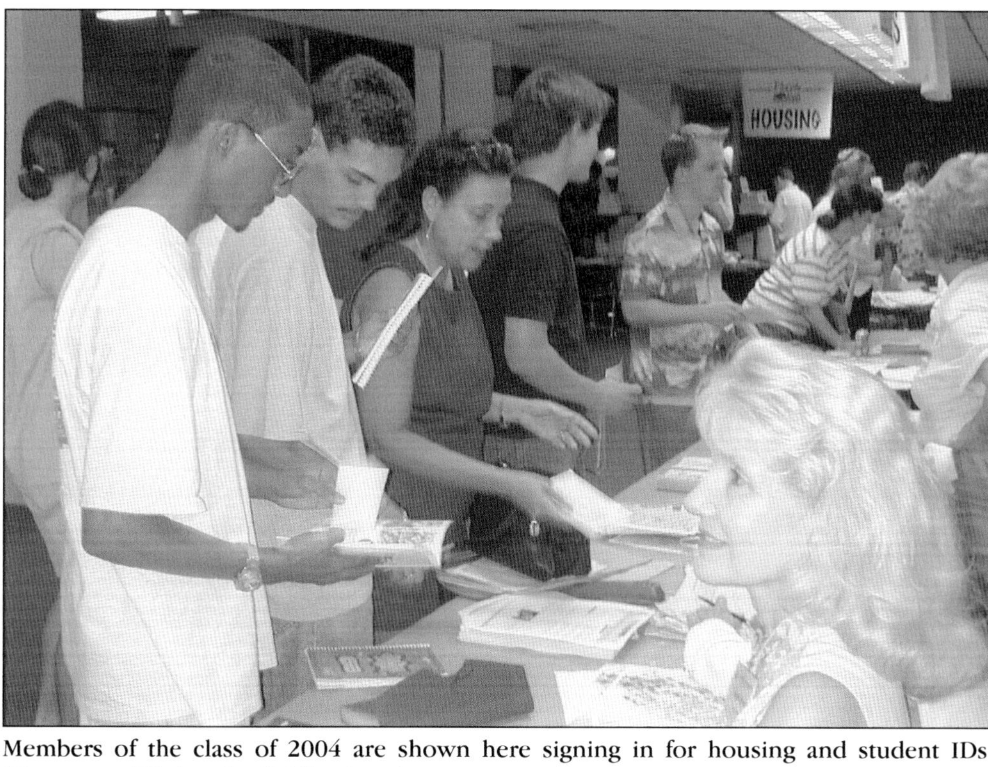

Members of the class of 2004 are shown here signing in for housing and student IDs. (Courtesy of University Publications.)

Bibliography

Cleveland, Weona. "Short Stories of Days Gone By of 'Old Melbourne'." In *The Melbourne Centennial Book*. Melbourne: Chamber of Commerce, 1980.

———. *Crossroad Towns Remembered.* Melbourne: Florida Today, 1994.

Crepeau, Richard. *Melbourne Village: The First Twenty-Five Years (1946–1971).* Orlando: University of Central Florida Press, 1988.

Gannon, Michael (Ed.). *The New History of Florida*. Gainesville: University of Florida Press, 1996.

Patterson, Gordon. "A Special Place, Always." *Forum: The Magazine of the Florida Humanities Council*, 20 (Winter 1997/1998), 19-22.

———. "Countdown to College: Launching Florida Institute of Technology." *Florida Historical Quarterly*, 77 (Fall 1998), 163-180.

———. "Space University: Lift-Off of Florida Institute of Technology," *Florida Historical Quarterly, 79* (Summer 2000), 47-67.

Shofner, Jerrell. *History of Brevard County*. 2 vols. Stuart: Brevard County Historical Commission, 1995.

Tebeau, Charlton. *A History of Florida*. Miami: University of Miami Press, 1971.